Alexander Benlian

Content Infrastructure Management

GABLER EDITION WISSENSCHAFT

Markt- und Unternehmensentwicklung

Herausgegeben von
Professor Dr. Dres. h.c. Arnold Picot,
Professor Dr. Professor h.c. Dr. h.c. Ralf Reichwald und
Professor Dr. Egon Franck

Der Wandel von Institutionen, Technologie und Wettbewerb prägt in vielfältiger Weise Entwicklungen im Spannungsfeld von Markt und Unternehmung. Die Schriftenreihe greift diese Fragen auf und stellt neue Erkenntnisse aus Theorie und Praxis sowie anwendungsorientierte Konzepte und Modelle zur Diskussion.

Alexander Benlian

Content Infrastructure Management

Results of an empirical study
in the print industry

With forewords by Prof. Dr. Dres. h.c. Arnold Picot
and Prof. Dr. Thomas Hess

Deutscher Universitäts-Verlag

Bibliografische Information Der Deutschen Bibliothek
Die Deutsche Bibliothek verzeichnet diese Publikation in der Deutschen Nationalbibliografie;
detaillierte bibliografische Daten sind im Internet über <http://dnb.ddb.de> abrufbar.

Dissertation Universität München, 2006

D 19

1. Auflage Mai 2006

Lektorat: Brigitte Siegel / Britta Göhrisch-Radmacher

Der Deutsche Universitäts-Verlag ist ein Unternehmen von Springer Science+Business Media.
www.duv.de

Umschlaggestaltung: Regine Zimmer, Dipl.-Designerin, Frankfurt/Main
Druck und Buchbinder: Rosch-Buch, Scheßlitz
Gedruckt auf säurefreiem und chlorfrei gebleichtem Papier
Printed in Germany

ISBN-10 3-8350-0368-2
ISBN-13 978-3-8350-0368-2

Foreword

Information and communication technologies are leading to new forms of collaboration and interaction relationships inside and outside of companies. With regard to media companies, this impact is tremendous as resources, products, and processes are virtually immaterial allowing IT to permeate and restructure the entire value chain. However, especially in the print industry, where the impact of digitization on organization designs and business practices is fervently discussed, companies most often realize that the degrees of freedom gained by the emergence of new technologies must be substantiated with rationalistic decision logic. One of the key questions in media companies is the way how and where digital content should be stored to optimally support primary activities (or core processes). However, state-of-the-art literature in MIS research falls short of giving answers to this question, as hardly the allocation of hardware, software, or databases has been treated so far – mostly just from one single (or even no) theoretical perspective.

These research deficits are taken up by the work at hand, which basically pursues two objectives: the description and explanation of content allocation arrangements in publishing companies. Based on a research framework that integrates strategic, economic, and contingency-based perspectives, Mr. Benlian examines the relevance and significance of different explanatory factors for the distribution and integration of media content. Empirical evidence is obtained from the rigorous method of structural equation modelling which assesses the suggested hypotheses by evaluating sample data collected from a questionnaire-based survey of 115 German publishing companies. The research findings are promising: Content allocation is primarily influenced by technological factors. Specific strategic and operational variables, however, do also play a significant role, whereas the investigated organizational variables have less impact. At the end of the work, practical guidance is given by providing IS managers with a benchmark against which they can reassess the design of their own content allocation configuration.

Altogether, this research work represents a sizable contribution to the discussion of centralizing or decentralizing digital resources in media companies, as new explanatory aspects are introduced and different theoretical perspectives are combined to shed light on the allocation problem. For that reason, I hope that this work is going to receive the response in academia and practice it deserves and that it helps companies to align their content infrastructure according to the specific contingencies they are facing.

Prof. Dr. Dres. h.c. Arnold Picot

Foreword

Content reutilization is a crucial concept in the slowly emerging theory of media management. It encompasses the idea and the conditions under which original pieces of content are bundled and redeployed across several product lines on the production side and across several distribution channels on the market side of media companies. Multi-Channel or Cross-Media Publishing, Online Content Syndication and Windowing are just few examples for media management concepts in which content reutilization plays a pivotal role. Content reutilization thus represents a cornerstone in media companies' increasingly important digitization strategies. Current empirical findings back up this trend in the media industry: More than 50% of German and more than 60% of US print publishers have already adopted the most common content reutilization practices with a tendency towards even higher penetration rates in the near future.

Despite the growing adoption and support of this management concept, one may not forget that the implementation of content reutilization is only feasible in practice if a technical infrastructure is provided that efficiently supports complex content workflows. Former research endeavors have already performed substantial analyses investigating the question *how* media-neutral content should be stored and retrieved by means of XML and the Semantic Web. The question *where* content should be allocated according to a comprehensive strategic, organizational, and economic analysis, however, has been neglected in the state-of-the-art literature so far. Exactly this research gap has been filled by Mr. Benlian's work, which addresses an important aspect in the implementation of media companies' current digitization strategies.

The doctoral thesis at hand is rooted and embedded in the works of the research group Content Lifecycle Management (CoLiMa) of the Institute for Information Systems and New Media at the Ludwig-Maximilians-University in Munich. In general, the guiding principle of CoLiMa is the transformation of the media industry's value chain through information and communication technologies. In particular, CoLiMa investigates and evaluates new content reutilization options along the entire lifecycle of media content.

By means of a structural model, which is based on a combination of three theoretical lenses, Mr. Benlian paints a differentiated picture of content allocation behavior in publishing companies. The descriptive results revealed the predominance of centralized content allocation arrangements in today's and future media companies – a finding that could not be taken for granted especially in the face of predominantly decentralized organization designs in the print industry. The analytical results show that the type of content and the type of sub-industry (book, magazine, or newspaper) have a significant impact on the decision on centralized or decentralized content allocation in media companies. By contrast, transaction costs and organizational variables seem to have no predictive power. The empirical study is grounded in a survey of 115 media companies of different sub-segments of the German print industry that was conducted in cooperation with the Association of German Book Publishers between March and May 2005.

In total, Mr. Benlian has provided an above-average dissertation thesis, which produced relevant findings both from a scientific and practical point of view. Furthermore, it is important to note that Mr. Benlian has chosen a methodological approach that is common in the international research on the Management of Information Systems (MIS), but has unfortunately been neglected in the German research discipline "Wirtschaftsinformatik" so far. Due to these two reasons, I hope that this thesis will strike a chord in the respective research and management communities.

Prof. Dr. Thomas Hess

Preface

In the face of growing digitization and modularity of content in the media industry, media companies find themselves challenged to exploit the gained degrees of freedom in the management of their most valuable asset. Opportunities abound in reutilizing, bundling and pushing content through diverse media channels leading to higher returns on investment by spreading out additional revenues over first copy costs. However, although many scientific works have tackled the problem of properly allocating data, processing power or IT-related decision rights in the past, no approaches have taken up the topic of media content allocation so far, leaving researchers and managers in the dark.

The thesis at hand attempts to address this research gap by throwing light on this pressing issue from various theoretical perspectives. In the first part of the thesis, different theoretical lenses stemming from the area of Management and Organization Science are sifted through for their appropriateness of shedding new light on the issue at hand. Hypotheses about content allocation are then deduced resulting in a structural model which integrates adequate theoretical perspectives. In the second part, the structural model is examined empirically on the basis of a sample of newspaper, magazine, and book publishing companies. Eventually, the results and findings of the study are interpreted and synthesized into a big picture distinguishing between implications for academia and practice.

Besides this short preview of relevant issues in this thesis, which hopefully will arouse readers' curiosity at least a little bit, I would like to thank everyone involved in the development and fine-tuning of this research work. First and foremost, I wish to express my gratitude to my supervisor Prof. Dr. Thomas Hess who thoughtfully guided my research endeavors. He has not only accompanied the entire research process with fruitful advice and inspiration, but also enabled my visiting scholarship at the School of Information Management & Systems, University of California at Berkeley, which gave me the opportunity to have enlightening discussions with Prof. Yale Braunstein. Furthermore, I would like to thank Prof. Hans-Bernd Brosius whose dedicated comments helped me to improve the design and measurement instrument of my research study.

Beyond these credits to my academic advisors, I wish to express my gratitude to a number of people that also supported me during my time at the Institute for Information Systems and New Media (WIM). In particular, I want to thank my colleagues Dr. Bernd Schulze, Dr. Andreas Müller, Dr. Markus Anding, Benedikt von Walter, Dr. Bernhard Gehra, Michael Samtleben, Thomas Wilde, Florian Stadlbauer, Barbara Rauscher, Christoph Grau and Dr. Christoph Hirnle for not only being helpful and supportive in all matters of daily work life, but also in establishing a social environment that has made my time at WIM very enjoyable. Last but not least, I'd like to give a special thanks to Monica Reitz, Michal Gruninger, Florian Mann, Barbara Ostrup, Patrick Schmidt, and Stefan Wurm for being a great support in coping with the well-known difficulties that come along with empirical studies.

This work is dedicated to my wife Nina who is a strong pillar and source of motivation in my life. She is the main reason why I always remained focused and determined in my efforts to accomplish such a challenging task.

Alexander Benlian

Overview of Contents

Table of Contents

List of Figures

List of Tables

List of Abbreviations

AKEP	Arbeitskreis Elektronisches Publizieren
BVDB	Börsenverein des Deutschen Buchhandels
BDZV	Bund Deutscher Zeitungsverleger
CIP	Comparative Institutional Performance
CT	Contingency Theory
ET	Evolutionary Theories
ISNM	Institute for Information System and New Media (Ludwig-Maximilians-University of Munich)
MBV	Market-Based View
MIS	Management of Information Systems
NIE	New Institutional Economics
PAT	Principal-Agent Theory
PLS	Partial Least Squares
PT	Power Theory
PRT	Property Rights Theory
RBV	Resource-Based View
SEM	Structural Equation Modeling
TAC	Transaction Costs
TCT	Transaction Cost Theory
VDZ	Verband Deutscher Zeitschriftenverleger

1 Introduction

1.1 Problem statement and motivation

The advent of digital technologies and standards (e.g. CMS and XML[1]) has dramatically changed the way how media content is distributed and exchanged over digital channels. New and more efficient options for the retrieval, transformation, and deployment of content point to a higher mobility and a greater potential for the reutilization of content, opening up avenues to streamline production and bundling processes. However, until recently, the technological landscape of publishing companies could be characterized as an archipelago of content islands or, even more severely, as a jumble of heterogeneous and often incompatible point-to-point-connections that could not be exploited efficiently for content reutilization activities such as cross-media or multi-channel-publishing (McKenney/ McFarlan, 1982; Vizjak/ Ringlstetter, 2001). Although often highly penetrated with digital networks and heterogeneous application systems, the majority of media companies still have not tackled the problem of how to strategically and economically leverage (i.e. store, integrate, and retrieve) digital content in production and bundling processes. However, especially in the print industry, where content reutilization strategies are hotly discussed and slowly gain momentum (AKEP, 2004, p. 45), companies realize that the degrees of freedom gained by the emergence of new technology must be substantiated with rationalistic decision logic. Potential efficiency gains might otherwise not be exploited.

In the MIS field, a sizable body of literature has taken up the question of how to link IT- and organization-related structural variables. During the last thirty years, numerous research studies have been undertaken to explore the logic underlying the allocation of IS decision making (e.g., Brown/ Magill, 1998; Boynton/ Jacobs/ Zmud, 1992), information systems (e.g., Heinrich/ Roithmayr, 1985; Rockart/ Bullen/ Leventer, 1977), hardware (e.g., Bacon, 1990; Laskey, 1982), and data (e.g., Jain et al., 1998; Cash/ McFarlan/ McKenney, 1992). Some of these research papers draw on evolutionary concepts suggesting that the allocation of most IT resources oscillates unevenly between domination of centralization and decentralization following the (temporarily) prevailing market technology (e.g. Peak/ Azadmanesh, 1997). From the majority of papers, organizations could learn that the actual allocation decision depends upon several different context factors and is therefore complex. A generally applicable decision for a centralized or decentralized content allocation scenario that is made independently of both idiosyncrasies and contingencies of firms would therefore ignore the differences between organizations. The research papers advocating

---

[1] The diffusion rate of XML in the German book publishing industry has nearly doubled in the last two years (Benlian, et al., 2005).

context-sensitive explanations of content allocation have primarily been originated in the Anglo-American research community and show a considerable methodological and theoretical range and depth. Especially conspicuous is the abundance of conceptual works based on contingency-theoretical thinking that have been applied to explain why organizations centralize or decentralize IT resources. Since the mid 90's, however, a slight shift can be observed from conceptual towards more empirical works that also took alternative explanatory approaches (e.g., economic or strategic) into considerations. This may not only indicate that focusing on just one stream of reasoning may not be appropriate to deal with the complexity of the allocation decision, but also that research has already reached an advanced state.

In spite of the maturing field in the research on the determinants of the allocation of IT-related artifacts, *two main research gaps* become apparent when one attempts to transfer the findings to the allocation of content in media companies. *First* and foremost, as media content is not only key input factor but also output in publishing firms, it differs tremendously from the allocation logic of classical IT resources. However, no work has taken up the question so far why *media content* is allocated in publishing companies. Although first descriptive investigations have shown a significant variance in the allocation of content in print companies (Benlian et al., 2005), there is still a lack in confirmatory and explanatory research based on a large-sample method. *Second*, although the MIS research on the allocation of IT-related resources has reached a mature stage of development, it has not come up yet with a comprehensive framework that integrates multiple reference theories in a way that recognizes the existing varied body of literature. Besides narrowing down on a specific IT resource (i.e. media content) in a specific industry (i.e. publishing companies), the blending of multiple theoretical lenses could thus shed light on content allocation practices on a more extensive level.

In accordance to the observed research gaps, business and IT practitioners seem to lack a solid foundation for how to decide upon the allocation of media content. Often the emphasis is either on leveraging synergies between media channels (e.g. cross-media publishing) or reducing production costs (e.g. replace media-specific by multimedia editors). The wider consequences of such a one-sided decision process often appear much later when organizations already are locked in IT investments and realize that other factors should have been taken into account simultaneously. These problems are often rooted in an unreflected allocation decision. All the more it seems imperative to draw on several theoretical resources that help rationalizing on content allocation in order to know which levers to manipulate to ensure an effective and efficient storage, retrieval, and delivery of media content.

Altogether, both theoretical deficiencies and practical shortcomings stated above provide the motivation for this work. Before they are addressed in the subsequent chapters though, research questions and objectives as well as the research methodology of this study are briefly outlined.

1.2 Research questions and objectives

In throwing light on selected factors that seem to affect how organizations seek to distribute media content, the study at hand attempts to address the aforementioned research gaps. Accordingly, core scientific objective of this study is to examine the overall pattern that explains the heterogeneous content allocation behavior of publishing companies in practice[2]. The research seeks to develop and specify a comprehensive framework that helps to understand consistent and inconsistent relationships between influencing factors and the allocation of content. The desired theoretical enhancements are inextricably interwoven with a second, more normative objective of this work. It is also intended to provide practitioners with recommendations for a sophisticated and rationalized content allocation decision.

In order to break down the overall objectives of this study into more digestible pieces, Table 1.2-1 gives an overview of underlying research questions that basically follow the scientific aims of describing, explaining, and predicting (Kerlinger/ Lee, 2000, p. 11; Eberhard, 1999, p. 16).

---

(1) *Describing (Phenomenological research focus)*: How is media content being allocated among editorial units of publishing companies?

(2) *Explaining (Causal research focus)*: Why can we observe variances in the allocation of content in publishing companies? To what antecedent factors can the allocation of media content in publishing companies be attributed?

(3) *Predicting (Prescriptive/Normative research focus)*: What can publishing companies do to influence the allocation of media content? What impact does the manipulation of antecedents of the allocation of media content have?

Table 1.2-1 : Research questions of overall research project

The first research question addresses the necessity to delve into conceptualizations about forms of content, content allocation, and publishing organizations. This phenomenological research step is not only expedient to develop a common language and understanding for the object and unit of analysis of this study. It also serves the purpose to reduce complexity by concentrating research endeavors on selected and specified aspects most pertinent to the research goal. Eventually, the descriptions of relevant phenomena form the conceptual pillars on which the process of theory development of this study is built on.

---

[2] An explanation for why *publishing* companies are addressed will be given in chapter 2.2.

The second research question points to the investigation of hypothesized causal relationships between selected antecedent factors[3] and the content allocation behavior in
publishing companies. Hence, a major goal is to uncover consistent patterns (i.e. invariabilities) for the research sample[4] under investigation. Valuable insights into content allocation behavior can be gained, if the overall research sample is examined
from angles stressing different aspects of content allocation. Consequently, by varying the type of content and the form of content allocation a more differentiated picture
can be painted. To reduce the complexity that would be caused by too many variations, but still enable focused model building, this study will concentrate on two forms
of content (productive vs. archived) and content allocation (content distribution vs.
content integration) respectively. Even more interesting findings can be gathered, if
the research sample is not only considered as one inseparable entity, but also as a
union of rather homogeneous subsets. In the context of this study, especially book,
magazine, and newspaper companies lend themselves as 'partitions' that are worth
studying more deeply.

The third research question of this study refers to the entreaties frequently expressed
by practitioners as well as social scientists[5] that scientific findings of applied empirical
research should not exist for their own sake. They should rather be translated into
recommendations for professionals in order to offer guidance in everday decision-
making. For that reason, this study will explicitly make a plea for relevance by breaking down the practical implications of empirical findings into context-dependent, im-
plementable action. The outputs of this study may support practitioners in ways such
that they are utilized to justify and rationalize content allocation decisions.

1.3 Overview of research methodology

As outlined in the problem statement, research into the factors that affect the allocation of IT-related artifacts has already reached a mature state. In an analysis of state-
of-the-art papers in the field of IT-related resource allocation, it was found that a variety of conceptual and exploratory studies and a few studies that rigorously test hypotheses do already exist. A summary that assigns related research papers to pre-

---

[3] Although it is impossible and therefore not intended to develop an exhaustive or total explanatory
model, profound and instructive insights should be provided from different theoretical angles.

[4] If certain statistical conditions are met, the findings for the research sample may even be inferred to
the underlying population.

[5] Especially in MIS research, researchers claim that IS academic research lacks relevance to practice and should therefore take efforts to improve on communicating the fruits of IS research more
effectively to IS professionals (Benbasat/ Zmud, 1999, p. 8; Lee, 1999, p. 32). This famous "rigor
vs. relevance" issue is not only hotly discussed in MIS research, but has also stirred controversy
among researchers in Management Science (e.g. Nicolai, 2004, pp. 99ff.).

vailing research methodologies in the state-of-the-art literature is given in Table 1.3-1[6].

Reference methodologies			
Empirical		Non-Empirical (Theoretical)	
(I) Exploratory	(II) Inductive	(III) Conceptual	(IV) Mathematical
17	8	20	1

Table 1.3-1: Applied reference methodologies in state-of-the-art literature

While conceptual contributions have dominated the discussion about this research topic so far, since the mid 90's, however, a tendency towards more empirical work can be observed. This pattern of development in the application of research methodologies further backs up the notion that research on the allocation of IT-related artifacts is no longer in its infancy, but has reached a level of maturity that allows for the usage of theory-testing instead of theory-creating methods (Friedrichs, 1990, pp. 50ff.).

Consequently, it is not seen critical to explore totally new concepts. Instead, the focus is on the integration of existing theories and the systematic assessment of the resulting comprehensive model. Accordingly, a confirmatory empirical approach, grounded on a functionalist-positivist research paradigm (e.g., Morgan, 1980; Burrell/ Morgan, 1979), is preferred in this research study. More specifically, the methodology applied in this study refers to the research tradition of theoretical empiricism (Wold, 1989b) which tries to harmonize two antagonistic philosophies: the world of idealism and empiricism. In order to gain knowledge about phenomena in the world, idealism, on the one hand, demands to deductively derive propositions between constructs being investigated through reasoning and theory building. On the other hand, empiricism posits that knowledge can solely be attributed to and verified by experience. Allegedly, there is a great chasm between these two ontological worlds. The objective of the theoretical empiricism is to bridge this chasm and to dissolve the supposed antagonism by connecting both philosophies: "*In synthesis, theoretical empiricism shares with empiricism the determination to learn primarily from experience, and with idealism the importance attached to ideas and reason*" (Dagum, 1989, p. 146).

---

[6] The detailed analysis of the state-of-the-art literature concerning research methodologies can be looked up in Appendix A.

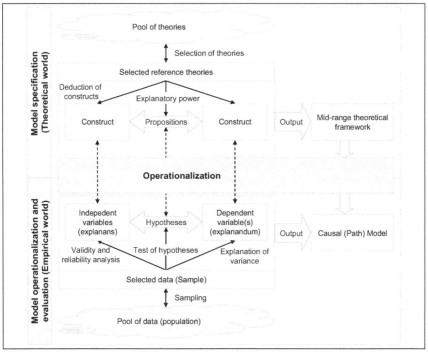

Figure 1.3-1: Methodology of research study

Hence, a research methodology which is based on the philosophical underpinnings of the theoretical empiricism has to harmonize two different worlds. As illustrated in Figure 1.3-1, this is realized by breaking down selected theoretical constructs and propositions, which are the output of reasoning, to measurable variables and hypotheses that, in turn, are paving the way to the empirical world.

The operationalization of constructs marks the transition from the theoretical to the empirical world and enables that a theoretical view of phenomena can be submitted to empirical examination. Structural equation modeling (SEM), which is later introduced as central statistical method of this study (see 4.1), does not only provide an advanced way of operationalizing theoretical constructs. It also allows rigorously testing multiple hypotheses simultaneously, corresponding perfectly to the multi-theoretical and primarily confirmatory nature of this research study[7]. The structural logic presented in Figure 1.3-1, which also manifests itself in the terminological as

---

[7] This research study actually represents one of the first attempts to enhance the awareness for this kind of confirmatory methodology in the German "Wirtschaftsinformatik" research community. An ancillary objective of this study is therefore to transfer SEM as an enriching statistical technique from MIS to Wirtschaftsinformtik research for the adequate investigation of multi-theoretical problems.

well as methodological foundations of SEM, provides orientation to researchers throughout the research process and also forms the guiding thread woven all the way through the research study at hand.

1.4 Organization and evolutionary context of study

The organization of the study at hand follows the structure of scientific model building which is closely intertwined with theoretical empiricism (e.g., Wold, 1989b; Dagum, 1989). This research approach, which has emerged in Econometrics in the 1930s and been adopted in several other research disciplines (e.g. psychology, communication research), suggests four research steps (Lohmöller, 1989a, p. 3), which need not follow consecutively, but may also incorporate feedback loops[8]. First, the conceptual foundation is laid by introducing and clarifying major concepts of the study. Second, a research model is specified drawing on a theoretical background. Third, the specified model with its theoretical constructs is translated into measurable variables. In order to test the theoretical model against the empirical world, statistical data is collected on the investigated phenomena by means of an appropriate measurement instrument.

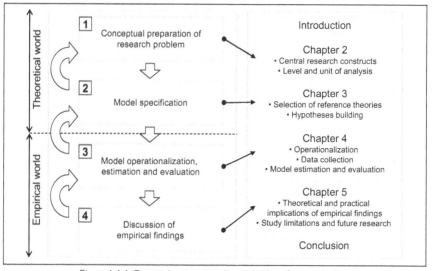

Figure 1.4-1: Research process and organization of research study

---

[8] The four steps in the model building process are predominantly successive. Nevertheless, iterative cycles are common as, for instance, research constructs can theoretically be enriched through empirical insights.

After the model estimation and evaluation phase has been accomplished, the findings of the comparison between the theoretical framework and the empirical model are discussed and dovetailed with existing related work. Figure 1.4-1 shows how the organization of this study aligns with the four steps of scientific model building. As illustrated above, the study is divided into six chapters. After having provided an overview of the research problem, the study objectives, and the methodology in this introductory chapter, the model specification process will conceptually be prepared by laying the terminological foundation in chapter 2. While chapter 2.1 defines and clarifies the dependent research construct under investigation, the context, level, and unit of analysis are specified in chapter 2.2.

In chapter 3, a theoretical model will be developed based on selected reference theories. Before the actual development of the causal model can begin though, the process of selecting reference theories will be outlined (see chapter 3.1). Furthermore, the selection criteria for why including or omitting reference theories during the model building process will be explicated (see chapter 3.2.1). Based on these criteria, a pool of theories will be examined more closely for their appropriateness in the explanation of content allocation behavior (see chapter 3.2.2). In addition to the top-down approach of sifting out relevant theories, the selected theoretical lenses are also benchmarked against theories primarily used in state-of-the-art literature (see chapter 3.2.3). In order to make all of the rather theoretical concepts more tangible, an abstract framework is finally introduced that attempts to glue the selected reference theories together by addressing their common logic in explaining content allocation (see chapter 3.2.4). In a next step, each selected reference theory will be examined for explanatory factors which contribute fruitfully to the explanation of content allocation (see chapter 3.3). The impacts of these determinants on the content allocation behavior of publishing companies are finally suggested as hypotheses which altogether form a theoretical framework of content allocation.

In chapter 1, the hypotheses will be tested in an empirical study. This requires the transistion from the theoretical to the empirical world (Figure 1.4-1), which means that the theoretical constructs have to be operationalized entailing all the requirements and technical specificities of the research method employed (see chapters 4.1 and 4.2). Subsequently, details about the data collection phase are given in chapter 4.3 including questionnaire design, sample selection, mailing procedure, and survey response. Finally, the presentation of relevant sample characteristics (see chapter 4.4) is followed by the model estimation and evaluation phase (see chapter 4.5).

In chapter 1, the model findings are discussed and interpreted. This includes not only a discussion of different facets of content allocation behavior, but also major theoretical and practical implications for academia and practice. Finally, in chapter 6, the study will be summarized and a final conclusion will be drawn.

Before the actual research study unfolds in the upcoming chapters, the evolutionary context of this study shall be depicted here briefly. The doctoral thesis at hand is rooted and embedded in the works of the research group *Content Lifecycle Management (CoLiMa)* of the Institute for Information Systems and New Media at the Ludwig-Maximilians-University in Munich. The overarching framework of the CoLiMa research group is the transformation of the media industry through information and communication technologies. In particular, the concept of content reutilization represents the connecting link between the specific research projects. The study at hand is conceptualized as a cross-sectional, sampling-based empirical research project, which investigates efficient content allocation practices in publishing firms considered a major prerequisite for content reutilization. The preparatory works of Markus Anding (Anding, 2004), Lutz Köhler (Köhler, 2005), and Bernd Schulze (Schulze, 2005) on content reutilization have motivated and influenced this research study to a great extent. The findings of this study will also be an input for upcoming research projects aiming at the semantic analysis of content modules from a micro perspective and the industrialization of content production and bundling processes from a macro perspective.

2 Conceptual foundations

"No matter what problem you want to work on and no matter what method you will eventually use, your empirical work must begin with a careful consideration of the research problem"
(Simon, 1978, p. 98)

Developing a theoretical framework for the explanation of varying content allocation scenarios is impossible without clarifying the fundamental terms of the research question, i.e. in particular of the research variable, under investigation. The following chapter takes up this issue by providing a brief overview of the definitions of core research constructs (chapter 2.1) and the unit and level of analysis (chapter 2.2).

2.1 Media content and content allocation

As outlined in chapter 1.2, central research objective of this study is *to explain the allocation of content in publishing companies.* Putting the structure of the sentence on a more abstract level, the general terminology describing allocation problems suggests a pattern for defining and clarifying the most relevant terms (see Figure 2.1-1).

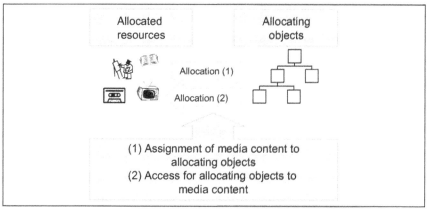

Figure 2.1-1: Terminology of the content allocation problem

When considering allocation problems on a general basis, resources (e.g. budget, staff) are either (1) assigned to or (2) accessed by allocating objects (e.g. organizational units, subsidiaries). In classical MIS research, allocated resources are hardware components or databases (e.g., Ahituv/ Neumann/ Zviran, 1989, p. 399) on a technical level and application system development or planning decision authority (e.g., Olson/ Chervany, 1980, p. 59) on an organizational level. In this study, *content* is considered the core resource of media companies to be efficiently allocated. While the basic understanding of media content and the process of content allocation will be explicated in the following two chapters, the allocating objects here coincide with the object of analysis (i.e. publishing companies) and therefore are granted a special attention in chapter 2.2.

2.1.1 Media content

A considerable number of definitions for the term *content* have been applied both in theory and practice so far (e.g. Shapiro/ Varian, 1998). One of the most elaborated definitions in recent years, that merges economic, technical, and legal aspects, views content as *"[...] a purposeful and individually protectable representation of implicit information whose creation is largely due to the editorial capabilities of human intelligence"* (Anding/ Hess, 2003, p. 14). To convey an abstract notion about content in general, this definition works well. As definitions of terms have to be suitable and practical in the context where they are applied, this definition, however, seems to be too broad in meaning, i.e. too much types of content would be included into the analysis at hand[1]. Hence, this rather abstract definition of content must be boiled down to a more appropriate format. While some aspects of the general definition also apply here, others must be put in more concrete terms to understand which types of content are investigated when talking about their allocation.

To derive a selection logic why concentrating on certain types of content and not on others, a classical content workflow will briefly be introduced (see Figure 2.1.1-1).

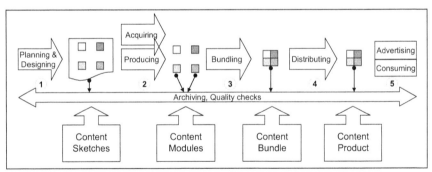

Figure 2.1.1-1: Content workflow and content types

On an abstract level, media content[2] is planned, designed, produced, bundled, and finally distributed (Rawolle, 2002, p. 11). At each step of this prototypical workflow, content is checked for its quality and archived in corresponding repositories. Accord-

---

[1] Especially in empirical studies, theoretical constructs should be defined as concrete as possible, as they have to be translated into operational definitions at a later stage in the research process.

[2] The specificities of media content as opposed to data (especially with respect to media types) are comprehensively discussed in Benlian/ Hess, 2004, p. 9 and will therefore not be mentioned here.

ing to these different steps, content can on the one side be distinguished with respect to its *granularity* (i.e. whether it is an idea, a sketch, a module, bundle, or a product) and *materiality* (i.e. whether it is digital or analog). On the other side, a destinction can be made regarding the *age of content* (i.e. whether the content runs through the workflow for the first time or is being retrieved from an archive[3]) and the *target market* which should be served (i.e. whether the content aims at the recipient or advertising market).

In this study, only content that already has taken shape or has materialized and technically can be utilized in the production or bundling process should be considered (i.e. *modules and bundles*), since ideas or sketches are either still tacit (i.e. implicit) or for the most part very unstructured and therefore not efficiently distributable in publishing companies. In addition to that, content products that are already attached to or deployed in special media carriers (e.g. DVD, CD-ROM) or digital networks (e.g. Internet) should not be taken into account, since they are no longer eligible for the production or bundling process at this late stage. Consequently, the focus of this study explicitly lies on the production and bundling stages of the content workflow (see Figure 2.1.1-1 Nr. ② and ③), whereas the distribution and consumption stages are excluded from the analysis.

Furthermore, since media content is increasingly produced, edited, and bundled digitally throughout the media industry, while analog content storage is more and more abandoned, focusing digital content allocation is all the more forward-looking and pertinent to the research question under investigation. Another crucial reason for narrowing the perspective to digital content is the fact that analog content would entail different underlying assumptions about the economics of allocating media content rendering a theoretical model even more complex.

Both currently used (i.e. productive) and formerly archived content is granted special attention in this research study, since both types of content are most often objects of different allocation strategies. While archived content tends to be kept in central repositories due to its out-of-date character, productive content is created for a new first copy of a content module or bundle and therefore most often doesn't reside at one central spot. As the consideration of both content types is especially expedient for theoretical juxtaposition and crucial for practical implications, the distinction of both variations will be a centerpiece of the empirical analysis in later chapters (see chapter 4.5.4).

Last but not least, a further restriction with regard to editorial as opposed to advertising content should be made. As the production and bundling of advertising content

---

[3] An archive can be defined as repository or collection of different types of content modules, which are no longer in current use, but are kept in long-term storage, as they may be required at a later stage in the future.

usually follows a different logic than editorial content, for the sake of simplicity we explicitly do not pay attention to ad content[4].

The following morphological box summarizes the types of content focused in this study (see the highlighted boxes in Table 2.1.1-1).

Types of content according to ...	Instances			
... media type	Text	Picture/Photo	Audio	Video
... granularity	Idea or Plan	Module	Bundle	Product
... materiality	Analog		Digital	
... content age	Archived		Productive	
... target market	Editorial content		Ad content	

Table 2.1.1-1: Types of content focused in this study

Based on the morphological box as a form of explicating the types of content considered in this study, the broad definition from the outset of this chapter will be adapted to better fit into this context:

For the purpose of this study, content is considered as a purposeful, digital representation of implicit information in the form of currently produced and archived modules or bundles that cater to consumer (i.e. readership) markets and whose creation is to the most part due to the capabilities of editors.

2.1.2 Content allocation

The objective of this study is to provide some rational explanations for the question of whether allocating content centrally or decentrally. Before being able to decide upon such a question, one has to know *how* content can be allocated in media companies, i.e. what forms of content allocation exist. As allocation scenarios can vary in the way resources are allocated to allocating objects, another relevant question is when the level of content allocation is higher in one allocation scenario or another.

---

[4] As the research at hand focuses content exchanges within the boundaries of a firm, any considerations about the association of content to property rights are not included into the analysis either. It is rather assumed that the distribution of property rights within a firm doesn't exert a significant influence on the *inhouse* allocation of content. As legal issues of media content are explicitly excluded, we will omit this aspect in our definition as well as in our model building process in following chapters.

From an orthographical point of view, *allocation* can be derived from the Latin word "allocare" and basically means "to assign objects to one or multiple *locations*" (Webster's Revised Unabridged Dictionary, 2005). In economics, for instance, allocation means to find locations for resources where they can efficiently be leveraged or utilized according to a specific optimal (e.g. Pareto-optimal) output (e.g. Varian, 2002, p. 544). In the context of the content allocation problem at hand, "locations" can be interpreted in terms of geographical coordinates or as places where objects are allocated (e.g., persons, organizational units, or countries). Taking up these notions, the allocation of media content may preliminarily be comprehended as *the process of assigning content to one or multiple locations*.

In order to further illuminate the meaning of allocation for the context of this study, the allocation construct will be made up of two dimensions[5] (see Figure 2.1.2-1).

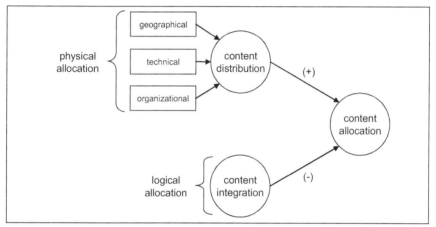

Figure 2.1.2-1: Physical and logical dimensions of content allocation

The first dimension is called content distribution and consists of three semantically overlapping concepts: geographical, technical, and organizational distribution (Mertens, 1985, p. 20; Heinzl, 1993, p. 22). While geographical distribution translates into different spacial locations of stored content (local vs. global), organizational distribution refers to the extent to which media content is parceled out among and integrated into organizational units (business units vs. corporate level). Finally, technical distribution is conceptually closely intertwined with the geographical aspect, but rather focuses on the distribution of physical IT components (e.g. hardware, software, and network components) that store, move, and manipulate media content. The second dimension, called *content integration*, represents the level of connectivity between distributed content, i.e. the intensity to which content modules are logically

---

[5] These dimensions are conceptually motivated by the two constituent meanings of allocation as illustrated in Figure 2.1-1.

linked in an organization. To put it in different terms, as the flip side of the distribution dimension, content integration describes the extent to which content workers have access to media content.

On the basis of all possible combinations between the physical and logical dimension of content allocation, a theoretical typology (Bailey, 1994, pp. 17ff.) can be developed (see Figure 2.1.2-2).

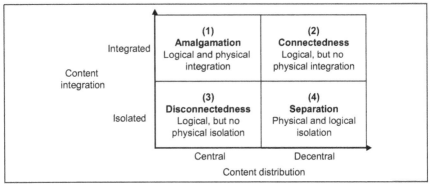

Figure 2.1.2-2: Typology of content allocation

While the allocation scenario of logically linked, but physically separated media content can be termed as a state of *connectedness* (2) (e.g. federated database in a network), both the combination of logically and physically integrated content can be called *amalgamation* (1) (e.g. local database with one consistent data scheme). The constellation, where distributed content modules are both physically and logically isolated from one another, can be referred to as *separation* (4) (e.g. isolated databases in geographically separated organizational units), while logically disconnected, but physically centralized pieces of media content can be labeled as *disconnectedness* (3) (e.g. local database with inconsistent or no data scheme).

After having pointed out the major allocation constellations being investigated in this study, it is imperative to know how content integration and content distribution relate to the allocation construct in order to know what constitutes a higher or lower degree of allocation. Basically, high levels of content allocation go with high levels of content distribution (i.e. towards a decentralization of content) and low levels of content integration (i.e. towards an isolation of content). Hence, content allocation behavior relates positively with content distribution and negatively with content integration (see signs in brackets in Figure 2.1.2-1). As the connectivity aspect outweighs the distributional aspect in the conceptualization of this study (i.e. the possibility of editors to access integrated data is considered more influential on the degree of content allocation than the actual physical distribution), allocation constellations (1) - (4) can be ranked[6] from the lowest (i.e. most centralized) to the highest (i.e. most decentralized) degree of content allocation:

$$(1) \prec (2) \prec (3) \prec (4)$$

Before delving into the process of theorizing about the allocation of content, the abovementioned *allocating objects*, that coincide methodologically with the object (or unit) of analysis in this study, will be explicated together with the level of abstraction on which the objects will be analyzed. In addition, context issues will be elaborated in order to demarcate the boundaries of time and space for the statements to be deduced in this research study.

2.2 Publishing companies

According to WHETTEN, research studies that strive for developing sound theoretical models should provide an answer to the question on what level and about which research objects scientific statements are being formulated (Whetten, 1989, p. 491f.). Making the level and unit of analysis explicit not only strengthens organizational theory development and research (e.g. Klein/ Dansereau/ Hall, 1994, p. 224), but also influences the nature of theoretical constructs and propositions as well as the data collection, analysis, and interpretation at later stages[7].

Basically, theories can address individuals (e.g. the behavior of managers) or groups of individuals as level of analysis. In organizational research, individuals are frequently aggregated to organizational units (i.e. departmental level), organizations (i.e. firm level), or groups of organizations (i.e. corporate group level), in order to yield theoretical statements on a higher level of abstraction and complexity. Relating these possible levels of analysis to the core research questions investigated in this study, content allocation behavior can be examined within the confines of an editor's workplace, of an editorial department, of a publishing company, or an entire corporate publishing group. As the objective of this study is to explain differences with respect to the content allocation behavior of media companies that operate independent production and bundling processes, the *level of analysis* most pertinent to address the research questions deduced in chapter 1.2 is the *firm or company level* (see Figure 2.2-1). With *publishing companies* as central *unit of analysis*, reference theories in later chapters will exclusively address the allocation of media content on the level of

---

[6] As the typology of content allocation is a theoretical construct that will be operationalized as an index of the dimensions of content distribution and integration, it is crucial to make the step from a categorical (with dichotomous variables) to a quasi-dimensional (with ordinal or continuous variables) world.

[7] KLEIN ET AL. put it as follows: *"Greater appreciation and recognition of [level issues] will [...] enhance the clarity, testability, comprehensiveness, and creativity of organizational theories."* (Klein/ Dansereau/ Hall, 1994, p. 196)

the individual firm, thus comprising the allotment of content not within[8], but among editorial units.

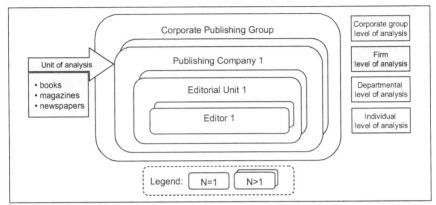

Figure 2.2-1: Unit and level of analysis

Furthermore, the study at hand will limit its research focus to publishing companies (i.e. book, magazine, and newspaper companies) in a first step (see Figure 2.2-1). As one sub-type of media companies, which most basically can be defined as enterprises that purchase, produce, bundle, and distribute media content[9] (Schumann/ Hess, 2005, p. 1), publishing companies differ greatly from broadcasting (TV and radio) and new media (Internet, Intranet, and Extranet) companies not only with regard to the quality and quantity of utilized media content (Benlian/ Hess, 2004, p. 9), but also with respect to the structure of the value chains (Wirtz, 2005, p. 171 and p. 222; Heinrich, 2001, pp. 250ff. and 321ff.). For the sake of simplicity, this research study will commence the analysis of content allocation behavior by focusing on content portfolios of publishing companies that exhibit the most static and time-independent features relative to the content portfolios of broadcasting and new media companies[10]. In doing so, basic findings might be a foundation and starting point for future research on content allocation behavior in other sectors of the media industry.

Although the restriction of the research focus on publishing companies is a means to reduce the complexity in the process of analyzing content allocation behavior, the diversity and heterogeneity of different types of publishing companies must not be

---

[8] In the case that a publishing company consists of just one editorial unit, the firm and departmental levels of analysis obviously coincide.

[9] A generic representation of an activity chain (or content workflow) in media companies in the form of a content workflow is illustrated in figure 2.1.1/1.

[10] Although the generizability of research findings is restricted when confining the investigation of content allocation behavior only to specific sub-types of media companies, the developed system of hypotheses is much more substantial and profound with respect to the selected unit of analysis. Following research projects can thus take up the research findings at hand and compare them to other industries.

underestimated. All three main sub-types of publishing companies (i.e. book, magazine, and newspaper companies) differ in value chain functions, publication output periodicity, and also in media product characteristics and thus imply not only structural but also process-related variations (Wirtz, 2005, p. 105ff. and pp. 205ff.). While editorial departments in book publishing companies rather represent loosely coupled organizational units (or even just one unit) that tend to edit and bundle monolithic content modules[11] on a non-periodical basis, magazine and newspaper companies usually exhibit higher levels of coordination between organizational units due to higher content modularity[12] and shorter publication cycles. Further discriminant characteristics between book publishers on the one side and magazine and newspaper publishers on the other side can be found in the depth of the published content and the structure of the value chains. Newspaper publishers typically cannot spare the time to get to the bottom of a topic, i.e. to present in-depth, exhaustive, and highly specialized issues. Their goal is rather to get to the point of highly current news as quickly as possible and to provide a full coverage of topics which are of public interest[13]. The value chains of these publishing sub-types are also distinctive inasmuch the scope of content production and bundling is concerned. Book publishing companies most frequently edit manuscripts which are handed in from contracted authors. The orginal content is therefore not produced within the confines of the publishing company. It is rather edited, proofread, and sometimes trimmed or extended by a specialized editorial team leading to a limited number of interfaces among editorial units which are responsible for different book genres. This structural feature of book companies usually entails a lower degree of content transactions between editorial units and can be regarded as one reason why book publishing firms tend to be more diversified than magazine and especially newspaper companies.

All of these organizational and content-related differences can be considered a source of variations between publisher sub-types in how content is produced and bundled. An interesting point of analysis of this research study will therefore be to investigate whether the organizational distinctions will also translate into different levels and mechanisms of content distribution and integration.

---

[11] Manuscripts of books are the most frequent types of content in book publishing companies. They most often consist of related, successive chapters, which cannot be separated for the sake of understandability. For marketing pitches, however, excerpts of the book's content are sometimes reutilized in several media channels (e.g. on the publisher's Website or on the back cover of print copies).

[12] Articles in magazines or newspapers are the most widespread content modules in magazine and newspaper publishing companies. They can be characterized as self-contained entities that do not or only slightly refer to other parts of the overall bundle. That is why those content modules can easily be separated and detached from their original context and redeployed in another one.

[13] Exceptions are special interest magazines that can be referred to as a hybrid between books and newspapers. While striving to provide in-depth knowledge of highly specialized topics, it most commonly comprises only loosely coupled articles that could be split up from one another without confusing the readership.

Although the logic of explanatory perspectives on the allocation of media content may apply to different contextual and temporal constellations, the study on hand concentrates on publishing companies in *Germany from a snapshot-like, cross-sectional point of view[14]*. Future replication studies may compare and transfer major research findings to various other contexts. Although examining the degree of content allocation over time (i.e. from a process theoretical point of view) would provide valuable insights into the transition from one to another content allocation scenario, the emphasis of this study lies on the explanation of observable differences in the degree of content allocation at any point in time (Mohr, 1982, p. 54). The content allocation problem should be highlighted from a variance theoretical perspective whose objective is to explain and predict a particular instance of an outcome independently of time (see Figure 2.2-2).

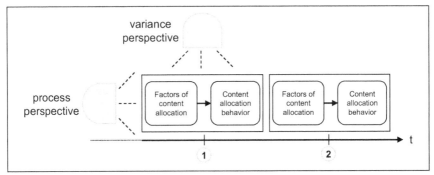

Figure 2.2-2: Variance versus process structure

Accordingly, this research study is not process-, but state-oriented (vgl. Simon, 1969, p. 111-112). Future longitudinal studies, however, should ideally complement these findings shedding further light on how content allocation configurations come about and develop over time.

The variance perspective illustrated above is nothing more than a lifeless body or "skeleton". Thus, theoretical flesh still has to be put on. That is, the particular variables and the logic of their relationships need to be ascertained. This may be viewed as the core of theorizing. Having laid the conceptual foundations of the research problem in this chapter, the development of a theoretical model on the allocation of media content will be taken up next.

---

[14] Asking where and when a theory applies refers to contextual and temporal conditions that "*[...] set the boundaries of generalizability, and as such constitute the range of the theory*" (Whetten, 1989, p. 492).

3 Causal model specification

Basically, a theoretical framework consists of statements about relations between broadly defined constructs within a set of boundary assumptions and constraints (see Figure 1.3-1 and Whetten, 1989, p. 492). Thus, the core of theorizing may be considered as finding answers to the questions of how and why research constructs are interrelated. The objective of building a *theory* is to understand the systematic reasons for a particular occurrence or non-occurrence of a phenomenon (Sutton and Staw, 1995). It *"[...] tries to make sense out of the observable world by ordering the relationships among elements that constitute the theorist's focus of attention in the real world"* (Dubin, 1976, p. 26).

In this chapter, a conceptual framework (i.e. causal model) will be developed on the basis of relevant reference theories that provide either an economic, strategic, or situational explanation for the makeup and existence of specific content allocation scenarios in publishing companies. From a theory-building standpoint, this study adopts the view of theoretical pluralism (Groenewegen/ Vromen, 1996, p. 372; Spinner, 1974, pp. 74ff.), which is based on the proposition that the explanation of organizational phenomena should not be constrained by any single theoretical perspective (Ang/ Cummings, 1997, p. 251). Rather a combination of theories can give a richer understanding of the phenomeon under investigation than any of them does in isolation. Accordingly, the objective of the framework development presented in this study is to provide different explanations as to why content allocation scenarios differ, or to put it more pragmatically, to substantiate and support content allocation decisions.

Before specific theoretical lenses and their conceptual contributions to the allocation phenomenon will be presented in chapter 3.3, the basic question of why particular and not other reference theories are chosen will be addressed. To this end, a general selection process will first be introduced in chapter 3.1 that discloses each selection step that lies ahead. Then, in chapter 3.2, the logic for the selection of specific theoretical lenses will be explicated, before the selection itself will finally be executed.

3.1 Generic selection process of theoretical lenses

During the development of a theoretical framework several selection steps have to be taken into consideration as depicted in Figure 3.1-1.

First, relevant reference theories have to be sifted out from a pool of theories based on a particular logic (filter 1). Then, relevant constructs have to be chosen from the reference theories (filter 2), as not all constructs may theoretically contribute to the research problem. Having selected relevant research constructs from multiple theoretical lenses, the research constructs (i.e. the independent variables) are related to the central research construct (i.e. the dependent variable) of the study resulting in a system of hypotheses.

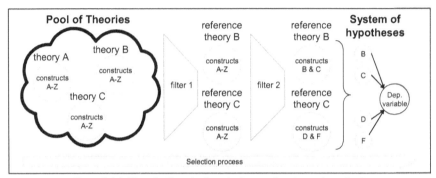

Figure 3.1-1: Steps for the selection of reference theories and constructs

In chapter 3.2, the logic for selecting particular reference theories will be outlined by explicating the criteria that have to be fulfilled by a theory to be included into this analysis and thus be eligible for becoming a reference theory (see filter 1 in Figure 3.1-1). In chapter 3.2.4, a conceptual umbrella will be presented that integrates and comprises the logic of possible eligible reference theories. While introducing and discussing the nuts and bolts of the selected reference theories in chapter 3.3, relevant research constructs will be analyzed and chosen on the basis of their adequacy in explaining variances in the dependent research variable (see filter 2 in Figure 3.1-1).

3.2 Logic and selection of reference theories

Basically, there are two approaches how to limit the range of possible reference theories: Either one inductively examines various theoretical perspectives with respect to their contributions to the content allocation problem ("bottom-up") or adequate reference theories are selected deductively ("top-down"). In this study, a combination of both selection approaches will be taken. First, selection criteria that are derived from the research problem will be presented in chapter 3.2.1. Second, theories that fulfill these criteria will be picked and evaluated in 3.2.2. Theories that do not meet the criteria will be excluded from the analysis. Third, the body of related literature will be reviewed in chapter 3.2.3 benchmarking the chosen reference theories against theories primarily used in the state-of-the-art literature with the aim to add further sources of explanation.

3.2.1 Selection criteria for reference theories

The point of departure for selecting reference theories should be the phenomenon that is sought to be explained (Seth/ Thomas, 1994, p. 187), i.e. the logic for deriving reference theories should stem from characteristics of the research problem itself. As outlined in the problem statement, the objective of this study is to theorize on relevant determinants of allocating media content in publishing companies. In this regard, those theories have to be included into a multi-theoretical framework that makes a significant contribution to the explanation of better deploying resources in a central or in multiple locations. In particular, the selected theories should pose some kind of rationality that may serve as evaluative criteria on whether to centralize or decentralize media content, and provide some background information on how the features of these criteria may be affected.

Deriving selection criteria from the research problem at hand, reference theories basically have to provide:

(a) (at least bounded) rationalistic explanations for
(b) the allocation of media content
(c) within the boundaries of publishing companies.

As this study is basically rooted in the paradigm of the reutilization of media content[1] that builds on traditional concepts of industrialization (e.g. automization, systematization and modularization), the focus will be laid on theories that emphasize rationalistic as opposed to irrationalistic efficiency criteria (a). Accordingly, potential reference theories must offer a logic for the allocation of content that follows rational reasoning in the sense that the comparatively superior (i.e. more efficient) allocation option[2] will prevail. Accordingly, theories referring to irrational (e.g. social or political) arguments that rigidly eschew rational views of organizations are not considered in this analysis[3].

Generally speaking, the allocation of media content is an organizational problem, since different structural content arrangements that go along with different production and bundling processes are compared and evaluated. Organizational problems can

---

[1] As mentioned before (see chapter 1.4), the preparatory works of Anding, 2004, Köhler, 2005, and Schulze, 2005 on content reutilization have motivated and influenced this research study to a great extent.

[2] In this study, we follow the definition of MILGROM AND ROBERTS who mean by an *efficient* option a situation for which there is no available alternative that is universally preferred in terms of the goals and preferences of the people involved (Milgrom/ Roberts, 1992, p. 22).

[3] Although irrational theories are left out from the analysis, it does not mean that relaxed behavioral assumptions of (bounded) rational theories (e.g transaction cost or principal-agent theory) are not useful for theorizing about the allocation of content. As long as these assumptions influence a rational efficiency mechanism, they definitely deliver further insights into the allocation process.

typically be subdivided into a coordination and motivation problem (Picot/ Dietl/ Franck, 2002, p. 7f.). While the *coordination* of input factors can be interpreted as the way of efficiently (i.e. rationally) organizing value-added activities, the *motivation* dimension refers to the fact that employers have to construct incentive systems in order to hedge against the risks that employees behave "irrationally" through shirking or cheating. As mentioned before, the allocation of media content should be analyzed from a rational point-of-view, i.e. the *coordination* aspect should primarily be focused. Potential reference theories should therefore be able to theoretically address coordination, i.e. allocation, problems within an organizational context (b).

Last but not least, potential reference theories should regard firms not as black, but as white boxes behaving heterogeneously with respect to their value creation and decision-making. As the research objective of this study is to explain why organizations behave differently with regard to the allocation of media content in publishing companies, reference theories should hold explanatory power with regard to structural phenomena occurring within the boundaries of firms (c).

3.2.2 Selection of reference theories

In this chapter, reference theories are derived from a pool of theories that belong to core and contiguous streams of research in organization and (strategic) management science[4]. Based on the selection criteria above, theoretical paradigms and corresponding sub-theories will briefly be evaluated for their usefulness in contributing to the allocation problem (see Table 3.2.2-1).

Theoretical paradigm	Sub-theories
(1) Neoclassical Economics	
(2) New Institutional Economics:	Transaction cost theory
	Principal-agent theory
	Property rights theory
(3) Strategic Management:	Market-based view
	Resource-based view
(4) Organizational theories:	Behavioral/Power theory
	Contingency theory
	Evolutionary theory

Table 3.2.2-1: Theoretical paradigms and corresponding sub-theories

---

[4] As the research problem at hand can be considered an organizational problem that addresses managerial issues about the allocation of resources, organization and management science represents the most adequate underlying pool of theories (see Figure 1.3-1).

(1) Neoclassical economics:

In neoclassical microeconomics, a firm is basically treated as a production function transferring inputs into outputs in a profit maximizing way (Cournot, 1924; Marshall, 1890). Preferences of customers and the underlying technology are assumed to be constant, i.e. input-output relations are analyzed under ceteris-paribus conditions. All firms potentially have access to the same production techniques without incurring switching or other frictional costs. As firms act as homogeneous entities, heterogeneous behavior – as it is the case in content allocation – cannot be explained by traditional production economics. In contrast to micro economics, the production techniques in this study, i.e., the actual way the content production and supporting allocation processes are performed by a particular organization, are not assumed to be homogeneous across all organizations. The production functions may rather vary independently from size and scope. Therefore, it may be concluded that production costs vary as well and are indeed a crucial factor when it comes to content allocation decisions. This is, however, only if the neoclassical assumption of firms being homogeneous entities is being relaxed. The relaxation of behavioral assumptions is a cornerstone of the New Institutional Economics which will be taken up next.

(2) New Institutional Economics:

New Institutional Economics (NIE) has been developed in response to the restrictive assumptions of neoclassics, in which the heterogeneity between firms – that are treated as a "black box" – is assumed away. Relaxing the strict assumptions about individuals' rationality and behavior posited in Neoclassical Economics, NIE purposefully incorporate into their analysis frictional costs that more realistically represent *"costs of running the economic system"* (Arrow, 1969, p. 48), that is, costs of coordinating and motivating. The focus of NIE rests on the analysis of coordination mechanisms in socio-economical exchange relationships, using transactions, property rights, and principal-agent relationships as central units of analysis (Richter/ Furubotn, 2003, p. 53-55). The three corresponding and most developed strands of NIE are briefly introduced and evaluated next.

In *transaction cost theory* (TCT), firms are viewed as a *governance structure* (Rindfleisch/ Heide, 1997, p. 32) that can take the shape of a market, hierarchical, or any hybrid organizational arrangement in between (Ouchi, 1980, p. 130). Depending on the magnitude of frictional (i.e. transaction) costs that are incurred when performing value-creating activities within the respective governance mode, the organizational structure that causes comparatively lower transaction costs will prevail (Milgrom/ Roberts, 1992, p. 29). According to WILLIAMSON, transaction costs are *"[...] comparative costs of planning, adapting, and monitoring task completion under alternative governance structures"* (Williamson, 1981, p. 552f.). Although the transaction cost approach has traditionally investigated contractual problems at the interface between two independent firms (e.g. make-or-buy[5]), some few articles have fruitfully transferred transaction cost logic to phenomena occuring within the boundaries of firms (vgl. Jost, 2001, pp. 33ff; Windsperger, 2001, pp. 155ff.; Ménard, 1996, pp. 149ff.; Ménard, 1997, pp. 30ff.; Picot, 1991, pp. 336ff.). Applied in this vein, transactions tend to occur in decentralized structures within firms when doing so is most efficient, while they are executed in centralized structures within firms when doing so minimizes the costs of carrying them out. As the transaction cost approach explicitly provides both economic criteria (i.e. transaction and production costs) for comparing different allocation structures within the boundaries of a firm and insights into context factors[6] that impact the magnitude of these criteria (see Figure 3.2.2-1), the theory seems highly relevant for this study.

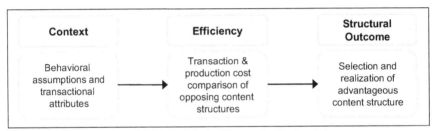

Figure 3.2.2-1: Basic logic of Transaction Cost analysis

In contrast to TCT, the *principal-agent theory* (PAT) focuses the relationship between principals and agents as central unit of analysis (e.g, Jensen/ Meckling, 1976). Accordingly, the main focus of the theory is not to explain why and how to enter into relationships with other stakeholders, e.g., external suppliers, but how to design resulting contractual relationships in an efficient way. The efficiency criteria are called agency costs that emerge when the principal allocates decision rights to the agent. Assuming that the agent has information advantages over the principal, the principal sets incentives in order to assure that the agent behaves in her/his interest (Picot/ Dietl/ Franck, 2002, pp. 86ff.). When calculating the magnitude of these incentives, the anticipated agency costs are considered. They are the sum of monitoring and bonding costs, including issues such as residual loss (Jensen/ Meckling, 1976, p. 308).

In reference to the content allocation problem, the principal may be devised as the management of the publishing company, while editorial units and editors may play the role of agents. For example, one can think of a situation where agents try to store and keep produced content within the boundaries of their editorial units intending to maintain or even extend their power in the company (i.e. they maximize their individ-

---

[5]   Examples for the application of transaction cost theory to make-or-buy problems are Dibbern, 2004, Ang/ Straub, 1998 and Picot/ Maier, 1992.

[6]   The context factors represent behavioral assumptions and transactional attributes in TCT which will be portrayed more thoroughly in chapter 3.3.1.3.

ual utility function). To encounter these tendencies, managers may try to undermine these activities by setting up standards or procedures (i.e. reducing information asymmetries) for storing media content centrally imposing sanctions when being violated. In the context of principal-agent models, that content allocation structure will prevail that minimizes agency costs for monitoring agents and implementing further incentive mechanisms. However, as there is little latitude and reason for agents to behave opportunistically[7] with respect to the storage of media content, the PAT may at best be used complementary to transaction cost theory in order to explain the phenomenon of content allocation.

Property rights theory (PRP) regards firms as a nexus of contracts, treaties, and understandings, in which it is indifferent whether the contracting partners are own employees or external vendors (Alchian/ Demsetz, 1972, p. 779; see also Barzel, 1997, pp. 3-15). The emphasis is laid on the interconnectedness of ownership rights, incentives, and economic behavior (Furubotn/ Pejovich, 1972, p. 1137). As opposed to the TCT and the PAT, PRT explicitly incorporates – besides transaction costs – external effects as efficiency criteria to compare and evaluate different property rights arrangements. A transaction is defined as the transfer of property rights (Picot/ Reichwald/ Wigand, 2003, p. 50), which are the rights of individuals to the use, alteration, income, and transfer of resources.

Tranferring this notion to the research problem at hand, one can think of the recommendation of property rights thinking that firms should deploy media content centrally as the transaction costs for controlling and enforcing associated property rights would be comparatively lower. In this regard, organizations should store media content centrally in order to hedge against the risk to lose property rights by the opportunistic behavior of employees passing content along to third parties. Overall, however, as the PRT rather focuses on the allocation of property rights than on the allocation of media content, and therefore strongly incorporates welfare considerations into the analysis, it mainly adopts a macro-analytical perspective. For that reason, PRT may

---

[7] In NIE literature, the authority system of hierarchies is said to be the more efficient structural mechanism to safeguard against opportunistic behavior than formal authority through market contracts: First, firms have more powerful control and monitoring mechanisms available to detect opportunism and facilitate adaptation. Second, organizations are able to provide rewards that are long term in nature to reduce the payoff of opportunistic behavior. Third, the organizational atmosphere promotes a culture of solidarity and team spirit as well as socialization processes that may create convergent goals between parties and reduce opportunism ex ante (Rindfleisch/ Heide, 1997, p. 32). In summary it may be said that hierarchies (i.e. rule-driven systems) are more transaction cost efficient than markets (i.e. price-driven systems) when opportunistic behavior in asset-specific transactions may potentially be high, as they cope more easily with the reduction of shirking or cheating costs of employees through the imposition of direct or indirect behavioral constraints (e.g. incentive systems).

indirectly provide some instructive suggestions for the allocation of media content[8], but it does not offer an efficiency criterion for why media content should be deployed centrally or decentrally.

(3) Strategic Management:

The *market-based view* (MBV) of strategic management is rooted in the theory of industrial organization that attempts to combine macro- and micro-economic perspectives for the analysis of different industries. Main concern of industrial organization and the embedded MBV is to analyze the structure of industries and its impact on the conduct and finally on the performance of organizations (so-called "structure-conduct-performance-paradigm") (Bain, 1968, p. 329; Porter, 1981, p. 611). Although the originally unilateral influence of industry characteristics on the behavior of organizations was mitigated[9] at later stages (e.g., Philips, 1976), the mainly deterministic character of this perspective on strategic management still hold. As the MBV of strategic management regards individual firms as homogeneous black boxes rather reacting and adapting to given industry characteristics ("outside-in-perspective") than independently leveraging own resources and capabilities, it bears less potential to theorize about the allocation of media content within the boundaries of firms.

While in the MBV, the achievement of competitive advantage of organizations can be attributed to the capability of more efficiently positioning oneself in a competitive environment that is determined by structural forces of the particular industry (e.g., Porter, 1979), the *resource-based view* (RBV) highlights the relevance of an organization's unique resource base (e.g., Wernerfelt, 1984). In contrast to MBV, *"it is the heterogeneity, and not the homogeneity, of the productive services available or potentially available from its resources that gives each firm its unique character"* (Penrose, 1959, p. 75) and the potential for gaining competitive advantage. In the context of RBV, resources are material or immaterial (intangible) input factors, while capabilities or competencies represent functional techniques and mechanisms that integrate, allocate, and deploy resources within organizational processes (Amit/ Schoemaker, 1993, p. 35). Applying the concepts to our study, the RBV provides efficiency criteria that do not focus cost aspects as the TCT does, however, it rather stresses strategic and operational contributions to competitive advantage, i.e. above-normal rents. Furthermore, the RBV lends itself to provide relevant terminology and insights for the content allocation problem. Not only can content be interpreted as a unique resource

---

[8] One possible supportive argument would be to interprete the allocation of content as usage rights with associated positive and negative external effects. On the one hand, the centralization of content would entail positive external effects, because the usage rights of each editorial unit would be extended to a greater content base (the social value of content for the whole publishing firm would outweigh the private value for the editorial units). On the other hand, the negative external effects of content centralization may occur through increased interdependencies between editorial units that would potentially hamper the efficient coordination of production and bundling processes.

[9] In the modified structure-conduct-performance-paradigm, at least mid- and long-term repercussions from market conduct and performance are taken into consideration.

for media companies, but the allocation of content can also be taken as a unique capability (i.e., as a source for competitive advantage) that differentiates organizations
from one another on a particluar market (Powell, 1992, p. 119). How and why organizations differ can be analyzed with a set of resource characteristics that come along
with the rich RBV literature. Last but not least, the RBV starts its analysis within the
boundaries of a firm, explicitly taking an "inside-out perspective" on strategic management. Altogether, the RBV seems to be a relevant approach to add further explanations for why content is better deployed centrally or decentrally (see Figure
3.2.2-2).

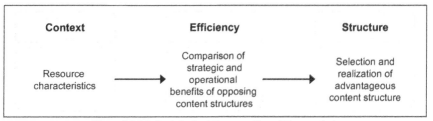

Figure 3.2.2-2: Basic logic of Resource-Based View analysis

(4) Organizational theories:

Organizational theories pursue to explain the emergence, existence, and the func-
tioning of organizations (Kieser, 2001, p. 1). As organizations are highly complex social entities that are confronted with diverse problems within and at the boundaries of
organizations, it is nearly impossible to integrate the various interesting objects of
analysis under one overall conceptual umbrella (i.e. an organizational supertheory).
That is why different and manifold organization theories have emerged to explain
organizations from different theoretical angles[10]. In the following, three organization
theories that had the greatest impact in organization research and are also the most
relevant ones for this study will be presented[11].

Behaviorism[12] in its original form is primarily based on the works from SIMON (Simon,
1957) and CYERT AND MARCH (Cyert/ March, 1963). Its main focus is to explain
decision making processes within organizations. In contrast to neoclassics and industrial organizations, SIMON holds that a firm's decision makers are "boundedly

---

[10] Seminal works in the methodological and ontological comparison of different organization theories
were written by Morgan, 1980 and Burrell/ Morgan, 1979.

[11] Sub-theories of NIE, in particular the TCT, are frequently interpreted within the scope of organization theories as well (e.g., Picot, 1992). For the purpose of this study, though, an analytical separation between theories that provide economic, strategic, and residual efficiency criteria was performed to clearly distinguish between different explanatory sources of content allocation.

[12] The basic ideas in behavioral organization theories stem from the learning approach to psychology
which states that the observation of behavior is the best way of investigating psychological and
mental processes (e.g. Watson, 1913; Skinner, 1938).

rational", that is, they are "intendedly rational but only limited so" (Simon, 1965, p. XXIV). Accordingly, a decision maker may not be a "maximizing" but a "satisficing animal" (Simon, 1959, p. 277). The firm is treated as a political coalition that consists of a sum of individual decision makers that all have their own objectives and expectations (Cyert/ March, 1963, pp. 19-21). The theory has been applied to analyze decision processes in depth. As a theoretical strand within behavioral research in organizations, *Power Theory* explicitly focuses on the role of power and politics in organizational decision making. Power can be defined as a party's potential to influence the behavior of another party in certain situations, whereas politics is the manner in which power is exercised (Pfeffer, 1981, p. 7; Tushman, 1977, p. 207). The motives for political processes in organizations are manifold: the fear of losing one's face, the striving for prestige or predominance is engendered by the existence of divergent interests and a scarcity of resources (Morgan, 1986, p. 148; see also Pettigrew, 1973). Although Power Theory contributes to the explanation of decision-making *processes* within organizations by analyzing the interests, behavioral motives, and power interdependencies of different parties (Abell, 1975, pp. 10-37), it does not provide any concrete criteria that may be used to compare alternative content allocation *states*. It is noteworthy, however, that it may provide valuable insights into the *process* of content allocation (see the process structure in Figure 2.2-2), as editorial units are potentially reluctant to share content with others trying to cement their own power and political clout in the publishing company. However, the theory does not offer a consistent *rational* logic for decision-making in organizations and thus does not provide a rationale for why media content is allocated centrally or decentrally. As little prior empirical research about the impact of poltical or power factors on the allocation of IT resources has been conducted[13] and preliminary pretests to this study have shown that an inter-departmental tug-of-war for media content apparently does not play a significant role[14], an analysis of the research questions from a power perspective will be omitted.

Classical *contingency research* (CT) has examined the question why organizations design their structures as they do (e.g., Burns/ Stalker, 1961; Woodward, 1965; Lawrence/ Lorsch, 1967). Contingency research projects were in search of organizational states or conditions, so-called situational or contingency factors, that are associated with the use of certain design parameters of organizations (Mintzberg, 1979, pp. 215ff.). Comparative studies across organizations have shown that much of the variation in overall organizational structure is explained by organizational context and domain (Van de Ven/ Ferry, 1980, p. 88). Central to structural contingency theory is the proposition that the structure and process of an organization must fit its context

---

[13] The conceptual papers of Bloomfield/ Coombs, 1992 and Markus/ Pfeffer, 1983 point to this lack of empirical investigations.

[14] The problem of receiving socially desirable answers from interview partners to the question of whether turf battles have an impact on the current content allocation may also be an aspect potentially distorting real phenomena.

(i.e. characteristics of the organization's culture, environment, technology, size, or task), if it is to survive or to perform efficiently (Drazin/ Van de Ven, 1985, p. 515). Consequently, the extent of congruence between context and structure provides a rationale for a proper design of structural relationships. Since CT is primarily concerned with the investigation of structural alignment problems inside of organizations, it provides an adequate analytical framework for the allocation of content.

Although the analysis of the fit between context and structure is most relevant and therefore accepted as reference theory, the investigation of the performance effects of the resulting fit would be beyond the scope of this study. Therefore, the contingency theory is better treated as a congruence theory[15] (Drazin/ Van de Ven, 1985, p. 516) in this study omitting the link between the context-structure-fit and efficiency (see Figure 3.2.2-3[16]).

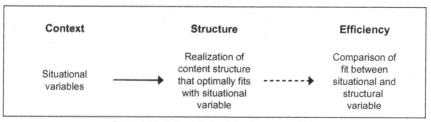

Figure 3.2.2-3: Basic logic of Contingency analysis

Evolutionary theories (ET) are based on the biological theorem of natural selection where a firm is conceptualized as a pool of routines, behavioral programs, and problem-solving capabilities. Depending on the respective maturity phase in the organizational lifecycle, firms develop specific characteristics with regard to their structure, leadership style, and administrative systems (Daft, 1989, pp. 188). Accordingly, each firm is subject to the stages of variation, selection, and retention (McKelvey/ Aldrich, 1983, p. 114). While in the variation phase, organizations adopt specific routines, processes, and structures that can be developed intentionally, unconsciously or even totally spontaneously, the environment of the organizations decides upon which organization offers sustainable combinations of variations in the selection phase. Those variations which turn out to be sustainable will finally be retained by the organization. Since all firms go through different learning processes, they are able to develop distinctive capabilities and identities. This view is fundamentally different from neoclassics and industrial organization economics, where the firm is merely treated as a homogeneous entity without a past (Knudsen, 1995, p. 180). However, ET is also in contradiction to institutional economics, as it rigorously denies that se-

---

[15] The difference between contingency and congruence theory will be more thoroughly elaborated in chapter 3.3.3.1 when presenting the logic of contingency-based thinking.
[16] The basic pattern of contingency research in MIS research is adopted from Weill/ Olson, 1989, p. 63.

lection processes of organizations are rational or at least boundedly rational, and that they result in efficient solutions. Accordingly, for advocates of ET, intentional interventions of organizational designers are all but possible variations. Since the natural selection processes and not organizational designers decide upon the relevance and survivability of these organizational variations, ET does not provide any rationale for why and how a firm should centralize or decentralize media content[17]. For that reason, it will not be considered in further steps of theory building.

Having selected the three most relevant reference theories out of a pool of theories, the related work is analyzed for formerly applied reference theories.

3.2.3 Applied reference theories in the state-of-the-art literature

In order to reflect upon the deductive selection process in chapter 3.2.2, the state-of-the-art literature was analyzed for pre-existing reference theories applied in the context of IT-related allocation problems (see Table 3.2.3-1). In total, 40 research papers published in major IS and management journals as well as in international conference proceedings were reviewed and assigned to the following main categories of reference theories: (I) economic, (II) strategic, and (III) organizational (contingency-based) reference theories[18] (see Appendix A for the detailed synopsis). Additionally, a residual category was introduced to capture those papers that did neither implicitly nor explicitly refer to a theory[19]: (IV) Non.

Reference Theories			
(I) Economic	(II) Strategic	(III) Contingency-based	(IV) Non
4	6	26	11

Table 3.2.3-1: Reference theories applied in state-of-the-art literature

---

[17] However, ET may lend itself as an explanatory complement to the concept of technological and cultural path dependencies within organizations, as it stresses the importance of firm-specific developments in the past that may constrain the behavior of firms in the present or future. As path dependencies are subsumed under the contingency theory in this study, ET won't be included in this analysis though.

[18] This structuring approach stems from Dibbern, 2004 who in turn adopted the Cheon/ Grover/ Teng, 1995 approach. Papers with technical arguments in the content allocation decision were assigned to the organizational category, since the variable "Technology" represents a major situational variable in contingency research (e.g., Hickson/ Pugh/ Pheysey, 1969; Lucas/ Baroudi, 1994).

[19] The re-analysis of state-of-the-art literature in the field of IT-related resource allocation could identify only few studies (e.g. Bloomfield/ Coombs, 1992) investigating the effects of power on the allocation of data. Furthermore, when power constructs were considered, no study could really determine whether centralized departments tended to resist decentralization tendencies in order to retain a high degree of power (e.g. Olson/ Chervany, 1980, p. 65). This supports the view advocated in this study to shed 'selected' rays of light on the allocation problem from a rationalistic perspective.

As can be inferred from Table 3.2.3-1, the number of papers using one or more reference theories (29 papers) exceeds the number of papers without a well-defined theoretical foundation (11 papers).

Altogether, 4 papers could be identified drawing on economic reference theories and 6 papers referred to strategic approaches to compare different allocation scenarios. However, the prevalent theory referred to in former studies on the allocation of IT-related resources (26 papers) is the contingency theory that functions as a theoretical foundation for studies relating contingency variables with structural variables.

Although the TCT and RBV have not been applied explicitly to investigate IT-related resource allocation problems, economic and strategic arguments were raised to comparatively evaluate centralized and decentralized allocation scenarios. With respect to cost aspects, for instance, production cost differences between centralized and decentralized data storage options were evaluated (Nault, 1998; Gurbaxani/ Whang, 1991). VON SIMSON, in turn, juxtaposed the economic advantages and disadvantages of organizing the IS function centrally or decentrally, reconciling both allocation modes by suggesting a hybrid solution that would offer both efficacy and local responsiveness (von Simson, 1990, p. 160). Exploring the relationship between competitive strategy and IS structure, TAVAKOLIAN used the MILES AND SNOW typology to investigate contingency-like hypotheses (Tavakolian, 1989; Miles/ Snow, 1978). Another contingency study, carried out by SAMBAMURTHY AND ZMUD, investigated the relationship between economies of scope – namely the diversification mode, diversification breadth, and the exploitation strategy for scope economies – and the locus of authority of a firm's IT decision making (Sambamurthy/ Zmud, 1999). Last but not least, several other studies evaluated the association between organizational (e.g. Fiedler/ Grover, 1996; Leifer, 1988) as well as technological variables (e.g. Ahituv/ Neumann/ Zviran, 1989) with IT-related structural constructs drawing on contingency-like approaches.

Summarizing, the reference theories selected in chapter 3.2.2 seem to represent adequate and relevant approaches to this study. While the CT is a theoretically well-grounded organizational framework to analyze allocation problems, TCT and RBV rather represent extensions to pre-existing economic and strategic reasoning that nevertheless may deliver some new insights into the allocation of media content. Although a brief outline of the state-of-the-art in the allocation of IT-related resources has already been given above, a more profound analysis will follow when elaborating on each selected reference theory.

In the course of selecting the foregoing theories, the basic reasoning of TCT, RBV, and CT stood out in their appropriateness and relevance to explain the allocation of media content. Accordingly, as the logic of comparing different structural arrangements turned out to be a promising approach to grasp content allocation problems, its abstraction to a more universally applicable level appears to be fruitful for the comprehension of the ensuing theory development.

3.2.4 Framework of comparative institutional performance

In the process of analyzing different theories, three reference theories stood out in their appropriateness and relevance concerning the research problem at hand. Studying more thoroughly the basic logic of these reference theories (see Figures 3.2.3-1 to 3.2.3-3), the framework of "Comparative Institutional Performance" (CIP) emerged as a promising umbrella that spans the logic of all of the reference theories identified in the previous selection process. While the TCT compares different alloca-tion arrangements on the basis of transaction and production costs, the RBV and CT lend themselves as well to evaluate opposing allocation scenarios by comparing stra-tegic and operational benefits as well as the magnitude of fit.

Such an umbrella framework can be called 'comparative institutional performance' insofar, as it compares performance[20] or efficiency criteria that each potential struc-tural arrangement would experience in organizing the in-house allocation of content (Hennart, 1994, pp. 194ff.). As the sole investigation of the relationship between evaluative criteria and the degree of content allocation would have a lacking in ex-planatory substance, it is also of importance to know under which circumstances con-tent is better deployed centrally than decentrally and vice versa. That is, how the comparative performance variables are affected by influencing the determinant fac-tors. Those independent variables are most often provided within the respective theo-retical framework giving insights into the contingencies of the dependent variable.

The basic structure of the CIP framework to explain heterogeneous behavior in con-tent allocation is illustrated in Figure 3.2.4-1. It will serve as an underlying structural framework to guide theory building.

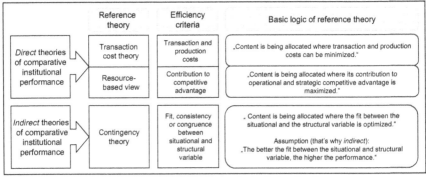

Figure 3.2.4-1: Framework of comparative institutional performance

---

[20] Although performance is not used as a dependent variable in this study, it represents the central evaluative criterion in the form of comparative cost, benefit, and alignment advantages of alternative content allocation modes. Empirically speaking, performance plays the role of an intermediating variable.

While the TCT and RBV compare different allocation arrangements on the basis of costs and benefits, contingency theory investigates optimal allocation constellations by analyzing the extent of fit between situational variables and a structural variable (in this case the content allocation structure). Accordingly, the TCT and RBV can be subsumed under the framework of CIP as *direct* theories, whereas the CT represents an *indirect* theory of the framework of CIP (see Figure 3.2.4-1), since it is implicitly assumed that the optimization of alignment between situational and structural variables produces higher performance (see Figure 3.2.2-3).

As illustrated above, the evaluative performance criteria play the crucial role in ultimately deciding upon whether choosing the centralized or decentralized allocation option. More specifically, it may be said that they represent decision criteria for decision-makers who finally influence the structural arrangements to be formed. Viewed in this vein, if one frames the content allocation problem as a decision process, a decision maker would first formulate the decision problem (1), compare the opposing decision alternatives on the basis of relevant efficiency criteria (2) and then decide in favor of the more efficient decision option (3). Figure 3.2.4-2 illustrates the three steps of decision-making with respect to the allocation of content.

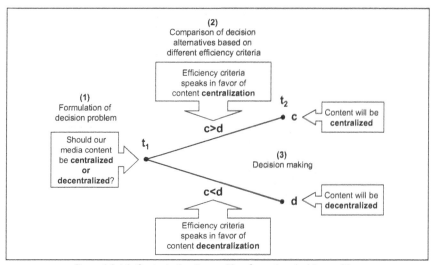

Figure 3.2.4-2: Content allocation problem framed as decision problem

In order to substantiate the CIP framework and its inherent decision logic as illustrated above, it will subsequently be filled with concrete constructs and interconnecting relationships emanating from theoretical lenses which were selected in chapter 3.2.2. That is, after having laid out the underlying logic of selected reference theories, the process of theorizing on content allocation behavior can begin.

3.3 Hypotheses from selected theoretical lenses

In general terms, hypotheses represent assumed cause-and-effect relationships between variables and reflect the chain of causality to shed light on heterogeneous
phenomena from different theoretical perspectives. Moreover, *"[...] they serve as crucial bridges to link the theory with data"* (Sutton/ Staw, 1995, p. 376). That is, they
specify the theoretical relationships that are to be tested empirically at later stages of
the research. From the three salient theoretical lenses selected in previous sections,
hypotheses will be deduced to understand and predict why firms behave differently
with respect to the allocation of media content. The building of hypotheses begins
with TCT (chapter 3.3.1), procedes with RBV (chapter 3.3.2), and concludes with CT
(chapter 3.3.3). Although each theory provides its own set of variables, it may occur
that some variables overlap between theories resulting in supportive or contradictory
hypotheses. These inter-theoretical relationships, i.e. the alignment and interplay of
the selected theoretical perspectives, will be taken up in chapter 3.4. Finally, the hypotheses will be synthesized into a comprehensive whole that serves as a mid-range
theoretical framework about the allocation of media content (chapter 3.5).

3.3.1 A transaction cost perspective on content allocation

In the following chapters, the origins, typical application fields, and the basic logic of
TCT with reference to the content allocation problem will be presented (chapter
3.3.1.1). Then, the efficiency criteria of TCT, namely transaction and production
costs, will be defined in the context of content allocation (chapter 3.3.1.2), as they
have to be clearly separated from each other. Finally, the attributes of transaction
costs will be analyzed for their applicability to the context of content allocation. In this
vein, relevant constructs will be selected (see filter 2 in Figure 3.1-1), defined, and
their impacts on the content allocation decision will be hypothesized (chapter
3.3.1.3). At the end of this chapter, a synopsis of deduced hypotheses will be presented (chapter 3.3.1.4). Figure 3.3.1-1 illustrates the organization of the following
four chapters.

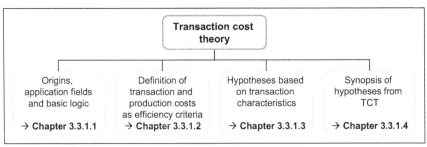

Figure 3.3.1-1: Organization of TCT analysis

3.3.1.1 Origins, application fields, and basic logic of TCT

TCT belongs to the NIE paradigm, which, over time, has supplanted traditional neo-classical economics, as more realistic behavioral assumptions were introduced into the economic analysis[21]. While neoclassical economics has largely ignored the concept of the firm by viewing it strictly as a production function, TCT explicitly treats the firm as a governance structure. One of COASE's initial propositions was that firms and markets are alternative governance structures differing in their transaction costs (Coase, 1937, p. 389) – where by transaction cost ARROW referred to the "*costs of running the system*" (Arrow, 1969, p. 48). Accordingly, the transaction-cost approach is based on the premise that the existence of different organizational forms, whether they are markets, bureaucracies, or clans, is primarily determined by how efficiently each form can mediate exchange transactions between parties (Ouchi, 1980, p. 130). Over the past two decades, WILLIAMSON has added considerable precision to COASE's general argument by identifying the types of exchanges that are more appropriately conducted within firm boundaries than via the market. To evaluate different governance or exchange arrangements, WILLIAMSON introduced characteristics or determinants of cost differences of which asset specificity, frequency, and uncertainty[22] are the most important ones (Williamson, 1975, 1985). While the focus of prior transaction cost analyses primarily has been laid on the comparison of hierarchy, market, and hybrid governance structures (e.g., Ouchi, 1980), an increasing number of research papers have applied the comparative institutional analysis to different intra-firm governance problems[23] (e.g. Ménard, 1996, 1997; Jost, 2001, pp. 301 ff.; Picot, 1991). Instead of the juxtaposition of hierarchical and market-based transactions, intra-firm transactions in centralized and decentralized organizational arrangements (e.g. employment contracts (Vázquez, 2004; Picot/ Wenger, 1988) or firm capital structure (Kochhar, 1996)) are compared and analyzed for a delta in transaction costs. On both accounts, PICOT ET AL. come to the conclusion that TCT represents an appropriate approach "*[...] to investigate and justify observable tendencies of centralization and decentralization*" (Picot/ Reichwald/ Wigand, 2003, p. 260).

Both in intra- and inter-firm transactional relationships, the general logic of transaction cost analysis can be interpreted as a performance comparison of different institutional arrangements, as it entails the comparative examination of the cost effects of

---

[21] The transfer from neoclassical thinking to NIE was a step towards relaxing the stringent assumptions of perfect rationality of individuals, perfect markets, and information symmetry.

[22] WILLIAMSON has called these three factors "attributes" of transactions, as may be seen from the following statement: "*Firms seek to align transactions, which differ in their attributes, with governance structures, which differ in their costs and competencies, in a discriminating (mainly transaction costs economizing) way*" (Williamson, 1991, p. 79).

[23] WILLIAMSON explicitly did not confine transaction cost analysis to inter-firm contractual relationships arguing that "*[...] substantially the same factors that are ultimately responsible for market failures also explain failures of internal organizations*" (Williamson, 1973, p. 316).

transactional attributes on the exchange performance for each governance mode[24]. In order to comprehend the application of TCT-analytical thinking in the context of this study, the comparison of centralized versus decentralized content allocation based on transaction costs can be illustrated mathematically as follows[25]:

$$Ca^* = \begin{cases} Ca_c \Leftrightarrow TAC_c < TAC_d \\ Ca_d \Leftrightarrow TAC_d < TAC_c \end{cases}$$

$$with \quad TAC_c = TAC_c(Z;e_c) = \alpha Z + e_c \quad and$$

$$TAC_d = TAC_d(Z;e_d) = \beta Z + e_d$$

Table 3.3-1: Basic logic of transaction cost comparison

While Ca^* is the final outcome in the process of choosing between two opposing content allocation arrangements (Ca_c stands for a central and Ca_d for a decentralized allocation scenario), TAC_c and TAC_d represent the costs of the transaction within the respective content allocation scenarios and thus form the decisive evaluative criteria. In general, transaction costs can be represented as a linear combination of different attributes of the transaction: Z is a vector of exogenous variables affecting the magnitude of the transaction costs, whereas α and β are coefficients representing the extent of the variables' respective impact. Following the terminology of transaction cost economics, such a vector is constituted of relevant characteristics of the transaction – namely asset specificity, transaction frequency, and uncertainty – explaining transaction cost levels under alternative governance choices. Finally, e_c and e_d are error terms that may reflect either variables that have not been considered or misperceptions (i.e. 'blind spots') on the part of investigators about the true values of TAC_c and TAC_d.

While the primary focus in TCT is usually on transaction costs, WILLIAMSON notes that production costs need to be considered as well. In fact, he argues that it is decisive to consider the sum of production and transaction cost differences between the firm and the market (Williamson, 1981, 1985). For that reason, before deducing hypotheses on content allocation behavior from a TCT perspective and based on the analysis of a transaction's attributes (vector Z), the concepts of transaction and production costs have to be clarified, which are crucial for the comprehension of comparative institutional analysis.

---

[24] Or as WILLIAMSON put it: "*The overall objective of this exercise essentially comes down to this: for each abstract description of a transaction, identify the most economical governance structure – where by governance structure I refer to the institutional framework within which the integrity of a transaction is decided*" (Williamson, 1996, p. 169).

[25] For a more developed formalized presentation of this trade-off see Masten/ Meehan/ Snyder, 1991.

3.3.1.2 Transaction and production costs in the allocation of content

Before specifying the terms transaction cost and production costs in the context of content allocation, it is imperative to clarify the meaning of 'transaction'. A transaction is commonly understood to be an outcome of two social entities in an exchange relationship (Leblebici, 1985, pp. 101f.). On an abstract level, a transaction can be defined as the contractual transfer of property rights that temporally and logically preceeds the exchange of goods or services (Michaelis, 1985, p. 72; Commons, 1931). On a more specific level, assuming that all property rights are already distributed and fixed, a transaction can be conceptualized as the transmission of goods or services via a technically separable interface (Williamson, 1990a, p.1).[26] Accordingly, transactions represent the transition from one to another step of an economic activity chain. In the context of content allocation, a (hierarchical) transaction can be characterized as the organizational linkage of two successive production steps, which in turn represent elements of a content workflow (see Figure 3.3-2 which is based on Hohberger, 2001, p. 28).

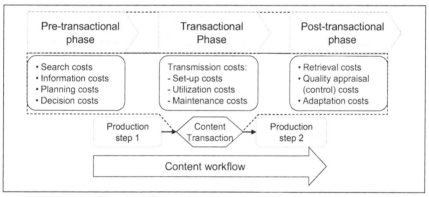

Figure 3.3-2: Transaction costs in the allocation of content

In a narrow sense, the transaction of content can be considered as the mere physical transmission of content between exchange partners[27]. In a broader sense, however, which is also advocated in this study, preparatory or managerial activities (e.g. planning, coordinating, and decision-making) before and finalizing activities (e.g. quality control, format conversion) after the physical content transmission are included into the analysis. In summary it may be said, the problem of content allocation can be

---

[26] OUCHI elaborates on this notion of transaction by specifying transactions as the exchange of goods or services between different departments in companies or between different companies (Ouchi, 1979).

[27] The exchange partners may represent one and the same person, if content is searched in a repository leading to a circular exchange relationship.

conceived as different ways of transacting media content between organizational units in a publishing company, causing varying levels of transaction costs.

The total cost of an economic activity (in this context the production and bundling of media content) can be expressed as the sum of production and transaction costs. According to MILGROM AND ROBERTS, *"[...] the former depend only on the technology and the inputs used and the latter depend only on the way transactions are organized"* (Milgrom/ Roberts, 1992, p. 33). Although this broad definition gives a rough idea about each type of costs, the terms "transaction and production costs" have to be demarcated more clearly from each other for the context of this study. Basically, transaction costs are frictional costs occurring at a technically separable interface between two exchange partners[28]. WILLIAMSON defines transaction costs as *"[...] comparative costs of planning, adapting, and monitoring task completion under alternative governance structures"* (Williamson, 1981, p. 552). Along the three phases of a content transaction (see Figure 3.3-2), these planning, monitoring, and adapting costs can be concretized. While transaction costs arise due to the coordination of content demand and content supply (e.g. research costs for finding and selecting the most adequate content modules or bundles) in the pre-transactional phase, they emerge as costs for the retrieval, adaptation (e.g. conversion), and quality appraisal of content in the post-transactional phase. During the transaction phase itself, transmission costs are incurred in the form of network set-up, utilization, and maintenance costs[29]. As transaction costs are subject to behavioral imperfections of individuals, namely bounded rationality and opportunism, they vary in different structural settings. To put it more concretely, deploying content centrally engenders different behavioral reactions of editors as opposed to the decentralized deployment of content, which in turn leads to different levels of transaction costs. The other way round, it may also be said that transaction costs arise in order to safeguard against the behavioral imperfections of an exchange partner.

By contrast, production (and bundling) costs are independent of specific behavioral assumptions. They include all costs that arise for performing the actual activities necessary to complete the tasks associated with the production and bundling of content. More specifically, they comprise the costs for all input factors that are needed in order to reach a desired output (Albach, 1981, pp. 717ff.). Within the process of producing and bundling media content, labor accounts for the lion's share of input factor costs (Schumann/ Hess, 2005, p. 82 and pp. 137f.). Labor or personnel costs refer to

---

[28] In the context of content allocation, theses exchange partners are editors on a micro-level, editorial units on a macro-level.

[29] The explanations of MILGROM AND ROBERTS give further insight into the comprehension of transaction costs in this study: *"The transaction costs of coordination [...] include not only the direct costs of compiling and transmitting information, but also the time costs of delay while the communication is taking place [...]. Because this communication can never be perfect, there are also transaction costs of maladaptation that occurs because decision makers have only insufficient or inaccurate information"* (Milgrom/ Roberts, 1992, p. 29).

the money spent for the combined working hours of all individuals involved in the process of producing and bundling the first copy of content products (Zerdick et al., 2001, pp. 165f.). The actual means of production, e.g. the required hardware and software tools, rather play a subordinate role and thus represent only ancillary costs.

After having defined the different costs of producing and transacting content, the next chapter will first analyze how different allocation modi affect the determinants of transactions. Then, hypotheses will be deduced about how selected determinants of transactions in turn influence comparative transaction and production costs.

3.3.1.3 Deduction of hypotheses based on Transaction Cost Theory

Basically, the comparative institutional analysis in TCT is performed by assessing the sources of transaction costs, i.e. by tracing back the variance in transaction costs to the influencing attributes of transactions[30]. Following this course of action, the relations between characteristics of transactions and transaction costs will be analyzed within the scope of content allocation. Finally, pertinent and insightful associations between attributes of transactions and transaction costs will be proposed as hypotheses.

WILLIAMSON's microanalytical framework basically rests on the interplay between two main assumptions of human behavior (i.e. bounded rationality and opportunism) and three key dimensions of transactions (i.e. asset specificity, frequency and uncertainty) (Williamson, 1973, pp. 317ff.). While the behavioral assumptions are attached to individuals, the key dimensions of transactions are environmental factors that directly influence the extent of transaction costs (see Figure 3.3.1.3-1). Typically, the frequency of a transaction lowers transaction costs due to economies of scale, while the other two parameters have an increasing effect – whereby asset specificity carries most influence (Williamson, 1981, p. 555).

---

[30] WILLIAMSON describes the comparative analytical logic of TCT as follows: "*Transaction cost economics is based on discriminating alignment hypotheses, according to which transactions, which differ in their attributes, are aligned with governance structures, which differ in their cost and competence, so as to effect an economizing result*" (Williamson, 1999, p. 1090).

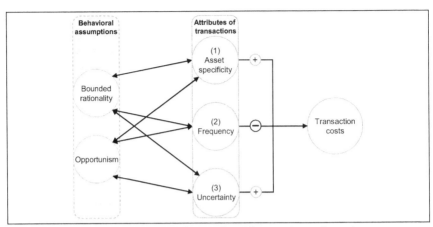

Figure 3.3.1.3-1: Impact of transaction attributes on transaction costs

In the following, the attributes of transactions and their impact on transaction costs will be presented in general. Then, they will be assessed for their adequacy to explain the allocation of content. Behavioral assumptions are discussed in the context of those transactional dimensions which are most obviously affected in the process of content allocation[31].

(1) Asset specificity

An asset is specific to a given exchange relation (or transaction) to the extent that it cannot be redeployed for use in another context without appreciable loss in productive value (Williamson, 1981, p. 555). Accordingly, highly specific assets represent sunk costs outside of the specific exchange relationship where it is deployed. Asset specificity has come to be the central concept in WILLIAMSON's transaction cost theory. It is claimed that transaction-specific assets introduce contractual difficulties, which are the principle reason for replacing market contracts with employment contracts. As a result, the basic explanation for the existence of hierarchy is the presence of a significant economic advantage to the use of specific, rather than generic, assets. WILLIAMSON distinguishes four major types of asset specificity: site specificity, physical asset specificity, human asset specificity, and asset dedication (Williamson, 1989, p. 143)[32]. Parties to a contract may be reluctant to invest in economically desirable specific assets due to concerns about recovering the costs of the nonredeployable asset, either because of demand uncertainty or contract termina-

---

[31] The interaction of behavioral assumptions and transaction dimensions is described in detail in Rindfleisch/ Heide, 1997 and will therefore not be elaborated any further.

[32] As only content specificity as a subform of immaterial asset specificity is taken up in this study, the other types are not further considered.

tion[33]. By removing contractual concerns, vertical integration (or centralization) can realize production efficiency gains.

In the context of producing and bundling content within the boundaries of a publishing company, the asset that is exchanged or deployed in different transactional relationships are content modules or bundles. In this realm, high content specificity means that content is highly adapted to the intended utilization, that is, the topic, structure, and layout are already closely adjusted to the particularities (and peculiarities) of a specific media channel. Accordingly, the value of the content is highest in a specific deployment channel. Hence, the transferability of highly specific content to other specific transactions (i.e. media channels or more broadly, customer needs) is limited, as high switching or adaptation costs (e.g. converting costs) would be incurred (Mahoney/ Pandian, 1992, p. 370; Bamberger/ Wrona, 1995, S. 8). By contrast, low content specificity means that content is not yet prepared for the intended usage purpose. The content – with respect to its topic, structure, and layout – is still independent of the final media channel. That means it is media-neutral. Consequently, the transferability of media-neutral content to several other media-specific transactions is much more flexible, as one would not incur switching costs. The transformation from media-neutral to any media-specific output format is not only efficiently supported by technological standards[34] (Rawolle, 2002, pp. 133ff.; Rawolle/ Hess, 2001, pp. 229ff.), but is also economically beneficial, as the content specification (e.g. the automatic transformation of an XML document to a PDF file) can be performed at almost zero marginal costs (Hess, 2005a, p. 62). Consequently, unspecific content seems to be technically and economically more flexible than specific content.

In contrast to classical transaction cost logic, where it is suggested to integrate highly specific assets into the hierarchy, it can be argued that a publishing firm is better off, if it allocates specific content decentrally. Due to the lower reutilization potential of specific content[35], it causes comparatively lower transaction costs in decentralized as opposed to centralized content allocation modes. If media-specific content is de-

---

[33] According to TCT logic, the reason underlying contract termination in market transactions is that the opportunistic behavior of the transaction partner may outweigh the efficiency advantages of market systems. The more specific the deployed assets in a market transaction, the more the exchange partners are locked into the transaction as switching costs would be very high. For that reason, the hierarchical organization (or vertical integration) of this transaction is preferred, since administrative fiat against opportunistic behavior exist that prevent "[...] self-interest seeking with guile" (Williamson, 1981, p. 554).

[34] The transformation from one to another media-specific output format is much more costly or even impossible, since information gets lost through the adaptation of content to a specific media channel that frequently can't be recuperated at a later stage (e.g. the transformation from a jpeg- to a gif-picture format).

[35] The term specificity is closely associated to the concept of content reutilization. In this study it is assumed that content specificity and the reutilization potential of content are negatively related, i.e., the more content is adapted to specific media channels, the lower is the potential of that content to be repurposed in other media channels.

ployed in a central location, storage, transmission, and coordination costs will be incurred due to the necessary interaction between the central network node (e.g. central IT department) and the corresponding peers (i.e., editorial units). In this regard, the peers (or editorial units) at the outer boundaries of the firm network act as sensor units that identify relevant information from their corresponding markets (e.g. customer preferences, media channel particularities). If there is no need to share media content across peers (i.e. content is highly specific), the company has a comparatively cost advantage if it keeps content nearest to the particular output channel, since additional content transmissions to a central location would entail unnecessary transaction costs in the form of inflexibilities (Dreyer/ Grønhaug, 2004, p. 489; Huber, 1990, p. 59).

On the other hand, unspecific content that is eligible for a high degree of content reutilization and which is based on topic-, structure-, and layout-related characteristics, will be more transaction cost-efficient when deployed centrally. This is mainly due to the consequences of the Baligh-Richartz-Effect, which basically says that the introduction of an intermediating (market) agent between a higher number of (content) demanders and suppliers reduces interface (or coordination) costs[36] (Gümbel, 1985, pp. 110ff.). As unspecific content entails a higher potential for reutilization, the number of interfaces between content demanders and suppliers will generally be at a high level. For that reason, a central storage and access point (i.e. the "intermediary") for unspecific content would comparatively outperform a decentralized deployment with respect to the transaction cost efficiency, since search, retrieval, conversion, and coordination[37] costs could be economized on the part of editors[38]. By the same token, a centrally organized information storage and management system leads to organizational intelligence that is more accurate, comprehensive, timely, and available when dealing with a plethora of cross-links (Huber, 1990, p. 63). In summary, it may be suggested that a central (in contrast to a dispersed) logic is more effective in coordinating a many-to-many-relationship, which can be attributed to the high potential of the multiple application of unspecific content.

---

[36] Centralized content allocation, for instance, simplifies the access to precise pieces of content at any level of granularity and enables editors to analyze and synthesize content within context of other pieces of relevant content more easily (Schek, 2005).

[37] The administration of highly reutilized content in one location reduces coordination expenses, as standardization costs in form of redundancies or inconsistencies between distributed content repositories do not have to be incurred to such an extent (Mertens, et al., 2005, p. 60; Fischer, 1999, p. 194).

[38] Editors researching for archived content modules and bundles are much more effective when looking up content at a centralized access point that provides standardized metadata and GUIs. Even in the case, that content is only logically, but not physically integrated, the organization of decentrally-deployed content would produce higher administration costs (e.g. exchange protocols). Organizing media content decentrally may, for example, cause additional governance structures to be implemented due to the necessity of more vigorous administrative controls (Leblebici, 1985).

Figure 3.3.1.3-2 (on the left) portrays the suggested relation between content specificity and content allocation.

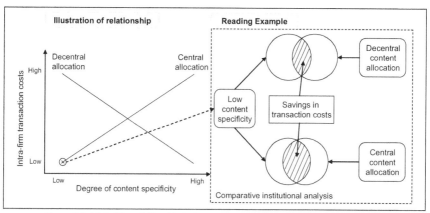

Figure 3.3.1.3-2: The relationship between content specificity and content allocation

The direction of the association between both constructs can be attributed to the comparative efficiency with which alternative generic forms of governance (here the central and decentralized options of content allocation) economize on transaction costs (see Figure 3.3.1.3-2 on the right).

According to WILLIAMSON, asset specificity has a profound impact on both transaction cost differences (ΔTAC) *and* production cost differences (ΔPC) between the firm and the market. Translated into the terminology of this study, this means that content specificity not only affects transaction cost, but also production cost variances between centralized and decentralized content allocation[39]. Analogous to transaction costs, it may be argued that production costs are lower, if unspecific content is deployed centrally as opposed to decentrally, because the input factor costs for the administration of a central repository (e.g. personnel costs, technical infrastructure costs) are comparatively lower than for the administration of a multitude of dispersed content repositories. This is, because economies of scale can be reaped from experience curve effects (Henderson, 1960, p. 3), as the knowledge and technology improvements for handling content search requests can more easily be accumulated and reused[40]. Furthermore, the findings of related research studies suggest that opportunities abound for gaining significant procurement discounts and other conces-

---

[39] In this study, production costs are examined not from a traditional neoclassical or micro-economical perspective (e.g., Marshall, 1890; Commons, 1931; Varian, 2002), but from a comparative institutional perspective. That is, the analytical focus lies on investigating the variance in production costs in dependence of the form of content allocation and not of input-output relations.

[40] Further arguments for the production cost advantage of centrally as opposed to decentrally deployed content are given in Benlian/ Hess, 2004.

sions from hard- and software vendors when content is concentrated at one location instead of being branched out (Taylor/ Tucker, 1989, p. 488).

Following the logic of TCT (see Figure 3.2.2-1), the sum of cost differences (ΔTAC + ΔPC) determines whether content should be allocated centrally or decentrally depending on the respective comparative cost advantage. In summarizing the indirect and direct effects on content allocation, the following hypotheses can be deduced:

Hypothesis 1a:	The more *specific media content* is, the higher the *comparative transaction cost advantage* of decentralizing as opposed to centralizing media content.
Hypothesis 1b:	The more *specific media content* is, the higher the *comparative production cost advantage* of decentralizing as opposed to centralizing media content.
Hypothesis 2a:	The higher the comparative *transaction cost advantage* of centralizing as opposed to decentralizing media content, the more media content will be allocated centrally.
Hypothesis 2b:	The higher the comparative *production cost advantage* of centralizing as opposed to decentralizing media content, the more media content will be allocated centrally.

(2) Transaction Frequency

Theoretical ideas about transaction frequency stems from the classical notion that an increasing number of transactions between two parties entails trust-building and routine so that less costs are incurred in a hierarchical than in a market governance structure[41]. In analogy to this inter-firm perspective, transactions (e.g. content transactions) also occur between organizational units within the boundaries of firms. An increasing number of transactions becomes manifest in how strong organizational units are interdependent from one another, i.e. how strong the degree of interdepartmental integration is. THOMPSON was the first to introduce pooled, sequential, reciprocal, and team-work interdependence as increasing levels of interdependency (Thompson, 1967, pp. 55ff.; see also Van de Ven/ Ferry, 1980, pp. 166ff.). Classical organizational theory argues that the higher the interdependence between organizational units, the higher the necessity to integrate both organizational units due to transaction cost savings (Picot/ Dietl/ Franck, 2002, p. 73), which in turn can be attributed to routinization effects and economies of scale (Ménard, 1997, p. 37). In MIS research, FIEDLER AND GROVER, for example, have empirically validated the proposition that companies with IT structures that supported resource sharing and communication have more integrated organizational structures (Fiedler/ Grover,

---

[41] WILLIAMSON put it as follows: *"The cost of specialised governance structures will be easier to recover for large transactions of a recurring kind"* (Williamson, 1984, p. 206).

1996, p. 29). Building forth on these findings, JAIN ET AL. found that high intersite data dependence goes hand in hand with high concentration of IS resources (Jain et al., 1998, pp. 18f.).

The transaction of media content can be interpreted in the same vein. When the number of transactions between editorial units increases (i.e. the resource interdependence grows), the necessity to centralize or integrate media content increases as well, because significant transaction and production cost savings can be realized. According to this view, coordination is improved by increasing the amount and/or timeliness of information transmitted across editorial units whereby sharing information is supposed to go hand in hand with improved coordination (e.g., Clemons/ Row, 1993, p. 76). While transaction cost savings mainly translate into less coordination costs (e.g. less search and adaptation costs) between parties, production costs in the form of infrastructure and personnel costs are economized due to economies of scale and scope. In summary, content transaction frequency is positively related with the possibility to economize on transaction as well as on production costs, when content is allocated centrally as opposed to decentrally. Analogous to content specificity, content transaction frequency influences the allocation of content indirectly via the cost efficiency criteria (see hypotheses 2a and 2b). Altogether, the relations deduced above may be translated into the following hypotheses:

Hypothesis 1c:	The higher the frequency of content transactions between editorial units, the higher the *comparative transaction cost advantage* of centralizing as opposed to decentralizing media content.
Hypothesis 1d:	The higher the frequency of content transactions between editorial units, the higher the *comparative production cost advantage* of centralizing as opposed to decentralizing media content.

(3) Uncertainty

Uncertainty surrounding transactions primarily results from opportunism and bounded rationality of individual actors. While opportunism describes the human self-interest in taking actions, including cheating, lying, and infringing transactions (Williamson, 1993, p. 458), bounded rationality is the assumption that decision makers have constraints on their cognitive capabilities and limits on their rationality. Although decision makers often intend to act rationally, this intention may be circumscribed by their limited information processing and communication ability (Simon 1957). Thus, humans are inclined to show erroneous and deceiving behavior. Basically, it can be distinguished between a primary (or strategic) and a secondary (non-strategic) kind of uncertainty (Williamson, 1984, p. 62). While primary uncertainty occurs because of misleading and deceptive behavior of the interactors (behavioral uncertainty), secondary uncertainty results from a lack of communication (Koopmans, 1957, p. 147) and unpredictable environmental conditions. As suggested in the state-of-the-art literature, transaction costs rise, if the uncertainty surrounding the transaction increases.

Within the scope of this study, uncertainty plays a crucial role, as behavioral constraints of editors and the predictability of environmental conditions vary with the mode of content allocation. It can be argued that the processing capacities (i.e. the cognitive style) of editors can easily be overloaded, if pieces of media content are spread all over the company with a plethora of diverse metadata and access information (e.g., Taylor, 2004, p. 60)[42]. Moreover, uncertainty rises, if a multitude of interfaces must be taken into account in the production and bundling of media content. System availability or security issues play a crucial role concerning technological uncertainty editors have to cope with. In summary, the level of content allocation (i.e. the degree of content distribution and integration) thus causes different levels of transaction and production costs due to behavioral and technological uncertainty.

However, as uncertainty is also involved in the line of argumentation of the previous two factors[43] and will also be covered by technology-related contingency constructs in ensuing chapters (see the construct IT-imperatives in chapter 3.3.3), uncertainty will be subsumed under hypotheses developed in this research study. Hence, uncertainty will be treated implicitly as a determinant of content allocation, being captured by related variables.

3.3.1.4 Synopsis of hypotheses from Transaction Cost Theory

An overview of the constructs and relationships deduced from transaction cost theory is presented in Figure 3.3.1.4-1.

---

[42] That would mean that the bounded rationality varies in dependence of the type of content allocation.

[43] Content transaction frequency, for instance, partially covers uncertainty, as (behavioral) uncertainty decreases, if the number of content transactions between two transaction partners rises due to learning curve effects.

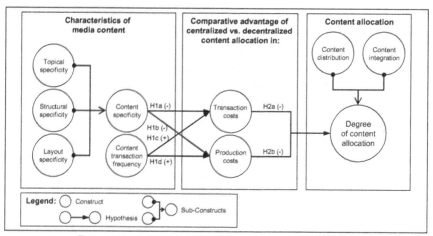

Figure 3.3.1.4-1: Partial causal model from Transaction Cost Theory

It shows that comparative cost advantages of centralizing as opposed to decentralizing media content will lead to a lower level of content allocation, which is formed by a physical (content distribution) and logical (content integration) dimension (see Figure 2.1.2-1). The cost differences in turn are contingent upon an organization's content characteristics, of which content transaction frequency and content specificity could be identified as the most relevant factors. The latter one is conceptualized as comprising three components: topical, structural, and layout specificity.

3.3.2 A resource-based view on the content allocation problem

In focusing merely on cost differences between alternative governance modes, transaction cost theory neglects that organizations can differ on other dimensions than costs. A pure cost comparison of alternative content allocation options implies that content can be allocated with equal benefits and at the same quality, no matter whether it is performed centrally or decentrally. It can be argued that the reasoning of resource-based theory begins where transaction cost theory has its limits and vice-versa. It is the strength of the RBV to include efficiency criteria other than cost aspects into its strategic analysis drawing on unique resources and capabilities of a firm.

Subsequently, the foundations and the basic logic of RBV will be outlined within the scope of the content allocation problem (chapter 3.3.2.1). In chapter 3.3.2.2, the efficiency criteria of the RBV, namely the strategic and operational contributory factors to competitive advantage, are presented and defined for the context of content allocation. Based on content-, market- and process-related characteristics associated with the content resources of publishing companies, hypotheses are deduced in chapter 3.3.2.3. Chapter 3.3.2.4 finally summarizes the hypotheses deduced within the framework of the RBV. The organization of the following chapters is depicted in Figure 3.3.2-1.

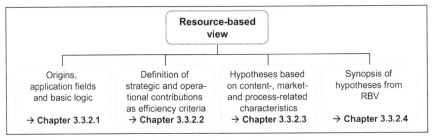

Figure 3.3.2-1: Organization of RBV analysis

3.3.2.1 Origins, application fields, and basic logic of the Resource-Based View

During the last twenty years, scholars have developed a resource-based framework for analyzing business strategy. Drawing heavily on Penrose's seminal work (Penrose, 1959), the RBV suggests that the firm can be conceptualized as a bundle of resources or capabilities that are heterogeneously distributed across firms enabling it to successfully compete against other firms (e.g., Wernerfelt, 1984; Barney, 1991). According to RBV, the sources of a sustained competitive advantage are inevitably linked to an organization's base of resources (e.g., Amit/ Schoemaker, 1993; Grant, 1991). An organization can only differentiate itself from current and potential competitors, if some of its resources are valuable, rare, inimitable, and non-substitutable (i.e., so-called VRIN attributes) resulting in a unique strategic value (e.g., Barney, 2001; Peteraf, 1993; Dierickx/ Cool/ Barney, 1989). These resources can be physical, such as unique equipment or innovations protected by patents, or intangible, such as brand equity, operating routines, or immaterial content. A few researchers have also stressed the distinction between resources and capabilities. For example, Grant states, "*A capability is the capacity for a team of resources to perform some task or activity*" (Grant, 1991, p. 119). Similarly, AMIT AND SCHUMACKER hold, "*Capabilities, by contrast, refer to a firm's capacity to deploy resources, usually in combination, using organizational processes, to effect a desired end*" (Amit/ Schoemaker, 1993, p. 35). Of particular importance is the application-specificity inherent in such resources. The same characteristics that enable a firm to extract a sustainable rent stream from these assets often make it nearly impossible for the firm to "transplant" or utilize them effectively in a new context.[44] Thus, a firm that has developed an advantageous resource position is protected to the extent that its resources are specific to certain applications. At the same time, this specificity

---

[44] There is a close link between specific resources and specific assets, as defined in transaction cost theory (Foss/ Knudsen/ Montgomery, 1995, p. 10).

constrains the firm's ability to transfer these resources to new applications (Montgomery/ Wernerfelt, 1988, pp. 625f.).

The RBV has traditionally been applied in the field of strategic management with research domains ranging from corporate diversification (e.g., Chatterjee/ Wernerfelt, 1991; Bamberger/ Wrona, 1996), human resources (e.g., Snell/ Dean Jr., 1992) to information technology (e.g., Mata/ Fuerst/ Barney, 1995; Powell/ Dent-Micallef, 1997; Byrd, 2001; Wade/ Hulland, 2004). Despite some inconsistent findings, the overall conclusion of nearly four decades of diversification research is that firms whose businesses are resource related achieve superior value, whereas firms whose businesses do not share any resources destroy value (e.g., Rumelt, 1974; Hoskisson/ Hitt, 1990; Ramanujam/ Varadarajan, 1989). With respect to structural (i.e. resource allocation) implications of RBV reasoning, it is also argued that just following a related-diversification strategy is not enough to generate superior performance. A firm must also adopt the appropriate organizational structure with adequate integration and differentiation mechanisms (Markides/ Williamson, 1996, pp. 357ff.; Nayyar/ Kazanjian, 1993, p. 736). This is where dynamic capabilities come into play whose value for competitive advantage lies in the resource (re-)configurations that they create (Eisenhardt/ Martin, 2000, p. 1106).

In the light of the RBV, content can be considered a strategic valuable resource and the allocation of content a capability (Altmeppen, 2000, pp. 47ff.). As the content portfolio of a media firm is an open system with content continuously flowing in and out, the allocation of content is not a static, but a dynamic process that has to be adjusted according to situational, strategic, and economic factors[45]. If content is leveraged efficiently, i.e. if it is provided in a timely manner to wherever it is needed in production and bundling processes, the allocation of content can be used to enhance existing resource configurations in the pursuit of (sustainable) competitive advantage. Rather than TCT that merely focuses on cost efficiency, it recognizes the fact that the resources themselves and the benefits that may result from their deployment may vary in alternative content allocation arrangements (Madhok, 1996, p. 577). Accordingly, what gives resource-based theory a distinctive character, is the consideration of the rent generating potential of specific assets in alternative governance modes. It therefore serves as an appropriate framework for the analysis of resource allocation problems.

In the following, two kinds of potential benefits based on the logic of RBV – the strategic and operational contribution to competitive advantage of allocating media content – will be introduced as efficiency criteria.

---

[45] Thus, content allocation is interpreted as a dynamic capability that exerts an influence on the value of content resources for it may lead to enhanced resource exploitation (Eisenhardt/ Martin, 2000, p. 1107).

3.3.2.2 Strategic and operational contribution to competitive advantage

(1) Strategic contribution:

In the early 1980s, researchers began to conceptually analyze how IT/IS can impact the competitive position of firms. PORTER and MILLAR have been among the first to argue that the deployment of IT would enable firms to both lower costs and enhance differentiation by either serving as performance driver or enabler of new business ventures (Porter/ Millar, 1985, p. 150)[46]. MCFARLAN used PORTER's five competitive forces model to analyze the organizational impact of IS (McFarlan, 1984). More recently, however, researchers tend to emphasize the complementary and supporting role of IS in generating a sustained competitive advantage (e.g., Clemons/ Row, 1991; Henderson/ Venkatraman, 1993). As many business strategies are increasingly dependent on specific underlying IT capabilities, ROSS, for instance, recommends to firms to develop organizational competencies in building a sophisticated IT architecture competency (Ross, 2003, pp. 31ff.). POWELL AND DENT-MICALLEF further suggest that *"[...] if IT per se do not provide distinctive advantages, then firms must use them to leverage or exploit firm specific, intangible resources such as organizational leadership, culture and business processes"* (Powell/ Dent-Micallef, 1997, p. 378). Similarly, CLEMONS comes to the conclusion that the *"[...] benefits resulting from an innovative application of information technology can be more readily defended if the system exploits unique resources of the innovating firm so that competitors do not fully benefit from imitation"* (Clemons/ Row, 1991, p. 289).

Two conclusions can be drawn from these insights. First, publishing companies can hardly create a sustained competitive advantage with the mere application of sophisticated IT/IS for the allocation of content. Second, however, they can (re-) use, (re-) deploy, and manage digital content in production and bundling processes with IT in a manner that the provision of pre-existing content modules and bundles is flexibly adapted to changes in the local and global content demand, organizational structure, and the underlying content portfolio. In this vein, the strategic contribution of IT-based content allocation to competitive advantage primarily consists of sharing media content among editorial units, which enables publishers to enhance existing resource configurations (Eisenhardt/ Martin, 2000, p. 1107). The sharing of content translates into economies of scale and scope, as carry-over effects within the same and spill-over effects between two distinctive media channels (or product lines) can be harnessed (Schulze, 2005, p. 138). If the dynamic capability of rapidly and flexibly ma-

---

[46] According to PORTER, firms employ different strategies in order to expand and defend their rents (or benefits) against current and emerging competitors in the market (Porter, 1985). In general, rents can be defined as the positive difference between the revenue that a firm creates through selling its products and/or services and the costs incurred by generating revenue. Firms that succeed in the market are said to have at least a short-term competitive advantage.

nipulating and redeploying content can be leveraged, the firm performance[47] can in turn be increased.

Within the scope of this study it is therefore argued that content can be efficiently leveraged when adequately being allocated either centrally or decentrally. In other words, the level of strategic contribution to competitive advantage alters between centralized and decentralized allocation scenarios which is, in turn, contigent upon distinguishing features in the capability to allocate resources efficiently. These characteristics may stem from the content portfolio, production processes, and/or market particularities. However, before these discriminating factors are further analyzed, the operational contribution of content allocation to competitive advantage – as another potential efficiency criterion – is specified next.

(2) Operational contribution:

Paradoxically, IS are often treated as strategic systems, although they do not clearly contribute to generate benefits or even a sustained competitive advantage (Byrd, 2001, pp. 41ff.). This phenomenon may partially be attributed to the difficulty or indeed impossibility to prove the direct and indirect impacts of IS to an organization's performance. Basically, the output of IS, the information, serves as an input for various organizational work processes (Leavitt, 1965, p. 1145). However, its impact is mostly invisible in the final products or services. Accordingly, the contribution of IS to sales and cost savings often can only vaguely be estimated. The perceived misfit between the investment into IT and the received benefits has been named the "productivity paradox" (Brynjolfsson, 1993, p. 14), and it has become an enduring challenge for both researchers and practitioners to proof the value created by IS (see e.g. Bharadwaj, 2000). In a recent review of the IT productivity debate, WILLCOCKS AND LESTER conclude that *"[...] an important part, but by no means all, of the uncertainty about the IT payoff relates to weaknesses in measurement and evaluation practice"* (Willcocks/ Lester, 2000, p. 551).

Accordingly, it is not surprising, that opposed to the benefits attained from the application of IS, failures in performing IS functions are more directly felt by IS users and clients, because they immediately affect their day-to-day work processes. Many organizational business processes are highly dependent on the functionality of IS. Consequently, any breakdown, mistakes, or bad performance of an organization's IS can severely threaten business operations. In a recent empirical assessment of the two dimensions of the strategic grid, the strategic importance of an organization's current systems portfolio has implicitly been treated as operational significance (Ragu-Nathan/ Ragu-Nathan/ Tu, 1999, p. 354).

---

[47] In this study, firm performance or rents are neither Ricardian rents nor monopoly rents (Mahoney/ Pandian, 1992, pp. 365ff.). They rather emerge from the fact that resources are deployed in a location where they can efficiently support primary activities in the content workflow. If content is leveraged in their first-best instead of their second-best use, so-called *quasi-rents* are yielded.

In this study it is argued that the allocation of digital content in publishing companies heavily relies on the performance features of IT/IS and therefore affects day-to-day operations. If the IT-based delivery and management of content is not performed properly, e.g., if new content sources are not integrated and provided in time, day-to-day business processes and thus the operational contribution to competitive advantage[48] can suffer severely causing delays and quality losses. By contrast, adequate and flexible content allocation management (e.g. more effective content access mechanisms) can be considered as a mean for process enhancements in the content workflow, as production and bundling steps are coordinated more efficiently among and between editors and editorial units, leading to time and quality improvements.

Overall it can be said that different modes of content allocation engender different levels of operational contribution to competitive advantage. Corresponding to the strategic implications of content allocation presented above, the operational contribution to competitive advantage does not only vary with the degree of content allocation, but is also influenced by the particular feature set of a publishing company's content portfolio, production processes, and market characteristics. These discriminating factors provide additional sources of explanation of why and how content allocation and operational benefits are related.

Having laid down the conceptual foundations to understand the meaning and application of strategic and operational contribution to competitive advantage in the context of content allocation, the next step is to analyze how these efficiency criteria are influenced by the contextual determinants which have already been mentioned above.

3.3.2.3 Deduction of hypotheses based on RBV logic

Within the scope of RBV reasoning, best practices of how to develop and handle resources or capabilities can be derived by analyzing their characteristics. In the context of content allocation, two major strands of the RBV literature seem to be relevant and instructive for theory building. On the one hand, the classical body of RBV literature draws on the VRIN characteristics (see Figure 3.3.2.3-1) of resources for designating companies as competitive advantageous or not (1). On the other hand, corporate diversification research from a RBV angle may deliver complementary insights into the centralization (e.g., sharing and pooling) or decentralization (e.g., separating and specializing) of content resources (2).

---

[48] The construct "operational contribution" will be introduced as to reflect the critical role of the influence of IT-based content allocation for an organization's business operations. In contrast to "strategic contribution", it captures the degree to which an organization's day-to-day business operations critically depend on the performance of IT-based content allocation.

(1) Strategic value of content:

Publishing companies primarily compete against each other by attracting and wooing the reader and advertising market on the basis of unique and salient media content. As a matter of fact, the structure of a content portfolio plays a superior role in differentiating publishers from one another (van Kranenburg, 2005, p. 23; Hess, 2005b, p. 136). Since content is not only input factor as in many other industries (e.g., bank or insurance industry), but also the central output, it represents the linchpin for strategic differentiation. In order to gain and defend a resource superiority over competitors, companies have to develop and manage resources in a way that the latter exibit the VRIN characteristics of strategic value[49], rareness, inimitability, and non-substitutability (Hoopes/ Madsen/ Walker, 2003, p. 890; Amit/ Schoemaker, 1993, p. 38; see Figure 3.3.2.3-1). While the last three characteristics can frequently not be met by content in the media industry, as it can easily be replicated, imitated, and substituted through modern IT/IS[50], the *strategic value* of content can be conceptually linked to the concept of content reutilization providing further insights into the allocation of content. In the media industry, strategic valuable content can be characterized through the potential of redeploying content in multiple utilization windows (Schulze/ Hess/ Eggers, 2004, p. 12).

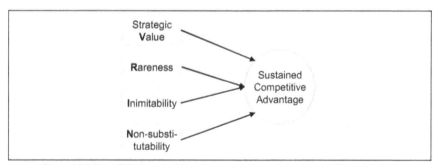

Figure 3.3.2.3-1: VRIN characteristics of resources for sustained competitive advantage

In this regard it may be suggested that the more valuable content is perceived, the higher the potential to repurpose content in other media channels, as more revenue

---

[49] Strategic value or significance of content will broadly be defined as the degree to which media content contributes to generate a sustained competitive advantage. A link to transaction cost theory is given through the linkage of the concepts of strategic value and asset specificity, as (above-normal) rent-generating resources are most often too asset-specific to allow contracting (Silverman, 1999, p. 1109).

[50] Of these four characteristics, only strategic value and inimitability are ultimately important. Rareness is important only if a resource is valuable and exists only if the resource cannot be imitated by competitors (Hoopes/ Madsen/ Walker, 2003, p. 890). As inimitability is not focused in this study as the content allocation decision is related to intra-firm problems, only strategic value strikes to the heart of the content allocation problem within a RBV analysis.

streams can be expected[51]. In order to completely unfold the potential of content re-utilization, it may also be argued that a central organization dominates a decentral organization of content. This is because content reutilization entails high task com-plexity, as different media channels have to be served simultaneously and/or subse-quently. Complexity costs do not only become manifest in search and retrieval costs, but also in the fact that the bundling of content modules is more efficiently supported by a central than by a distributed IS logic[52]. This is, because communication costs between dispersed interfaces outweigh the costs for a central storage and access point. Furthermore, with respect to product innovation potential, new content bundles are more effectively invented when strategic valuable content modules are not dis-seminated throughout the entire company, but kept centrally at one location, because it is less costly and therefore more probable that semantically relevant content mod-ules are adequately combined (Anding/ Hess, 2004, p. 10).

By contrast, media content that is perceived as less strategic bears less potential for redeployment. As there is no need or demand to cross-distribute content to various media channels, the multiple combination and utilization of content seem to be less adequate. Accordingly, content is more effectively stored locally (i.e. decentrally) than centrally, because a central storage and access point to content would entail higher communication costs, as content would have to be transferred to each particular local editorial unit. As the increased costs for installing and maintaining an additional cen-tral network node cannot be recouped by generating cross-media revenues, the de-centralized allocation of content seems to be relatively advantageous.

Overall, as it was argued that the placement of strategic content opens up avenues to strategically contribute to the bottom line of a company through the increase in cross-revenue potentials, it may be suggested that the *strategic contribution*[53] of me-dia content to competitive advantage is higher when allocated centrally than decen-trally and vice versa. The hypothesized relationship between the strategic value of content and the degree of content allocation via the reutilization potential is illustrated in Figure 3.3.2.3-2.

---

[51] The economic logic underlying the concept of content reutilization is either to minimize the unit costs of the first-copy by increasing the overall output or to skim off consumer rents more effectively by exploiting differentiation advantages (Schulze, 2005, p. 22).

[52] Technical aspects such as performance, reliability, and security issues essentially back these in-sights (Tanenbaum/ van Steen, 2002). Further light on the technical issues will be thrown in chapter 4.2.4 when analyzing contingency effects on content allocation behavior

[53] Since *strategic* valuable content is focused as discriminating characteristic in this RBV-related con-text, it is hypothesized that its allocation mainly affects the *strategic* contribution and less the *opera-tional* contribution to competitive advantage.

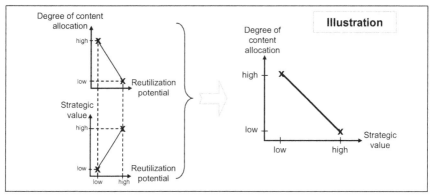

Figure 3.3.2.3-2: Relationship between strategic value of content and content allocation

Based on the foregoing analysis, working hypothesis I and hypothesis 3a can be deduced, referring to the relationships between perceived strategic value and the level of content reutilization as well as between perceived strategic value and the strategic contribution to competitive advantage.

Working Hypothesis I:	The *perceived strategic value* of media content is positively related with the *level of content reutilization.*
Hypothesis 3a:	The higher the *perceived strategic value* of media content is, the higher the level of comparative advantages in the *strategic contribution* of centrally- as opposed to decentrally-deployed media content.

(2) Concepts of relatedness, synergy, and complementarity:

Researchers building on the resource-based view (RBV) of diversification posit that the sharing of strategic resources among business units creates cross-business 'resource based synergies,' which in turn improve the overall value of the corporation (e.g., Farjoun, 1994; Markides/ Williamson, 1994; Robins/ Wiersema, 1995). They examine the link between resource relatedness[54] and firm performance to understand whether the synergies arising from the relatedness of resources make any difference in firm value[55]. Resource sharing indicates that the business units are using common factors of production and achieving economies of scope, which means that their joint

---

[54] Resource relatedness refers to the 'presence of similar activities and shared resources' across business units of a firm and represents a logic by which a firm's different lines of business (or industries) are interconnected (Davis/ Thomas, 1993, p. 1334).

[55] The majority of findings point to the superiority of related as opposed to unrelated diversification (e.g., Nayyar/ Kazanjian, 1993; Grant, 1988). Thus, "[...] more *"related"* diversification supports more extensive exploitation of application-specific resources than does unrelated diversification" (Silverman, 1999, p. 1109, p. 1110).

production costs are less than the sum of their standalone production costs[56]. Hence, the main type of synergy captured by 'resource relatedness' is subadditivity in production costs. However, as the value of a multibusiness firm is a function of both subadditive costs and super-additive values of the underlying resource combinations, the 'resource relatedness' construct does not adequately capture the superadditive value of the resource combinations (Tanriverdi/ Venkatraman, 2005, p. 100). By contrast, the economic theory of complementarities holds the explanatory power to account for the super-additive value of resource combinations. It defines a set of resources as complementary when doing more of any one of them increases the returns to doing more of the others (Milgrom/ Roberts, 1995, p. 181; Goold/ Luchs, 1993, pp. 7ff.). Complementary resources are not identical, but they are interdependent and mutually supportive. The returns obtained from the joint adoption of complementary resources are greater than the sum of returns obtained from the adoption of individual resources in isolation[57] (Milgrom/ Roberts, 1995, p. 184). Thus, the use of a complementary set of related resources across business units can create additional, superadditive value synergies that are not captured by resource relatedness.

In the context of this research study, the resource-based view (RBV) is considered to synthesize both the concept of related diversification and the economic theory of complementarities in order to argue that both the relatedness and the complementarity of resources can confer synergies between editorial units. Yet, despite the multiplicity of approaches to relatedness, the idea that relatedness encompasses several dimensions has not been adequately researched. Thus, the view of relatedness as multidimensional construct calls for an appreciation of combining different bases of relatedness (Farjoun, 1998, p. 611). Theoretically, existing relatedness constructs focus on cross-business synergies arising from the relatedness of certain functional resources: e.g., product relatedness (Rumelt, 1974), technological relatedness (Robins/ Wiersema, 1995; Silverman, 1999), marketing relatedness (Capron/ Hulland, 1999), managerial relatedness (Prahalad/ Bettis, 1986), and strategic relatedness (Tsai, 2004). The manifestations of resource relatedness in multiple functional domains indicate that firms may be seeking to exploit cross-business synergies in multiple functional resources simultaneously. Moreover, studies focusing solely on resource relatedness do not recognize that synergies can also arise from different, but complementary resources (Milgrom/ Roberts, 1995, p. 181), and that such a complementary bundle of resources can also provide unique value to a firm that is difficult to observe and imitate (Harrison et al., 2001, p. 680 ; Porter, 1996, p. 62).

---

[56] When businesses (a) and (b) share some common factors of production, they achieve 'synergies' or 'economies of scope' because their joint production costs are less than the sum of their stand-alone production costs: i.e., Cost (a, b) < Cost (a) + Cost (b) (Teece, 1980, p. 224). The term 'synergy' has also been used synonymously with the term 'economies of scope,' and conceptualized in terms of the sub-additivity of production costs.

[57] Superadditive value synergies between businesses (a) and (b) make their joint value greater than the sum of their standalone values: i.e., Value (a, b) > Value (a) + Value (b) (e.g., Nayyar, 1992, p. 220).

Against this background, the allocation of media content can be interpreted as a combinative capability[56], by which publishing firms synthesize knowledge and content resources across editorial units and generate new applications from those resources. In this regard, not only the characteristicis of the content portfolio (1) of individual editorial units offer a potential source of relatedness, but also their particular knowledge[59] about production processes[60] (2) and market characteristics (3). These specific knowledge bases have been singled out in the literature as particularly fundamental (e.g. Tanriverdi/ Venkatraman, 2005, pp. 101f.). In order to assess their interrelationships more thoroughly, the following working hypothesis may be deduced.

Working Hypothesis II	The higher the content relatedness across editorial units, the higher the market- and production process-relatedness across editorial units.

(1) Content relatedness refers to the degree of similarity of content according to its topic, structure, and layout across editorial units. The *similarity of content topics or genres* depends on possible semantic linkages or interconnections between content modules. As an example, business and technology as two types of genres are generally more correlated than business and sports. Thus, the probability will be higher that possible links between business and technology publications exist than between business and sports publications. Technological representations of semantic links between content modules are so-called ontologies[61] (e.g. Benlian/ Wiedemann/ Hess, 2004, p. 3229) which help instilling meaning into the underlying content structure for automated interpretation. *Structural similarity* between content modules refers to varying levels of structural organization. While a low level of structure goes hand in hand with a low level of systematization and an irregular positioning of content modules in a document, high levels of structure show high regularities in the organization of content modules. For example, recipies or program guides are types of content that are well-structured inherently, as their content modules are aligned to each other in a regular way that can easily be supported by automatizing technologies. Structural metadata is technically implemented through so-called Document Type Definitions (DTDs) or Schemes[62] providing a basic structural framework for a class of content bundles. Last but not least, the relatedness of layout characteristics represents the *similarity of design and visual elements of content*. A high similarity between content layouts is, for instance, manifested in the use of common fonts, colors, and spac-

---

[56] HENDERSON and COCKBURN use the term "architectural competence" to describe these dynamic capabilities (Henderson/ Cockburn, 1994).

[59] The knowledge relatedness of process and market characteristics is defined as the extent to which a publishing firm uses common knowledge resources across its editorial units.

[60] The similarity of tasks and activities and their impacts on transaction costs are further discussed in Picot et al., 2002, p. 237.

[61] Technical implementations of semantic ontologies are mainly based on XML standards. Examples for XML-based ontology standards are TopicMaps, OWL, and RDF.

[62] See for example http://www.w3.org/TR/xmlschema-1/

ing, which in practice are realized in the form of so-called stylesheets (e.g. Cascading Stylesheets for Web documents[63]). To sum up the previous descriptions, it may be argued that the higher the degree of relatedness of content modules across editorial firms, the higher the potential for cross-pollination and cross-reference, which is suggested to be realized more efficiently in centralized content allocation arrangements.

(2) The intra-organizational production processes of a multi-business publishing firm provide opportunities for exploiting similar product knowledge across multiple businesses and creating cross-business synergies (Teece, 1980, p. 226). Internal product knowledge primarily resides in (content) product platforms (e.g., Köhler/ Anding/ Hess, 2003, pp. 305ff.; see also Meyer/ Lehnerd, 1997 and Robertson/ Ulrich, 1998). A product platform is a set of designs, subsystems, interfaces, and components that enables the development of a family of derivative products. Likewise, a content process platform is a set of process technologies used in the production of a family of content products (Köhler, 2005, p. 22). Some companies seek to achieve higher product knowledge synergies by developing modular product architectures, flexible bundling practices, modules, and module libraries that can be exploited in multiple businesses (Meyer/ Lehnerd, 1997, p. 39; Völker/ Voit, 2000, p. 137)[64]. Synergies arising from the exploitation of common product knowledge across multiple businesses confer both efficiency and effectiveness benefits. When the business units share product designs, subsystems, interfaces, components, and content production and bundling processes, the firm can obtain 'asset amortization benefits' from economies of scope (Markides/ Williamson, 1994, p. 156). Reuse of existing product knowledge reduces production and bundling costs, speeds up new product development, and allows a firm to rapidly address new market opportunities (Schilling, 2000, p. 312; Meyer/ Lehnerd, 1997, pp. 209-212). Further, innovations of one business unit may spark ideas for other businesses and lead to asset improvement benefits across the firm (Markides/ Williamson, 1994, p. 156).

(3) Knowledge about the respective market refers to the needs, preferences, and buying behaviors of customers (Markides/ Williamson, 1996, p. 348). Since customer knowledge develops over long periods of time through learning relationships with customers (Woodruff, 1997, pp. 140ff.), it is costly to observe and imitate it. Exchanging knowledge about expressed and latent needs of each other's customers can allow business units of a multibusiness firm to cross-sell their content offerings to each other's customers or to develop new products and services. If the customers exhibit similar needs, preferences, and behaviors across different business units of the firm, the firm can reduce its overall marketing and advertising costs by redeploying not only content, but also its general marketing expertise and brands among those businesses (Capron/ Hulland, 1999, pp. 50f.). By contrast, editorial units with dissimilar

---

[63] See for example http://www.w3.org/Style/CSS/
[64] For an overview of general benefits of product modularity see Gershenson/ Prasad/ Zhang, 2003.

customer needs and behaviors have fewer opportunities to exploit cross-business customer knowledge synergies.

The abovementioned types of relatedness[65] can also be complementary to each other. Hence, their coexistence may create additional, super-additive value synergies that are not captured by any one of them in isolation. Conversely, the absence or weakness of one of them can diminish the value of the others, too. For instance, a multi-business publishing firm has an opportunity to use similar stylesheets, DTDs, and/or text components when customers exhibit similar needs, preferences, and purchasing behaviors across different editorial units. That is, if customer characteristics are similar across editorial units, related content bundles may be leveraged and cross-sold more effectively across product lines. Synergy effects may also arise between production process and content relatedness. The application of similar processes and technologies together with related content modules that are shared across editorial units can not only engender an even greater potential for content reuse and product innovation. It also bears the potential to leverage operational content workflows more efficiently, as so-called media frictions may be reduced due to common or integrated processes and technologies.

In total, if content, production process, and market-related characteristics are similar across different editorial units, the probability is much higher that content is cross-referenced or even exchanged for redeployment. Given this situation, it is argued that the strategic and operational contribution to competitive advantage is comparatively higher when content is shared among editorial units in a central content repository as opposed to multiple decentralized storage points[66]. Conversely, if the relatedness of content, production processes, and market characteristics among editorial units is low or even non-existant, the costs for the establishment and maintenance of a centralized content repository would not be made up by cross-business synergies. Hence, a decentralized content storage solution would be relatively superior in terms of the strategic and operational contribution to competitive advantage.

Altogether, inter-editorial synergies in a publishing company are conceptualized in terms of: (1) synergies arising from the relatedness of content, production process, and market knowledge resources across editorial units respectively; and (2) synergies arising from the use of a complementary set of these related resources across editorial units. Figure 3.3.2.3-3 illustrates the interrelationships discussed before.

---

[65] The relatedness factors applied in this study are slightly modified compared to TANRIVERDI's first order factors that actually refer to product, customer, and managerial knowledge relatedness (Tanriverdi, 2005, pp. 101-103).

[66] Once again, these synergy effects are either due to economies of scope (e.g. the innovation of new content bundles can be produced more easily if stored centrally) or economies of scale (e.g. the first copy of a content module can be used multiple times, so that fixed costs can be covered by an increased output level).

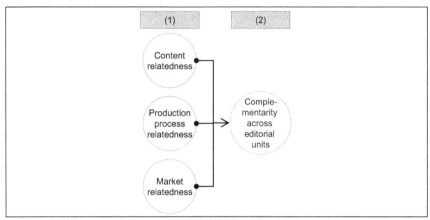

Figure 3.3.2.3-3: Relatedness factors forming the complementarity construct

Based on the theoretical relations described in the preceding chapters, working hypothesis II and hypotheses 3b and 3c can be deduced.

Hypothesis 3b:	The higher the level of related diversification across editorial units as indicated by a combination of content-, production process-, and market-relatedness, the higher the level of comparative advantages in the *strategic contribution* of centrally- as opposed to decentrally-deployed media content.
Hypothesis 3c:	The higher the level of related diversification across editorial units as indicated by a combination of content-, production process-, and market-relatedness, the higher the level of comparative advantages in the *operational contribution* of centrally- as opposed to decentrally-deployed media content.

Finally, to close the gap between the comparative evaluative criteria of strategic and operational advantage and content allocation behavior, hypotheses 4a and 4b are formulated.

Hypothesis 4a:	The higher the level of *strategic contribution* of centrally as opposed to decentrally deployed media content, the more media content will be allocated centrally.
Hypothesis 4b:	The higher the level of *operational contribution* of centrally as opposed to decentrally deployed media content, the more media content will be allocated centrally.

3.3.2.4 Synopsis of hypotheses from RBV

Altogether, the interrelationsips between RBV-motivated constructs and the degree of content allocation is depicted in Figure 3.3.2.4-1.

It shows that the comparative strategic and operational advantages of centralizing as opposed to decentralizing media content will lead to a lower level of content allocation, i.e. to a higher degree of centralization. The variances in the strategic and operational contributory factors in turn hinge upon the characteristics of a publishing company's content-, market- and process-related characteristics, with the interdepartmental complementarity being specified as a second-order construct.

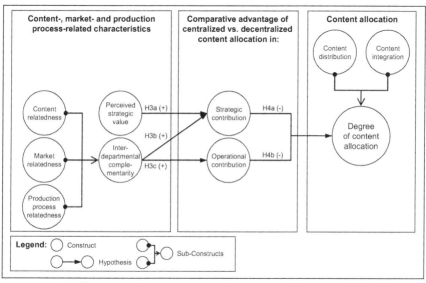

Figure 3.3.2.4-1: Partial causal model from Resource-based View

3.3.3 A contingency approach to content allocation

Subsequently, the last reference theory will be examined for its richness and comprehensiveness in shedding light onto the content allocation problem. First, just like in the context of preceding reference theories, the origins, typical application fields and the basic logic of Contingency Theory (CT) will be introduced (chapter 3.3.3.1). Second, the conceptual building block of CT research, the concept of fit, will be clearly defined for the context of this study (chapter 3.3.3.2), since there are several different notions and conceptualizations of this term in state-of-the-art literature. Third, a pyramid with hierarchical contingency factors will be introduced representing a frame of reference for analyzing multiple contingencies on the degree of content allocation. In this regard, relevant constructs will be chosen (see filter 2 in Figure

3.1-1), defined and their relation to the content allocation decision will be hypothesized (see chapter 3.3.3.3). Finally, a summary of deduced hypotheses will be presented in chapter 3.3.3.4. Figure 3.3.3-1 illustrates the organization of the chapters that follow.

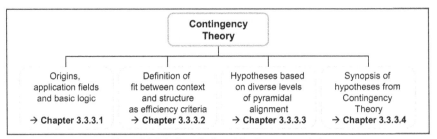

Figure 3.3.3-1: Organization of Contingency analysis

3.3.3.1 Origins, application fields, and basic logic of Contigency Theory

The contingency approach to the study of organizations developed beginning in the 1950's as a response to criticisms that the classical theories (i.e. Scientific Management, the Human Relations and Human Resources movements) advocated "one best way" of organizing and managing. Contingency theories, on the other hand, proposed that the appropriate organizational structure and management style were dependent upon a set of "contingency" factors (Hall, 1962, p. 297). SZILAGYI AND WALLACE appropriately describe, *"The contingency approach attempts to understand the interrelationships within and among organizational subsystems as well as between the organizational system as an entity and its environments. It emphasizes the multivariate nature of organizations and attempts to interpret and understand how they operate under varying conditions [...]"* (Szilagyi/ Wallace, 1980, p. 178).

In a seminal study following CT, BURNS AND STALKER studied the influence of environmental dynamics on organizational integration and differentiation (Burns/ Stalker, 1961). LAWRENCE AND LORSCH extended the works of BURNS AND STALKER by breaking their findings down to an organization's sub-units which were considered to be influenced differently by the dynamics of their particular sub-environments (Lawrence/ Lorsch, 1967). WOODWARD, in turn, studied the influence of technology on organizational structure (Woodward, 1965). Other classic studies include PUGH ET AL. (Pugh/ Hickson, 1969; Pugh/ Hickson/ Hinings, 1969; Pugh et al., 1968) and HAGE AND AIKEN (Hage/ Aiken, 1967; Aiken/ Hage, 1968), who focused on the interrelationships among various aspects of organizational structure. BLAU studied the impact of organizational size on structural centralization, specialization, and formalization (Blau, 1970). HICKSON ET AL. examined subunit power and its impact on organizational structure (Hickson et al., 1971).

Contingency (or configuration) theories have also received considerable attention in MIS research, where the most studied variables have been strategy, structure, size, environment, technology, task, and individual characteristics (Weill/ Olson, 1989, p. 63). The goal of all these studies was to be as descriptive as possible in delineating the relationships among sets of variables.

In general, contingency theorists assert that successful performance is the result of a proper alignment of endogenous design variables (such as organizational or MIS structure) with exogenous context or contingency variables (such as strategy, technology or organizational size)[67]. Accordingly, CT rests upon the assumption that a fit among the patterns of relevant contextual, structural, and strategic factors will yield better performance than when misfits occur (Doty/ Glick, 1993, p.1196). In a normative perspective, the principal research problem becomes one of identifying structural designs which are efficient, effective, and viable under conditions of changing context. Efficiency, effectiveness, and viability thus become the criteria against which different designs are validated (Klaas, 2004, p. 2; see also Burton/ Obel, 2004). Because of its comprehensible logic to bring situational and structural variables into alignment, CT remains the dominant approach to organization design (Lawrence, 1993, pp. 9ff.) and the most widely utilized contemporary theoretical approach to the study of organizations (Scott, 2003, p. 97).

Although the overall goal of CT is to explain context-structure-performance relationships, many structural contingency theories are in fact congruence theories, because they simply hypothesize that organizational context (whether environment, technology, or size) is related to structure (e.g. centralization, formalization, complexity) without examining whether this context-structure relationship affects performance. Classical arguments for omitting the link to performance emanate from natural selection and managerial selection perspectives that have surfaced from evolutionary theories (e.g., Nelson/ Winter, 1982). They provide some justification for viewing fit as a basic assumption underlying congruence propositions between organizational context and structure. In the natural selection argument, fit is the result of an evolutionary process of adaptation that ensures that only the best-performing organizations survive (Hannan/ Freeman, 1989, p. 91). An equilibrium between environment and organization is assumed to exist, at least over long periods of time, and only context-structure relationships need to be examined to assess fit (e.g., Fennell, 1980, pp. 485ff.), because an identity or isomorphic relationship between context and structure

---

[67] In CT terminology, variables such as differentiation and integration are termed contingency factors, or simply contingencies. A "contingent" proposition is one, which hypothesizes a conditional association of two or more independent variables with a dependent outcome (Fry/ Smith, 1987). In the case of LAWRENCE AND LORSCH (Lawrence/ Lorsch, 1967), differentiation, integration, and environmental uncertainty are independent variables influencing economic performance as dependent outcome. In this connection, it is assumed that successful organizations are aligned in a small number of typical patterns.

is presumed to exist for the surviving organizations (DiMaggio/ Powell, 1983, pp. 147ff.).

Following the abovementioned conceptualization of contingency theory, a rather congruence than pure contingency approach is adopted in this study. Since not the performance effects of the alignment between context and content allocation variables are the dependent variable, but the allocation of content itself, only the relationship between context and structure will be investigated (see Figure 3.2.2-3[68]), providing an implicit feedback logic underlying the reason for the association between context and structure (Drazin/ Van de Ven, 1985, p. 516).

The application of the CT approach for the investigation of organizational problems has never been free of criticism. Several authors in organization, management, and MIS research accuse CT research of being too inconsistent and imprecise in the use and measurement of the fit criteria (e.g., Weill/ Olson, 1989; Schoonhoven, 1981; Tosi Jr., 1984). Accordingly, one conclusion that emanated from the discussion about the future of CT research was that researchers should always clearly explicate the meaning of fit in the context of the respective study (e.g., Ensign, 2001; Venkatraman, 1989), which will be taken up next.

3.3.3.2 Definition of 'fit' in Contingency Theory

An extensive body of CT literature suggests that an organization's ability to achieve its goals is a function of the congruence between various organizational components. If the components "fit well", then the organization functions effectively, if they "fit poorly", it does not (Fry/ Smith, 1987, pp. 120ff.). Different notions about the meaning of fit[69] have been explored in the past, resulting in controversial discussions about the vagueness of the concept.

An intuitive access to the concept of fit is provided by NADLER AND TUSHMAN who argue that *"the congruence between two components is the degree to which the needs, demands, goals, objectives, and / or structure of one component are consistent with the needs, demands, goals, objectives and/or structure of another component"* (Nadler/ Tushman, 1980, p. 40). Their congruence model emphasizes the critical system characteristic of interdependence, and the importance of congruence of

---

[68] The basic pattern of the contingency approach in MIS research is adopted from Weill/ Olson, 1989, p. 63.

[69] For fit "congruency, consistency, and alignment" are synonyms, for misfit "incongruency, inconsistency, and misalignment".

the various system components as a necessary condition for organizational effectiveness[70] (Fry/ Smith, 1987, p. 121).

In their seminal paper, DRAZIN AND VAN DE VEN are the first to provide a clear classification scheme for alternative forms of fit in contingency theory (Drazin/ Van de Ven, 1985). They basically distinguish between the selection, interaction, and systems approaches to fit. While the goal in the selection approach is to investigate and understand the congruence between context and structure[71], the focus in the interaction approach is rather on explaining the variations in organizational performance from the interaction of organizational structure and context[72]. Finally, the systems approach to contingency research asserts that the understanding of context-structure performance relationships can only advance by addressing simultaneously the contingencies, structural alternatives, and performance criteria that must be considered holistically to understand organizational design. Unlike the selection and interaction approaches to fit, the systems approach thus emphasizes the need to adopt multivariate analysis to examine patterns of consistency among dimensions of organizational context, structure, and performance (e.g., Miller, 1981). Fit is therefore conceptualized as the internal consistency of multiple contingencies and multiple structural characteristics, which in turn affects performance characteristics[73].

In the context of this study, the concept of fit is treated as efficiency criteria. Although the performance effects of context-structure alignment are not explicitly investigated (see Figure 3.2.2-3), it is (implicitly) assumed that an increased consistency between context and structural variables will produce increased performance. That is, the more contextual and structural variables co-align, the higher the performance effects will be. As it is assumed that a decision maker (e.g. IT architect) will adhere to this rational causal agency (see Figure 3.2.4-2), he will manipulate the content allocation structure accordingly. Hence, the congruence perspective adopted in this study is best compatible with a *selection view of fit*, where fit is reflected by the interrelationship (or correlation) between organizational context factors and a structural variable, i.e. the content allocation structure (see Figure 3.3.3.2-1).

---

[70] In some instances, contingency theorists provide a priori theoretical reasons why such alignments should exist, including natural selection (i.e. the elimination of poorly aligned organizations) and organizational inertia.

[71] The concept of 'fit' is conceptualized as assumed premise underlying a congruence between context and structure, which is statistically tested with correlation or regression coefficients of context on structure (Drazin/ Van de Ven, 1985, p. 516).

[72] Here, fit is defined as the interaction between pairs of organizational context-structure factors. The interaction between these factors in turn affects performance. Statistically, the correlation between context-structure interaction terms and performance measures are examined in MANOVA or regression equations (Drazin/ Van de Ven, 1985, p. 517).

[73] Statistically, deviations from ideal-type designs are examined. The source of these so-called misfits originates in conflicting contingencies.

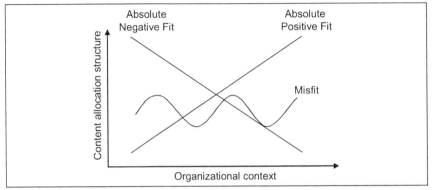

Figure 3.3.3.2-1: Fit as correlation between organizational context and structure

Having explicated the meaning of fit for the purpose of this study, potential organizational context factors will be analyzed in the following section referring to their impact on the content allocation structure.

3.3.3.3 Hypotheses from multiple levels of alignment

While early contingency research produced a large number of bivariate relationships, involving single contingency, later developments sought contributions through the integration of early research into more parsimonious models. In particular, it was recommended for future developments of the selection approach to fit to include multiple levels of organizational analysis (Drazin/ Van de Ven, 1985, p. 517). One approach relied on multicontigency models (e.g., Gresov, 1989; Burton/ Obel, 2004). MINTZBERG, for instance, introduced a more integrated view of contingency notions and proposed a multiple contingency model, which suggested that size, technology, environment, and management would affect the choice of an appropriate structure for the firm (Mintzberg, 1979, pp. 296-297).

In MIS research, several contingency antecedents were included into the analysis. In particular, strategy, structure, size, environment, technology, task, and individual characteristics are the most studied variables (Weill/ Olson, 1989, p. 63). The dependent variables cover a broad, but quite fragmented area of research, ranging from micro-analytical variables such as IS adoption and satisfaction to more macro-analytical factors such as IS structure, performance, and effectiveness (Larsen, 2003). Corresponding to organizational CT research, MIS research tends more and more to apply an integrated CT view on the investigation of structural IT problems (e.g. Sambamurthy/ Zmud, 1999, p. 261).

As the main objective in this study is to trace variations in the allocation of content to selected explanatory factors, it is most reasonable to pursue the trend in MIS research identified above. The assumptions underlying CT research studies that examined the singular effects of contingency factors are as though the investigated contingencies act in isolation in influencing the structural dependent variable. However, in reality, organizations are subject to the pulls and pressures of multiple, rather than singular, contingency forces. To investigate the relative importance of multiple CT factors is therefore a most crucial task in the advancement of theory building and in the exchange processes between academia and practice.

During the pre-test stages of this research study, several contingency factors were analyzed for their appropriateness to the research problem, of which six crystallized as most relevant and promising: Strategy, organizational structure, size, IT governance, IT-related path dependencies, and infrastructural IT-imperatives. Serving as an integrating frame of reference, a slightly adapted ISA-model of KRCMAR[74] (Krcmar, 1990) helped to impose a structure on strategy-, organization-, and IT-related contingencies (see Figure 3.3.3.3-1).

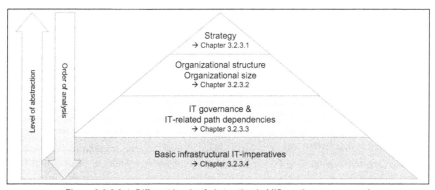

Figure 3.3.3.3-1: Different levels of abstraction in MIS contingency research

The topmost layer of the ISA-model is represented by the business strategy, which should penetrate and permeate every aspect of an organization. Ideally, it should provide directions for organization-building ("structure follows strategy"), which becomes concrete in organizational structures, processes and size (layer 2). Human or artificial resources (i.e. information systems) then fill out these structures and realize value creating processes (layer 3), which are in turn supported by a basic communication and information infrastructure (layer 4). If an organization is conceived in this vein, contingency variables become increasingly abstract from the bottom to the top, influencing the content allocation structure more and more indirectly. Additionally, it may be said that content allocation as structural variable is affected by numerous

---

[74] As a guideline for the management and development of information systems and architectures, the ISA-model boils down the different contingencies, an organization has to consider, to conceptually separated layers (Krcmar, 2003, p. 42). Analogous conceptual models are for example the architectural framework of ZACHMAN (Zachman, 1997) or, on a more abtract level, the concepts of Information Systems Management of St. Gallen (Österle/ Brenner/ Hilbers, 1992).

variables lying on upper and lower layers, because it is located in the midst and at the crossroads of multiple contingencies between strategic and technological variables. More specifically, if one has to decide upon the allocation of content, the organisation's strategic objectives, organizational requirements, as well as technological possibilities have to be taken into account.

The ISA-model not only functions as theoretical fabric for CT-related causal relationships, though, but also acts as a 'structural scaffolding' for further investigations of respective contingency variables identified in previous field research. Subsequently, CT-related hypotheses[75] are explored in the context of content allocation, following a top-down structure as indicated in Figure 3.3.3.3-1 ("order of analysis").

(1) Strategy:

The topic of business strategy and its relationship to MIS has become an area of considerable research interest. The majority of work analyzing the relationship between strategy and MIS has been in the form of definition of conceptual frameworks or case studies (e.g., Ives/ Learmonth, 1984; Henderson/ Venkatraman, 1992[76]). An example of an empirical study using strategy as a contingency variable is VITALE ET AL., who examined information assets and opportunities and how they were incorporated into a firm's strategic planning process (Vitale/ Ives/ Beath, 1986). A prominent paper about the linking of competitive strategy and IT structure was put forth by TAVAKOLIAN (Tavakolian, 1989) who adopted the MILES AND SNOW typology of defenders, prospectors, analyzers, and reactors as basic strategic types of organizations (Miles/ Snow, 1978). He empirically found out that an organization's IT structure (i.e. the degree of allocating IT resources) is significantly related to business strategies. Different IT structures seem to fit[77] different competitive strategies in current practice. Other studies (e.g., Miller, 1988; Floyd/ Wooldridge, 1990), investigating the relationship between competitive strategy and IT structure, drew on the typology of PORTER's two generic types that a firm may choose to follow in determining its course of competitive action (Porter, 1980; Porter/ Millar, 1985): The strategies of overall cost leadership and differentiation[78]. In addition to these two generic types of strategy, a firm can decide upon how broadly or narrowly a market (niche) is covered, so that both the differentiation and low-cost strategies can be applied to different lev-

---

[75] Furthermore, the contingency variables' moderating effects on the relationship between other theoretically derived variables and content allocation are theoretically explored.

[76] Strategic alignment models, for example, examine contingencies between different business- and IT-related variables either from an external (i.e. strategic) or internal (i.e. operational) perspective.

[77] The results further indicate that the IT of an organization with a conservative competitive strategy is more centralized than that of an organization with an aggressive competitive strategy. To be more specific, the user departments of a conservative organization have less responsibility for their IT activities than the user departments of an aggressive organization (Tavakolian, 1989, p. 314).

[78] Similarly, CONNER stated, *"obtaining [...] returns requires either that (a) the firm's product be distinctive in the eyes of the buyers [...] or (b) that the firm selling a identical product in comparison to competitors must have a lowcost position"*(Conner, 1991, p. 132).

els of market focus. In accordance with the studies centering around the MILES AND SNOW typology, authors basically suggest contingencies between the strategy of differentiation and IS decentralization as well as between the strategy of low-cost and IS centralization (Brown/ Magill, 1998, p. 181).

Following the stream of research drawing on PORTER's framework, the relationship between competitive strategy, as first contingency factor, and the content allocation structure should be examined. Relating to the strategy of differentiation, it may be said that publishing firms strive to skim off higher consumer rents as opposed to their competitors by individualizing and personalizing content products. Hazarding the cost disadvantages, this premium-product strategy usually leads to unrelated diversification and a decentralized organizational design (Govindarajan, 1988, p. 833). Thus, as editorial units are urged to produce individual and highly specific content (see chapter 3.3.1.3) to foster market awareness and responsiveness, inter-departmental synergy and content reutilization potentials are rare. Since there's no necessity for the exchange of content as a consequence of the differentiation strategy, it may be argued that content is allocated decentrally. Contrariwise, if a publishing firm takes on the competitive strategy of cost-leadership, it ideally aligns all its forces to realize economic efficiency through cost reduction. All organizational units, in particular those with value-creating tasks, should comply with and adhere to this directive. As the style of leadership is rather autocratic than democratic, the locus of decision-making is concentrated around one epicenter. In order to support and mirror the centralizing tendencies in the leadership and structure of the organization, it may be argued that IT-related activities are centralized as well. Due to rising complexity in the management of content[79], costs can be traced back more easily to a single than multiple sources of origin. Accordingly, it can be presumed that publishing firms consolidate media content in one corporate IS unit.

Based on the foregoing discussion, the following two hypotheses may be put forth:

Hypothesis 5a:	i) The more publishing companies employ a *strategy of low cost*, the more media content will be allocated centrally.
	ii) The more publishing companies employ a *strategy of differentiation*, the more media content will be allocated decentrally.

As could be seen in the line of reasoning presented above, strategic agencies are closely intertwined with organizational infrastructure and processes, whose impact on content allocation can be assumed to be even more compelling.

---

[79] A single point of content allocation, for instance, reduces storage and personnel costs.

(2) Organizational structure & size:

Proponents of the "organizational fit" concept argue that the variance in IT structures is attributable to the difference in overall organizational context variables in corporations (e.g., King, 1983; Ein-Dor/ Segev, 1982; McKenney/ McFarlan, 1982; Olson/ Chervany, 1980). They maintain that to avoid causing organizational friction, an organization should structure its IT systems to conform to its overall organizational context variables, such as organizational form, size, and decision-making (Cash/ McFarlan/ McKenney, 1992, p. 125).

Organizational form or structure is believed to directly affect the structure of IT systems (e.g., Fiedler/ Grover, 1996, pp. 30ff.; Lee/ Leifer, 1992, pp. 28f.; Hickson/ Pugh/ Pheysey, 1969, p. 392). In the functional organizational form, an organization's structure is aligned with basic business functions such as marketing, finance, and accounting. In the product organizational form, the activities are grouped around the product lines or customer groups (Laux/ Liermann, 2005, pp. 181ff.). In general, a centralized organizational structure capitalizes on efficiency, improved coordination, and economies of scale, clear responsibility, standardization as well as reduced managerial overhead. On the other hand, a decentralized organizational structure has such benefits as effectiveness, autonomy, flexibility, responsiveness, specialization, and attention to local needs. In this regard, a number of empirical studies could find out that an organization with a functional organizational form tends to rely on a centralized IT structure, because a centralized IT function fits the organizational philosophy of structuring activities around functional departments[80]. On the other hand, organizations with rather a product organizational form tend to have a decentralized IT function, because a decentralized IT function fits its organizational philosophy of distributing the functional activities around product-market divisions (Leifer, 1988, p. 68)[81].

Analogous to previous studies on the alignment of IT and organizational structure, it may be argued that the content allocation structure should fit the organizational form. Publishing organizations with a rather centralized organizational form will tend to control and gather resources at one single location in order to keep hardware and personnel costs at a low level. Centralizing tendencies will usually be expressed by a high degree of formalization and standardization of rules and procedures about the access to and use of content[82]. By the same token, to take advantage of economies of scale (and scope), multiple usages of content modules and bundles will be stimu-

---

[80] EIN-DOR AND SEGEV, for instance, looked at the degree of organizational centralization and its relationship to MIS centralization (Ein-Dor/ Segev, 1982).

[81] In an example of an empirical study, Olson analyzed the fit between organizational structure and the structure of the MIS services function (Olson/ Chervany, 1980).

[82] See for example the studies of DEWAR ET AL. or AIKEN AND HAGE who found out significant correlations between centralization, formalization, and standardization variables (Dewar/ Whetten/ Boje, 1980, p. 124; Aiken/ Hage, 1968).

lated and fostered. Accordingly, it can be hypothesized that organizational centraliza-tion, formalization, and standardization – these three organizational attributes will be aggregated to the 'level of bureaucracy' in further analyses – will go hand in hand with a tendency towards content centralization[83].

The other way round, if a publishing firm is highly decentralized with respect to its organizational form, it can be presumed that content will be disseminated across edi-torial units, which are themselves rather diversified. As with diversification, the mag-nitude and impact of bureaucracy usually decrease as well (Hall, 1962, p. 307), edito-rial units usually will have more autonomy to shape own content workflows with sepa-rate content repositories. Thus, it may be said, organizational decentralization exerts conforming effects on other organizational and technological phenomena such as the allocation of content.

Based on the previous rationale, the following hypothesis is deduced:

Hypothesis 5b:	The more *bureaucratic (centralized, formalized, specialized)* the organizational structure, the more media content will be allo-cated centrally.

As a second classical organizational variable, the impact of organization size on con-tent allocation structure will be examined. In organization theory, organizational size is often included as a contingency variable in empirical studies and is suggested to have an important moderating influence (e.g., Kimberly, 1976, p. 581). In his seminal theoretical work, BLAU investigated the impact of the size of organizations on struc-tural differentiation in companies[84]. One of his general propositions was that increas-ing organizational size generates structural differentiation at decelerating rates, which in turn enlarges the administrative component (Blau, 1970, p. 210; see also Baker/ Cullen, 1993, pp. 1252ff.). The underlying logic behind the enlargement of a central power is to counteract differentiation through integrative mechanisms[85]. One of those integrative mechanisms in bigger publishing firms, for instance, can be to create cen-

---

[83] More specifically, both the physical centralization of content as well as the logical access scope to content among editorial units will increase.

[84] This relationship has also been transferred to MIS research. KLATZKY found that organizational size was partially responsible for the decentralization that accompanied automation (Klatzky, 1970). CARTER discovered that organizational size moderated the relationship between MIS and organ-izational structure in a study of newspaper organizations (Carter, 1984).

[85] In developing a contingency theory of organization, LAWRENCE AND LORSCH introduced the basic concepts of differentiation and integration. As organizations interact with their external envi-ronment, they differentiate and develop specialized units that deal with sub-environments. Besides the formal division of labor, subunits develop different frames of reference and belief systems (Lawrence/ Lorsch, 1967; Kieser, 2001, pp. 179-180). In order to achieve unity of effort, differentia-tion requires integration for achieving organizational objectives. According to NADLER AND TUSHMAN, the dilemma of organization remains how to design and manage both differentiation and integration (Nadler/ Tushman, 1998, p. 14).

tral content repositories to tie different sub-units together and provide for a seamless content workflow.

To illustrate and exemplify the conceptual thinking of BLAU, which is also followed in this research study, two simplified network models with a centralized ("Client-Server") and decentralized ("Peer-2-Peer") mode of content allocation will be compared on a purely analytical basis (see Figure 3.3.3.3-2). It is assumed that organizations are only made up of network relationships that represent (globale) content transactions between editors ("network nodes") that potentially belong to different editorial units. Furthermore, it is assumed that the content portfolio is exhaustive in the organization, that is, every content request will be satisfied. Costs associated with each transaction for searching, transmitting, and retrieving content is assumed to be equal in both opposing network models. Fixed costs such as set-up or personnel costs should be neglected in this comparative analysis.

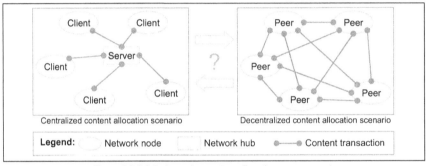

Figure 3.3.3.3-2: Opposing content allocation arrangements

Regarding a centralized network model, content is stored in one central repository ("content server"), to which several different editors or editorial units ("content clients") have access. If total exchange costs EC are computed, maximally n editors search and retrieve content from the central repository. Costs for content search queries to the content server ("search costs SC") and the provision of content to the content clients ("retrieval costs RC") thus have to be added up across editors. Assuming that in the *central* content allocation mode, one transaction for the research or retrieval of content costs c_c, overall exchange costs will maximally be:

$$EC_C = SC + RC = c_c n + c_c n = 2c_c n \tag{1}$$

Supposing a decentralized network model, content is disseminated among several equal network peers (i.e., editors or editorial units). That is, the so-called middleman, the content server or any other substitutional mechanism (e.g. index lists), does not exist in this Peer-2-Peer content allocation scenario. Since editors cannot exactly know where searched content is located, they may have to check every single peer in the decentralized network. As soon as the requested content is found, however, content will directly be transferred to the searching network node. In the worst case, search and retrieval costs accordingly run up to:

$$EC_d = SC + RC = (n-1)*c_d n + c_d n = c_d n^2 \tag{2}$$

If one simultaneously takes into account that search costs of decentralized content allocation equals those of centralized content allocation in the best case scenario (i.e. in a situation where all peers find content after the first search query), the following inequation can be formulated:

$$2c_d n \le EC_d \le c_d n^2 \tag{3}$$

Assuming equal unit costs for content search queries in both allocation scenarios (i.e. $c=c_c=c_d$), content allocation in decentralized networks is as expensive as in centralized networks only in the best case scenario. In all other cases, however, centralized content allocation will be more cost efficient than decentralized content allocation under the condition that

$$cn^2 > 2cn \Leftrightarrow n > 2 \tag{4}$$

As a consequence, the probability that decentralized content allocation becomes even more inferior to centralized content allocation rises with increasing network size n, which can be interpreted as a proxy for organization size in the context of this research study.

Although this network model has major limitations due to highly restrictive assumptions, it nevertheless illustrates that integrating mechanisms in the form of a central content repository reduce exchange costs tremendously with increasing organization size. Accordingly, due to the potential cost savings through the integration of media content and based on previous supportive empirical findings, the following hypothesis can be formulated:

Hypothesis 5c:	The greater the *organization size* of the publishing firm, the more content will be allocated centrally.

(3) IT governance and IT-related path dependencies:

A major contender to structure and size as a cause of structural differentiation is technology (e.g., Dewar, 1978). A variety of different notions of technology on different levels of analysis and its effect on organizational variables have been analyzed so far ranging from the seminal classification of operations technology of HICKSON ET AL. (Hickson/ Pugh/ Pheysey, 1969) to more specialized works such as about the relationship between the locus of IT decision making and the placement of IT resources (e.g., Kahai/ Snyder/ Carr, 2002; Weill/ Ross, 2004). The major objective underlying all these research endeavors was and still is to find out how technology and structural variables interact.

Special attention in MIS research has been paid to the relationship between IT governance and organizational variables (e.g., Sambamurthy/ Zmud, 1999; Peterson/ O'Callaghan/ Ribbers, 2000). Defined as the locus of IT decision-making authority[86] (Brown, 1997, p. 70; Sambamurthy/ Zmud, 1999, pp. 262ff.), discussions concerning IT governance have flourished across research communities. Posed as a question of centralization during the 1970s, IT governance drifted toward decentralization in the 1980s, and the recentralization of IT was a 1990s trend. As the network economy with P2P systems and mobile technology has already arrived, evidence suggests that decentralized IT management is, once more, leading IT-based business innovation towards decentralization (e.g., von Walter/ Hess, 2004). As business environments continuously change and new technologies evolve rapidly, how to govern IT to efficiently support core processes also represents an enduring and challenging question for media companies (e.g., van Eimeren/ Ridder, 2002; Stamer, 2002). Building forth on previous literature on IT governance, the effects of IT governance related activities on content allocation should be examined next.

Traditionally, three configurations have been distinguished for IT governance (Sambamurthy/ Zmud, 1999, p. 262). In each configuration, stakeholder constituencies take different lead roles and responsibilities for IT decision making. In the centralized configuration, corporate IT management has IT decision-making authority concerning infrastructure, applications, and development. In the decentralized configuration, division IT management and business-unit management have authority for infrastructure, applications, and development. In the federal configuration (a hybrid configuration of centralization and decentralization), IT authorities are divided up between corporate IT and division IT management in the respective business-units. In general, it is argued that centralization provides greater efficiency and standardization, while decentralization improves business ownership, flexibility, and responsiveness to local needs (e.g., Gordon/ Gordon, 2000, p. 8; Buchanan/ Linowes, 1980, p. 146)[87].

Based on this argument, it may be hypothesized that the content allocation structure in publishing companies is affected in dependence of the scope and extent of corporate IT's grasp on IT-related resources. That is, the more a central IT department is involved in the administration and support of content workflow activities in editorial

---

[86] Another more elaborated definition stems from WEILL AND WOODHAM, who defines IT governance as "*specifying the decision rights and accountability framework to encourage desirable behavior in the use of IT*" (Weill/ Woodham, 2002, p. 1).

[87] On the one hand, literature suggests that the federal configuration provides the benefits of both centralization and decentralization (e.g., von Simson, 1990, p. 162; see also Hodgkinson, 1996). On the other, research indicates that organizations adopt a federal configuration when pursuing multiple competing objectives (Brown/ Magill, 1998, p. 190).

units, the more it will attempt to consolidate different content sources at one location and enforce standardization. This proposition may, for instance, be supported by the empirical study of AHITUV ET AL., who found that the distribution of IT decision-making processes is (significantly) reflected in the degree of hardware distribution in an organization (Ahituv/ Neumann/ Zviran, 1989, pp. 393f.). Not only pure rationalistic criteria (e.g., less storage and maintenance costs) do play a role in the centralization endeavors of a central IT unit. State-of-the-art literature also draws on rather "soft" arguments such as power protection[88] (e.g., Bloomfield/ Coombs, 1992; Jasperson et al., 2002) or psychological or technological path dependencies to explain why the switching to an apparently more optimal allocation structure will frequently not be realized due to lock-in effects.

In general, path dependence exists when the outcome of a process depends on its past history, on the entire sequence of decisions made by agents and resulting outcomes, and not just on contemporary conditions. According to DAVID, path dependence *"[...] refers to a property of contingent, non-reversible dynamic processes, including a wide array of processes that can properly be described as 'evolutionary'"* (David, 2000, p. 2). In economic path dependence literature, it is argued that investments in the past, in the form of social and/or technological switching costs, are an impediment to change to a more effective form of resource allocation in the presence (Herrmann-Pillath, 2002, p. 232). Frequently investigated in economic papers are sub-optimal or inefficient technologies that can become locked in. In instances where there are significant network effects, these inefficiencies may even persist for extended periods of time (David, 1985, p. 336; Arthur, 1989, p. 130).

With respect to the content allocation problem at hand, path dependencies may moderate the decision of a central IT department, which has to decide upon the transition to a more optimal allocation option. Due to the existence of transaction costs in the transition between two different forms of governance structure, switching costs may arise that can outweigh the net benefits of the more optimal governance scenario without prior commitments (Leiblein/ Miller, 2003, p. 842). Two main sources of technological path dependencies are distinguished in the body of path dependence literature[89] (see Figure 3.3.3.3-3).

---

[88] As mentioned before (see chapter 3.2.2), effects of political or power-related motives on content allocation are not considered in this study.

[89] LANGOLIS AND SAVAGE emphasized that previous essays on path dependency have focused primarily on the lock-in of technical standards (Langolis/ Savage, 2001). As a result, this body of work has largely ignored the instances regarding the lock-in of standards relating to human behavior. More recent papers, however, have included behavioral forms of path dependence into their analysis (e.g., Barnes/ Gartland/ Stack, 2004).

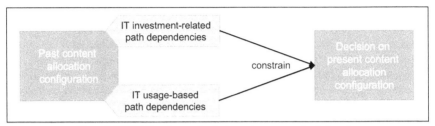

Figure 3.3.3.3-3: Two types of path dependency on content allocation

On the one hand, hardware, software, and network systems (i.e., IT-investment related path dependencies) that have been established and integrated into the organization in the past can hinder IT decision-makers in the presence to switch to better suited systems that may optimize content allocation. For instance, a publishing company that has implemented several decentralized local content repositories in its editorial units in the past may be reluctant to switch to a more optimal centralized content allocation solution in the presence, because of high expenses on new technical equipment. On the other hand, negative effects of path dependencies can emerge from IT users themselves (so-called IT-usage based path dependencies). Every organization to some degree exhibits more or less stable patterns of behavior based upon a structure of roles and specialized tasks (Perrow, 1970, p. 50). Editors of publishing companies, for instance, usually draw on a fix set of access rules and patterns to find and retrieve content. If they are accustomed to retrieve content from one content repository for a long time, a switching to different content access mechanisms in the wake of a change in content allocation will potentially prombt behavioral inertia and resistance (Barnes/ Gartland/ Stack, 2004, p. 373). Editors may even have problems to cope with the new content allocation configuration that they may consider burdensome and obstructive to the accomplishment of their work. Switching costs in the form of learning and training costs may occur that potentially play an important role in the resource decision-making of central IT departments.

Since path dependencies are generally discussed within the context of IT-related governance decisions in prior research activities, no direct link between path dependencies and content allocation is put forth. It rather may be argued that path dependencies – acting as a so-called moderating factor[90] – reinforce or attenuate the impact of IT governance on content allocation in dependence of the direction and strength of their effect.

---

[90] Several prior works in IS research emphasize the importance of identifying and quantifying moderating effects for the better comprehension of complex relationships (see for example Eggert/ Fassott/ Helm, 2005, pp. 102f.; Chin/ Marcolin/ Newsted, 2003, p. 193; Homburg/ Giering, 1996, p. 47).

In summary, the above analysis suggests the following hypotheses:

Hypothesis 5d:	The higher the *influence of a central IT department* on content allocation, the more content will be allocated centrally.
Hypothesis 5e:	i) The higher *IT investment-related path dependencies*, the more positively IT governance and the centralization of content are related. ii) The higher *IT usage-based path dependencies*, the more positively IT governance and the centralization of content are related.

When weighing a decision about the allocation of media content, which is an issue closely intertwined and highly permeated with technology, not only organizational requirements (i.e. editor's content processing needs) have to be taken into consideration. Factors that stem from technological imperatives also play a major role by delimiting the boundaries of efficient allocation scenarios.

(4) Infrastructural IT-imperatives:

The investigation of the influence of technology on structural (organizational) variables has a long tradition in management and organization science[91]. Technology has been seen as significant in developing comparative analyses (e.g., Perrow, 1967), in specifying how organizations interact with their environment (e.g., Newkirk/ Lederer, 2004), and in measuring the amount of explained variance in organizational performance (e.g., Melville/ Kraemer/ Gurbaxani, 2004; Santhanam/ Hartono, 2003).

In MIS research, three major streams of research about the fundamental relationship between IT (or computing) and organizational structure developed over the last decades (George/ King, 1991). One strand of research asserts that IT causes organizational *decentralization*, pointing at the growing potentials of network technologies and digitization for teleworking arrangements. A second group of researchers, advocating the opposite view, holds that computerization entails *centralization*, which is attributed to increasing possibilities of controlling and supervising organizational units due to growing information transparency. Last but not least, the technological imperative view regards "*[...] technology as an exogenous force which determines or strongly constrains the behavior of individuals and organizations*" (Markus/ Robey, 1988, p. 585). From this perspective, no consistent answer to whether organizational structure will be de- or centralized can be given. On the contrary, dependent on the optimal fit between organizational information and communication requirements and technical possibilities, an individual solution has to be found for each company. Viewed in this

---

[91] A brief introduction into the application of technology in the context of organization research is given in Gillespie/ Mileti, 1977.

vein, technical capabilities, or so-called IT-imperatives, can be interpreted in the terminology of contingency theory as a determinant factor influencing structural outcome variables in organizations via the feasibility of task fulfillment.

In the vast body of literature treating IT-related infrastructure[92] characteristics, a host
of different criteria have been put forth that (distributed) IT systems have to fulfill in
order to meet expected service levels and to support seamless organizational processes, of which five have emerged to be most relevant for the context of the content
allocation problem[93]: system reliability (and availability), performance, security, scalability, and extensibility (see Figure 3.3.3.3-4).

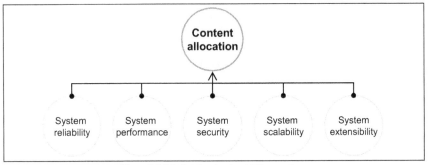

Figure 3.3.3.3-4: Infrastructural IT-imperatives

While *system reliability* refers to the capability of a system to fulfill required functions
with a certain probability[94], the availability denotes the average time a system fulfills
its functions correctly. As both criteria tap into the same underlying factor, i.e. the
system's robustness, they are often used interchangeably. The reliability of editorial
systems or content repositories, for instance, has a crucial impact on the effectiveness of day-to-day operations in publishing companies. If the availability of these systems is impeded, serious disruptions and delays in the production and bundling processes are the consequence. For that reason, a major strategy to hedge against risks
resulting from system breakdowns, is to distribute resources among several different
systems (i.e. resources are kept redundantly), so that another system can step in if
one system fails.

---

[92] IT infrastructure refers to the foundation for enterprise applications and services and is comprised of
data, network, and processing architectures (Duncan, 1995). An IT infrastructure influences the
reach and range of business opportunities available to firms in applying IT to shape global business
strategies (Keen, 1991).

[93] The selection of appropriate infrastructure characteristics is based on prior research works of the
author (Benlian/ Hess, 2004) and other relevant contributions in the MIS and computer science literature (see for example Weber, 1998; Dadam, 1996; Rofrano, 1992).

[94] A common measure to track system reliability of fault tolerance is, for instance, the mean time between malfunctions (e.g., Tanenbaum/ van Steen, 2002, p. 28).

System performance refers to the time-to-answer behavior (or latency time) of a system. In general, it is dependent both on the processing performance of the system[95] and on the transmission capacities of networks (Tanenbaum/ van Steen, 2002, p. 28). With respect to the allocation of content, the system's performance for content retrieval and editing activities can play an important role in the day-to-day business of publishing companies. Similar to system reliability, a lack in system's performance can do harm to organizational performance. To enhance the performance of systems, it is usually a common denominator among IT experts to pursue a centralization of IT-resources for that a remote access to resources is reduced to a minimum.

A *system's level of security* denotes a system's capability to protect and safeguard against unauthorized access to IT resources and certain kinds of damage or loss[96] (e.g., Straub, 1998; Loch/ Carr/ Warkentin, 1992). In the advent of Peer-2-Peer systems and increasing intrusion incidents of hackers, security measures became more and more a strategic factor for companies of all kinds of industries. Especially in the media sector, where property rights infringements have caused an industry disruption on a massive scale, different protective solutions (e.g. digital rights management systems) against the improper use of media content have been developed (e.g., Hess/ Ünlü, 2004; Bechtold, 2002). This rather market-oriented perspective also applies to content allocation endeavors within the boundaries of publishing companies. With media content disseminated across several different editorial units, the probability rises that one or more repositories fall victim to "denial of service"-attacks, content corruption, or even theft. On the other hand, if content is spread over several locations, system-integrated fail-safe and resilience measures can often more easily be realized. In any rate, serious reflections on the optimal security level of a company's systems therefore seem to be highly interrelated with the actual content allocation structure.

The last two IT-imperatives discussed here, *system scalability and extensibility*, are interrelated to some extent. While system scalability characterizes a system's capability to adjust to increasing levels of technical requirements[97] (i.e. without a fundamental reconfiguration of the system), system extensibility describes the costs and efforts that are incurred, if new IT-related resources have to be integrated into the existing system (e.g., due to an incorporation of another organizational unit). As pub-

---

[95] Hardware and software can represent sources for performance bottlenecks.

[96] Security once meant safe storage of materials, equipment, and money. Today the primary threat is to corporate data. The computing environment was historically controlled by a few knowledgeable professionals in a centralized batch processing mode. Physical security was of paramount importance. Today, almost unlimited access by a large, knowledgeable community of end users from desktop, dial-in, and network facilities creates a new and extremely vulnerable environment. The threats to data and system security include *"[...] natural and man-made disasters, errors by loyal employees, and the overt acts of competitors, hackers and creators of computer viruses"* (Loch/ Carr/ Warkentin, 1992, p. 174).

[97] Normally, increasing levels of technical requirements mean an increasing number of users or amount of resources that have to be processed.

lishing companies have to be responsive towards new technological developments (e.g., new distribution channels and devices) and customer preferences, farsighted investments into a system's flexible scalability and extensibility can be crucial. If both factors are not considered at an early stage of information systems planning, a lack of scalability and extensibility can do great financial harm to the day-to-day production and bundling processes. In this connection, the structure of content allocation may be an enabler or impediment to flexible system scalability and extensibility. Contingent upon the complexity of the respective installed system, either a centralized or decentralized content allocation structure is more easily scalable and extensible[98].

As could be seen in the previous theoretical analysis about the relationship between IT-imperatives and content allocation, in all cases, it can be assumed that the operational performance of a publishing company will be negatively affected, if a certain 'service-level agreement' can not be fulfilled. Taking all the discussed factors into account, it may be argued that content is centralized, if IT-imperatives tend to favor a centralized allocation structure and vice versa. That is, the alignment of IT-imperatives and the content allocation structure should be maximized, particularly to enhance the delivery of the existing content resources (Goodhue/ Quillard/ Rockart, 1988, p. 390). Accordingly, the following hypothesis is deduced:

Hypothesis 5f:	The more *IT-imperatives* are met in a centralized as opposed to a decentralized content allocation arrangement, the more media content will be allocated centrally.

3.3.3.4 Synopsis of hypotheses from Contingency Theory

To sum up, contingent effects between strategic, organizational, and technological variables and the content allocation structure have been investigated on different levels of abstraction. The resulting partial causal model is depicted in Figure 3.3.3.4-1. In general, it illustrates that that kind of content allocation structure in a publishing company will prevail that best fits the multiple contingencies affecting it.

---

[98] If content is spread over several highly integrated content repositories, which are connected via some sort of a bus system, new content repositories can easily be 'plugged and played'. Additionally, higher content processing requirements can be divided up among different content peers. On the other hand, if a decentralized system is in a messy state, with a host of differing standards in place, a centralized system may be more efficient due to the lower complexity.

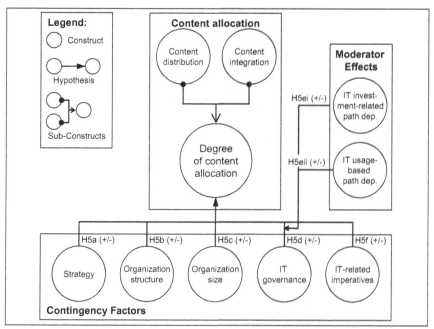

Figure 3.3.3.4-1: Partial causal model from Contingency Theory

Before the results of the theoretical analysis in previous chapters can be integrated into a coherent whole, the theoretical connections and intersections between TCT, RBV, and CT are explored in the following chapter.

3.4 Interplay and integration of reference theories

With TCT, RBV and CT, three theoretical lenses have been sifted out in previous selection processes stemming from different particular theoretical origins. This is consistent with the idea of theoretical pluralism (Spinner, 1974, p. 173), which supports the interplay and integration of multiple theories in order to examine a research problem from various angles. However, different reference theories provide different perspectives, lenses, and insights for the explanation of how media content is allocated in print companies. Although different reference theories are most often conceptually separated and argue on different levels of abstractions, semantic overlaps or incongruencies may occur. In those situations the question arises how to properly knit together perspectives and lenses from different theoretical backgrounds. In the context of this study, the remaining task to round off the theorizing process is to explicate the arrangement of the reference theories towards each other, clarifying the intertheoretical linkages between the partial frameworks.

The central starting point for shedding light on the theoretical interrelationships is the framework of Comparative Insititutional Performance (CIP) introduced in chapter 3.2.4. In the process of theorizing on the content allocation problem, it emerged as a structurizing framework for the formation and alignment of different theoretical constructs. Its overarching concept was to integrate theoretical lenses that concurred in their basic decision logic: Bi-polar allocation structures are compared and assessed on the basis of an evaluative criterion, of which the one with a comparative advantage will prevail. While all reference theories conform in this general structural decision logic, the concrete evaluative criteria themselves are complements rather than substitutes to each other. It may be argued that economic (i.e. cost-related) and strategic or operational (i.e. benefit-related) evaluative criteria can conceptually be linked to a purely rational cost-benefit-analysis, whereas organizational fit criteria tend to bear a less rational causal agency, emanating from the basic notion of structural alignment. Hence, a clear theoretical devidieng line can be seen in the type of evaluative criteria.

Accordingly, in the course of deducing contextual and evaluative constructs out of the respective theoretical lenses, it could be found that no constructs completely coincided in their meaning or directional link with other constructs. However, semantic overlaps as well as mutual conceptual enrichment between constructs of different reference theories emerged during the theory building process. To assess the reciprocal theoretical stimulations between the respective reference theories, each pair of theoretical interaction will be analyzed briefly (see Figure 3.4-1).

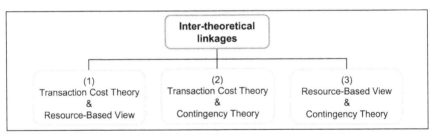

Figure 3.4-1: Inter-theoretical linkages between reference theories

(1) Transaction Cost Theory and Resource-Based View

In general, TCT and RBV are theoretical lenses, which arose from different theoretical backgrounds and research communities. However, not only in previous literature (e.g., Silverman, 1999; Hennart, 1994), but also in the mid-range theoretical framework developed in this study, conceptually fruitful interlinkages were found.

First of all, it was deduced, that the characteristics of a publishing firm's resource base, as manifested in its content portfolio, influences the final allocation decision via comparative cost and benefit effects. With the terminological notions about resources in RBV (see chapter 3.3.2.1) and the basic comparative institutional framework of

TCT (see chapter 3.3.1.1), conceptual parts of both theories could be fused and combined in one coherent framework[99]. In addition, the attributes of transactions were used to deduce more discriminating characteristics of media content (e.g. content specificity), fruitfully enriching and complementing resource-based thinking.

Another theoretical linkage between TCT and RBV may be seen in the proposition that above-normal rent-generating (i.e. perceived strategic) content tends to bear a great content reutilization potential and is therefore rather unspecific than specific. WILLIAMSON himself has recognized that specific assets cannot *"[...] be redeployed to alternative users and by alternative uses without sacrifice of productive value"* (Williamson, 1990b, p. 142). In the context of this research study, this suggests that lower perceived strategic content value translates into content decentralization. To reflect this conceptual conjunction, working hypothesis I, which suggests a significant relationship between perceived strategic content value and content reutilization, was introduced into the causal model.

(2) Transaction Cost Theory and Contingency Theory

To illustrate the interrelationships between TCT and CT in the causal model on hand, two examples should be provided. First of all, IT-related imperatives, representing a form of technological contingency factor, can also be interpreted as a source of comparative transaction and production costs, since, with different levels of compliance, they may cause different transaction and production costs in centralized as opposed to decentralized allocation modes. For that reason, it can be assumed that IT-imperatives may correlate significantly with comparative transaction and production costs.

As another example, a conceptual interplay also exists between content transaction frequency and organizational structure. As content transaction frequency represents a measure for the intensity of interdepartmental integration and sharing (Lee/ Leifer, 1992, pp. 32ff.), it captures organizational characteristics of publishing firms on a horizontal process (i.e. workflow) level. As a complement, the organizational structure covers the relationship between different vertical levels of hierarchy, as manifested by centralization, formalization, and standardization of decision-making in the form of working rules and procedures. Hence, organizational structure emphasizes, as the name implies, structural rather than procedural relationships.

---

[99] In this realm, it is notable that the impact of content specificity on comparative production cost advantages between content centralization and decentralization could have equally been deduced from transaction cost theory and resource-based theory. There are only differences in wording. While resource-based theory always refers to production cost advantages based on specific assets (Bamberger/ Wrona, 1996, pp. 135ff.), transaction cost theory emphasizes production cost disadvantages of the market (here of the decentralization of content) (Conner, 1991, p. 139). However, since specificity is primarily discussed as an attribute of transactions, it was attributed to transaction costs.

(3) Resource-Based View and Contingency Theory

Last but not least, examples for a conceptual cross-fertilization between RBV- and CT-related constructs can be uncovered as well. Technological path dependencies, for instance, can be interpreted as characteristics leading to sustained competitive advantage, which in turn is closely related to the concept of causal ambiguity in RBV research (e.g., Reed, 1990). Another, more obvious example of construct linkages between RBV and CT refers to the interaction between the business strategy of organizations and the perceived strategic value of content. As the evaluative appraisal of the own content portfolio also reflects the strategic business focus, both theoretical constructs can be considered as interrelated and may provide further insights with regard to their combined impact on content allocation. Finally, semantic similarities exist between the chosen business strategy and the level of diversification as manifested in the relatedness constructs. As diversification can be realized both in a cost leadership and differentiation strategy, both concepts are different enough to capture complement rather than redundant aspects.

Overall, it may be said that all three theoretical lenses, which are derived from different theories, but linked to the same dependent variable (i.e. content allocation), are complementary explanatory and predictive in the context of this study. That is, concertedly, they increase the ability to explain and predict the heterogeneous content allocation behavior of publishing companies.

3.5 Synopsis of hypotheses and path model

Having derived three reference theories and several hypotheses in previous chapters, the process of theorizing on the content allocation problem was rounded off by explicating theoretical conjunctions among reference theories. Before theoretical constructs and hypotheses are transferred into the empirical world and evaluated in the chapters to come though, the partial causal models with their intra- and intertheoretical linkages will be synthesized into a comprehensive framework. Table 3.5-1 recapitulates the collection of hypotheses from TCT and RBV developed in the course of theorizing on content allocation behavior.

No.	Hypotheses
Hypothesis 1a:	The more *specific media content* is, the higher the *comparative transaction cost advantage* of decentralizing as opposed to centralizing media content.
Hypothesis 1b:	The more *specific media content* is, the higher the *comparative production cost advantage* of decentralizing as opposed to centralizing media content.
Hypothesis 2a:	The higher the comparative *transaction cost advantage* of centralizing as opposed to decentralizing media content, the more media content will be allocated centrally.
Hypothesis 2b:	The higher the comparative *production cost advantage* of centralizing as opposed to decentralizing media content, the more media content will be allocated centrally.
Working Hypothesis I:	The *perceived strategic value* of media content is positively related with the *level of content reutilization*.
Hypothesis 3a:	The higher the *perceived strategic value* of content is, the higher the level of comparative advantages in the *strategic contribution* of centrally- as opposed to decentrally-deployed content.
Working Hypothesis II	The higher the content relatedness across editorial units, the higher the market- and production process-relatedness across editorial units.
Hypothesis 3b:	The higher the level of related diversification across editorial units as indicated by a combination of content-, production process-, and market-relatedness, the higher the level of comparative advantages in the *strategic contribution* of centrally- as opposed to decentrally-deployed media content.
Hypothesis 3c:	The higher the level of related diversification across editorial units as indicated by a combination of content-, production process-, and market-relatedness, the higher the level of comparative advantages in the *operational contribution* of centrally- as opposed to decentrally-deployed media content.
Hypothesis 4a:	The higher the level of *strategic contribution* of centrally as opposed to decentrally deployed media content, the more media content will be allocated centrally.
Hypothesis 4b:	The higher the level of *operational contribution* of centrally as opposed to decentrally deployed media content, the more media content will be allocated centrally.

Table 3.5-1: Summary of hypotheses from TCT and RBV

Finally, Table 3.5-2 summarizes the hypotheses derived from contingency theoretical thinking, integrating business strategic, organizational (structure and size) and technological (IT governance and IT infrastructure management) perspectives.

Hypothesis 5a:	i) The more publishing companies employ a *strategy of low cost*, the more media content will be allocated centrally. ii) The more publishing companies employ a *strategy of differentiation*, the more media content will be allocated decentrally.
Hypothesis 5b:	The more *bureaucratic (centralized, formalized, specialized)* the organizational structure, the more media content will be allocated centrally.
Hypothesis 5c:	The greater the *organization size* of the publishing firm, the more content will be allocated centrally.
Hypothesis 5d:	The higher the *influence of a central IT department* on content allocation, the more content will be allocated centrally.
Hypothesis 5e:	i) The higher *IT investment-related path dependencies*, the more positively IT governance and the centralization of content are related. ii) The higher *IT usage-based path dependencies*, the more positively IT governance and the centralization of content are related.
Hypothesis 5f:	The more *IT-imperatives* are met in a centralized as opposed to a decentralized content allocation arrangement, the more media content will be allocated centrally.

Table 3.5-2: Summary of hypotheses from CT

The resulting integrative framework, which is made up of the partial models of the respective reference theories (see Figure 3.3.1.4-1, Figure 3.3.2.4-1, and Figure 3.3.3.4-1), is illustrated in Figure 3.5-1. It may be viewed as a "mid-range theoretical framework of content allocation".

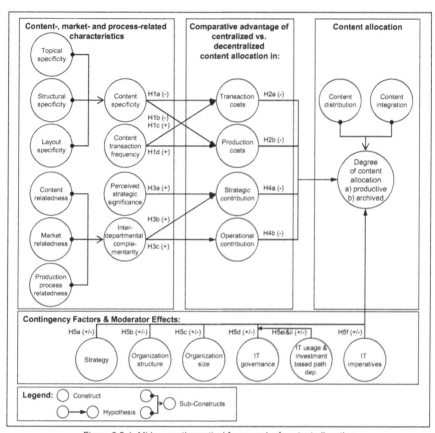

Figure 3.5-1: Mid-range theoretical framework of content allocation

4 Empirical test of the content allocation model

In this chapter, the mid-range theoretical framework on content allocation, which integrates different theoretical lenses into a coherent whole, will be subjected to an empirical test. This requires to transform the theoretical language into an observable language (Kerlinger/ Lee, 2000, p. 54). In other words, the constructs have to be operationalized as measurable variables. In doing so, it is necessary to satisfy both the theoretical and the empirical requirements. One method that provides a formal structure which allows the matching of theory and data is that of structural equation modeling (SEM). This statistical modeling technique provides rules on how to specify a variance-based theoretical framework in a way that recognizes the requirements of the statistical procedures that are applied to rigorously estimate and evaluate the parameters of the model.

The theoretical groundwork that was laid by developing the theoretical framework facilitates the model building process. However, in order to specify and subsequently test the framework, the requirements of the modeling technique have to be considered a priori. Therefore, the fundamentals of the SEM method will first be introduced in the following chapter (see chapter 4.1). Subsequently, the constructs of the mid-range theoretical framework on content allocation will be operationalized (see chapter 4.2). After the development of the measurement instrument, the conduct and analysis of the empirical study will be outlined. This includes the data collection (see chapter 4.3), the presentation of major descriptive characteristics of the sample data (see chapter 4.4), and the more extensive model estimation and evaluation process (see chapter 4.5).

4.1 Fundamentals of structural equation modeling

Within the last twenty years, structural equation modeling (SEM) techniques have become increasingly popular among social scientists (e.g., Chin, 1998a; Hildebrandt/ Homburg, 1998). They allow the rigorous statistical examination of theoretical relationships. Their popularity is essentially attributed to their ability to combine an econometric perspective, focusing on prediction, with psychometric modeling, which focuses on the measurement of not directly observable (i.e. latent) variables by multiple observables – also called indicators or manifest variables (Chin, 1998a, p. vii; Lee/ Barua/ Whinston, 1997, p. 120). The approach is primarily confirmatory in nature. It is generally used to determine whether a pre-specified model is valid, rather than to find a model by exploring the data – although it often includes some exploratory elements in the analysis (e.g., Chin, 1998a; Homburg/ Dobratz, 1991, 1992).

SEM techniques allow the researcher to simultaneously test the strength of the relationships between multiple latent variables and the reliability of the measures of the latent variables (Chin, 1998a, p. vii). The relationships between latent theoretical variables form the structural model, which sometimes is also called inner model (see Figure 4.1-1). The structural model equals a variance-based theoretical framework. Accordingly, the mid-range theoretical framework on content allocation, as illustrated in Figure 3.5-1, represents a structural model of content allocation. As an example, content specificity is hypothesized to have a direct negative impact on the comparative transaction cost advantages of centrally vs. decentrally deployed content (H1a-), and an indirect positive impact (two negative result into one positive relationship) on the allocation of content via comparative transaction cost advantages (H2a-).

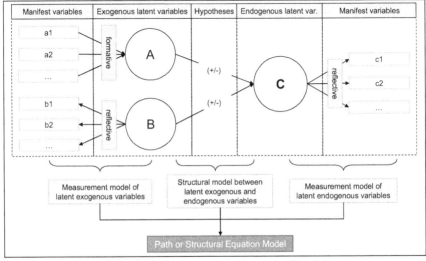

Figure 4.1-1: Measurement, structure, and path model

At that point of time, it is appropriate to note that the proposed directional links between latent variables are not truly causal in a theoretical sense, since the elimination of disturbing factors and a time lag between the cause of the independent variable and the effect on the dependent variable are not provided in cross-sectional studies (Brosius/ Koschel, 2005, pp. 178ff.). For that reason, correlations rather than causal links[1] lie behind path relationships. However, as it is assumed that theory and prior empirical findings back up the proposed directions, it is supposed that the resulting

---

[1] In fact, Popper (Popper, 1994) has generally rejected causality as to be "metaphysical". Instead he points out to a simple methodological rule. It suggests that researchers should not stop searching for general laws and comprehensive theoretical systems by (temporarily) eliminating false and (temporarily) accepting true relationships (Chalmers, 2001). SEM, which can be considered a research methodology in the tradition of Popper, therefore attempts to falsify hypotheses in causal models through the elimination of non-significant correlations. This also puts the theoretical meaning of the term "causal analysis", which is widely used as a synonym for SEM (Hildebrandt/ Homburg, 1998, p. 5), into perspective.

"causal" model is more plausible than any alternative model (Bortz/ Bongers, 1984, p. 396). From a methodological point of view, the term "causal" is less questionable. Here, it simply refers to cause-effect or stimulus-response relationships between variables (Lohmöller, 1989b, p. 16-21) in the sense that the researcher wants to account for the extent to which the variation in one (dependent) variable Y corresponds with the variation of another (independent) variable X.

With regard to the empirical examination of the structural model, the theoretical constructs need to be measured. That is, the instances of each latent variable have to be determined and operationalized. Unfortunately, most of the constructs in social sciences are not directly observable. They have a subjective rather than objective character. For example, the degree of content specificity can not be observed directly. Therefore, it has to be measured indirectly, e.g., by asking different questions. The more questions one is asking, the more complete will be the picture of the degree of content specificity. Asking multiple questions allows accounting for the potential measurement error ("noise") that is included in the respondent's answers. In other words, if only one measure is used, i.e., one question asked, it is implicitly assumed that the measure is perfect, i.e., without measurement error, which is a rather unrealistic assumption. Structural equation modeling recognizes the issue of measurement error. It allows to measure one construct with more than one item. Each measure of a construct is called indicator or manifest variable. The sum (or block) of indicators of one construct is called measurement model of the construct (see Figure 4.1-1).

The linkages between the indicators and their constructs are based on correspondence rules. Accordingly, one also speaks of correspondence hypotheses that link indicators with a construct. In general, two different correspondence rules (i.e. measurement modes) may be distinguished (Eggert/ Fassott, 2005, p. 36ff). On the one hand, the indicators can reflect the construct. In this reflective mode, each indicator is an alternative or redundant measure of the construct. That is, the indicators are interdependent. They "[...] covary as a consequence of their common content" (Fornell, 1989, p. 161). If the magnitude of one of the measures increases, the magnitude of the other indicators should increase as well (Chin/ Newsted, 1999, p. 310). Graphically, this is depicted by having arrows pointing from the construct to its indicators (see Figure 4.1-1). On the other hand, the measures could be designed in a way so that they form the construct. In this formative mode, the indicators are "[...] conceptually independent subdimensions of the concept" (Fornell, 1989, p. 161). That is, the indicators do not need to covary. Each indicator is "[...] defined as a portion of the object or event implied by the focal concept" (Fornell, 1989, p. 161). This is illustrated by drawing arrows from the indicators to their respective latent variable[2] (see Figure 4.1-1). Altogether, the combination of the structural model and the measurement models forms the whole path model (see Figure 4.1-1).

---

[2] BOLLEN provides an excellent discussion of the relationships between indicators for reflective (or "effect") and formative (or "cause") constructs (Bollen, 1984).

A second interesting feature that goes beyond the basic model specification in SEM is that of using second-order constructs. Second-order factors are aggregates of regularly measured first-order latent variables. They are linked to first-order latent variables just as latent variables are linked to their indicators. Therefore, the same correspondence rules as in case of linking indicators with latent variables need to be considered. One approach of modeling second-order constructs is that of repeated indicators, also known as the hierarchical component model by LOHMÖLLER (Lohmöller, 1989b, pp. 130-133). In this case, the indicators from all the first-order constructs are taken over by the second-order construct. However, it is also possible to use the estimated component scores of the first-order constructs as indicators of the second-order construct (see Figure 4.1-2).

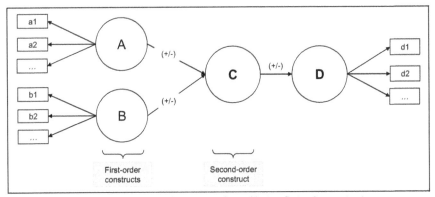

Figure 4.1-2: Second-order construct formed by two first-order constructs

The first-order constructs can either form (molar analysis), as is the case in Figure 4.1-2, or reflect (molecular analysis) the second-order construct (Chin/ Gopal, 1995). Beside their role as aggregates of a number of first-order factors, the second-order factors usually mediate the impact of a number of exogenous latent variables on one or more endogenous latent variables. They are especially useful within complex models, because they help to simplify the model structure and to better understand the semantic of the constructs[3].

Having provided a structural model in the form of the mid-range theoretical model on content allocation (see Figure 3.5-1) and explicated the statistical technique for its evaluation, the measurement models for both endogenous and exogenous constructs will be presented next.

---

[3] For more current examples of second-order constructs see Staples/ Seddon, 2004 or Zhu, et al., 2005.

4.2 Operationalization of research constructs

Each of the constructs from the mid-range theoretical framework needs to be measured with an item battery. As recommended in the MIS literature, existing measures from prior empirical studies that already have been utilized and validated are adopted whenever possible (Straub, 1989, p. 161)[4]. Measures are either formulated as questions, that need to be answered, or as statements, that need to be evaluated by the respondents[5].

The majority of the indicators are provided with (quasi-)continuous measurement scales. In particular, three different types were applied in the research study on hand. Most of the variables are measured on a five-point Likert scale ranging from "strongly disagree" to "strongly agree", with "neither agree nor disagree" as a mid-point[6]. In a few questions respondents are asked to provide percentages (ranging form 0% to 100%) or numbers. In one case, the semantic differential approach to measurement, which was first introduced by OSGOOD ET AL. (Osgood/ Suci/ Tannenmann, 1957) is adopted, where each response is located on an evaluative bipolar (negative-to-positive) dimension, using a seven-point Likert scale (Schnell/ Hill/ Esser, 2005, p. 175).

As outlined previously, the allocation object of this study is media content. More specifically, two different types of content, namely currently used (i.e. productive) and archived content are considered. Each variable in the mid-range theoretical framework that has a direct impact on the allocation of content, i.e. the efficiency criteria, therefore has to refer to both variables. That is, each respondent has to evaluate given statements both for *productive* and *archived content*. Exceptions to this are the contingency variables whose impact on content allocation should be assessed by investigating their covariance with both types of content irrespective of a concrete reference in the questionnaire (see Figure 3.3.3.2-1 for the interpretation of fit as cor-

---

[4] A valuable starting point and source for identifying useful empirical studies in MIS research is the meta-analysis of LARSEN who lists all relevant antecedents of information systems success (Larsen, 2003, pp. 219-246).

[5] When applying a multiple indicator approach the question arises, why measure a construct indirectly through the summation of a number of item scores rather than directly through the response to the score on a single question aimed directly at the construct in question? The answer is that the sum (or average) of a number of items should be more accurate than the response to a single question provided. Further, the construct of interest is often more abstract than the manifest items and respondents find it difficult to think about such abstract concepts. Accordingly, fresh participant responses should be elicited by using a variety of items within the same instrumentation (Straub/ Boudreau/ Gefen, 2004, p. 401).

[6] Usually, interval scaling is a major prerequisite for the estimation of SEM (Zinnbauer/ Eberl, 2004, p. 3). In organizational and sociological research practice, however, Likert scales, if equidistant, are accepted as "quasi-metric" scales (Jaccard/ Wan, 1996, p. 4). In order to not to violate the assumption of continuous variables in SEM too seriously, despite discrete item measurement, at least five scale points are recommended (Bagozzi, 1981, p. 380).Less than five points tends to constrain useful feedback. More than five scale points makes differentiation among individual points more difficult.

relation in this study).

Following the theoretical structure, as illustrated in Figure 4.2-1, the indicators can be semantically differentiated into four clusters.

- The first cluster is represented by those constructs that directly refer to the behavior under investigation: Archived and productive content allocation behavior from a current (or real) and ideal point-of-view consisting of content distribution and content integration (see chapter 4.2.1).

- The second cluster refers to comparative advantage constructs representing the efficiency criteria derived from TCT and RBV. More specifically, they represent estimates about different types of comparative advantages in allocating content centrally versus decentrally (see chapter 4.2.2).

- Contextual variables derived from TCT and RBV make up cluster three. They represent different characteristics of media content. The particular questions or statements capturing these constructs are only indirectly related to the issue of content allocation (see chapter 4.2.3).

- The fourth and last cluster comprises selected contingency variables, which are directly connected to the content allocation variables. They represent different factors characterizing the internal situation of a publishing firm with respect to its strategy, organization, and technology (see chapter 4.2.4).

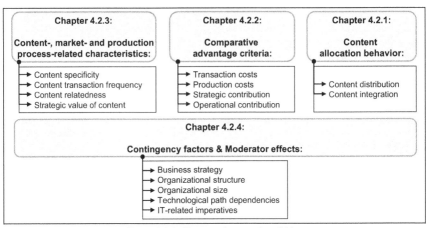

Figure 4.2-1: Clusters of research variables

In the following, the measures of the constructs for each of these four semantic categories will be presented. In each section, tables are provided that show the numbered abbreviations of the measures (item numbers), as used in the analysis, the working definition, as elaborated in preceding chapters, and shortened versions of the actual measures. The entire measurement instrument, in form of a 5-page questionnaire, is presented both in German and English in Appendix C.

4.2.1 Content allocation behavior

The current[7] degree of content allocation is the central dependent variable of the theoretical framework. For the purpose of this research, items measuring content allocation should on the one hand reflect the extent to which content is physically dispersed among editorial units in publishing companies. On the other hand, measurement items should tap into the logical integration of content as indicated by the scope of access to content of editors in and between editorial units.

To the knowledge of the author, no useful operationalizations of the construct have been provided in previous empirical studies so far[8]. To grasp the semantic universe (or content domain) of both sub-constructs, a rational scale development strategy was first employed to find adequate indicators (Fisseni, 2004, pp. 35ff.). This is, indicators for content distribution and content integration were derived based on prior theoretical works. While MERTENS was the primary theoretical source for content distribution categories (Mertens, 1985), ÖSTERLE ET AL. provided the conceptual underpinnings for content integration (Österle/ Riehm/ Vogler, 1996). After having generated an initial pool of different measurement items, the content, face, convergent, and discriminant validity[9] of both constructs was pilot tested with faculty members ("experts") as well as with undergraduate students ("laypersons") of the Institute for Information Systems and New Media (ISNM) at the Ludwig-Maximilians-University of Munich[10]. In a first round, 61 pretesters were asked to judge each item of the initial item pool for how strong it was semantically related to both factors on a 5-point Likert-scale. Additionally, the feedback on the face validity was noted down for future improvements. The results of this first pre-test round were used to trim and adjust the initial item pool. In a second round, 61 pretesters should directly assign measurement items to either content distribution or content integration. A factor analysis investigating the convergent and discriminant validity of the different sub-scales resulted in satisfactory values.

---

[7] For descriptive reasons, i.e. to identify potential gaps, respondents should also assess the ideal degree of content allocation for productive and archived content in their publishing firms.

[8] If pre-existing measurement items were not found in previous works, own scales were developed trying to closely adhere to the recommended procedures and steps in the literature (Netemeyer/ Bearden/ Sharma, 2003, p. 15; Fisseni, 2004; Hinkin, 1995).

[9] The definitions of these evaluative criteria in scale development can, for instance, be looked up in NETEMEYER ET AL. (Netemeyer/ Bearden/ Sharma, 2003).

[10] The procedures for assessing the theoretical content adequacy are mainly based on the works of SCHRIESHEIM ET AL. (Schriesheim, et al., 1993) and HINKIN (Hinkin, 1995).

Ultimately, three indicators for content distribution and four indicators for content integration were incorporated into the questionnaire (see Table 4.2.1-1). The first indicator of each sub-scale (Dist1 and Int1) should directly address the different options for content distribution and integration by approximating interval measurement (Kerlinger/ Lee, 2000, p. 635). Concepts in theoretical works (e.g. Lee/ Leifer, 1992, pp. 32ff.) and measures of empirical studies in MIS research (Lewis/ Snyder/ Rainer, 1995, pp. 211ff.) served as a foundation to develop the constructs. The next two measurement items (Dist2&3 and Int2&3) should objectively reflect the extent of centralized vs. decentralized content allocation. On the one hand, the average share of content being stored in central databases (Dist2), and the average share of content to which editors have access (Int2) should be assessed respectively. This way of measuring the dependent research variable is frequently used in MIS research for assessing the extent to which an IT-related resource is allocated in one or another way[11] and has yielded satisfactory results with regard to item reliability. On the other hand, it was assumed that the more content is integrated and stored centrally, the more resources (i.e. staff) are needed to take care for the content handling. Thus, respective indicators were formulated that asked for the total number of employees employed for the administration of central databases (Dist3) and for the configuration of access rights to content (Int3). As additional "yardstick" for content integration and for descriptive purposes, a measurement item was included that was supposed to account for the degree of content reutilization among editorial units (Int4). Here, it was likewise assumed that higher content integration goes hand in hand with increased content reutilization.

For descriptive reasons, a question was integrated at the beginning of the questionnaire asking for whether content is stored in-house or outsourced to an external service provider, delivering additional information on the organization of content allocation. Table 4.2.1-1 gives an overview on the definitions and operationalizations of variables concerning content allocation behavior in publishing companies.

---

[11] DIBBERN, for instance, used a similar indicator to measure the average percentage of IS functions (applications development and maintenance) allocated to external service providers in terms of the function's total budget, total person working days, and total number of people that participate in doing the work (Dibbern, 2004. p. 248).

Item #	Constructs, definitions, and indicators
Degree of (productive and archived) Content Distribution (Dist): reflective	
"Content distribution refers to the physical distribution of media content among editorial units in publishing companies."	
Dist1	Distribution of content among editorial units: from content stored in one central, organization-wide database to content disseminated across the workstations of editors in several different editorial units.
Dist2	Average share of content stored in central databases (in %).
Dist3	Total number of employees employed or responsible for the administration of central databases.
Degree of (productive and archived) Content Integration (Int): reflective	
"Content integration refers to the logical integration of content as indicated by the scope of access to content for editors in an between editorial units."	
Int1	Scope of access to content for editors: from content created by the entire publishing firm to content created by the individual editor.
Int2	Average share of content to which editors have access (in %).
Int3	Total number of employees that is employed or responsible for the configuration of access rights to content.
Int4	Percentage of content that is reutilized in other than the original media product.
In-house or Outsourced Content Storage (InOut): binary	
InOut	In-house or outsourced content storage.

Table 4.2.1-1: Measures of content allocation behavior

4.2.2 Comperative advantage variables

The notion of "comparative advantage" is closely related to that of "relative advantage", which has been thoroughly explored in the context of IT adoption in MIS research (e.g., Agarwal/ Prasad, 1998; Chin/ Gopal, 1995; Moore/ Benbasat, 1991). In the context of IT acceptance research, AGARWAL AND PRASAD note: *"Relative advantage captures the extent to which a potential adopter views the innovation as offering an advantage over previous ways of performing the same task"* (Agarwal/ Prasad, p. 562). Analogous to innovation theory, where a common hypothesis is that less expensive innovations go hand in hand with higher adoption probability (Rogers, 1983), the concept of comparative advantages in the context of content allocation may be defined as the extent to which an organization considers the centralized content allocation form as being superior to the decentralized allocation option. Comparative advantages can generally be assessed globally, or they can be related to particular evaluative criteria. Within the theoretical framework of content allocation, a number of evaluative criteria have been deduced from transaction cost theory, re-source-based theory, and contingency research. At the level of analysis chosen in this study (see Figure 2.2-1), they refer to the production costs, the transaction costs, the strategic and operational contribution to competitive advantage[12]. Each of these concepts can be operationalized by letting respondents weigh up advantages (or dis-advantages) of either ways of deploying content centrally or decentrally.

Production cost advantages:

Drawing on the definition and the measures from DIBBERN (Dibbern, 2004, pp. 151f.) and ANG AND STRAUB (Ang/ Straub, 1998, p. 552), three items have been derived and adjusted to the context of content allocation. They reflect the extent to which the input factor costs, in terms of time, effort, and money included in perform-ing the actual content production and bundling, are lower in a centralized than in a decentralized allocation mode. In recognizing the required theoretical interdependen-cies of the items (reflective mode), three measures have been created based on the following ideas. The costs emerging in the course of producing and bundling content are inevitably linked to personnel resources. Accordingly, the efficiency and the speed of working[13] are two redundant measures leading to items Pc1 and Pc2. At the same time, however, it is more likely that the efficiency and the speed of working in-crease, if an organization can realize economies of scale, which may be attributed to either a centralized or decentralized content allocation mode. The consequences are lower overall costs, which should be reflected by item Pc3.

Transaction cost advantages:

For the purpose of this study, the measures representing comparative transaction cost advantages should capture those (intra-firm or hierarchical) transaction costs that are incurred during the production and bundling of media content due to different modes of content allocation (see also Figure 3.3-2 illustrating different transaction cost categories). Drawing on previous conceptual works of RAWOLLE (Rawolle, 2002) and methodological contributions of DIBBERN (Dibbern, 2004, pp. 151ff.)[14], four measures were developed that reflect the extent to which the (frictional) costs in terms of time, effort, and money spent are lower, when content is allocated centrally as opposed to decentrally. In particular, these costs arise, when content is re-searched, exchanged, and/or administered (Tc1-Tc4). Table 4.2.2-1 summarizes the

---

[12] Although the fit between situational context factors and the structural variable 'content allocation' can be interpreted as evaluative criteria as well (see Figure 3.2.4-1), for the sake of consistency, its operationalization will be discussed in chapter 4.2.4.

[13] Further insights into items of expected efficiency and expected time savings were provided by the research study of Hiltz/ Johnson, 1990, pp. 743ff..

[14] The item development process was further backed up by taking into account the recommendations provided in Benham/ Benham, 2004, Wang, 2003, Boerner/ Macher, 2001, and Hohberger, 2001.

measures for comparative cost advantages.

Item #	Constructs, definitions, and indicators
Production Cost Advantage (Pc): reflective (Dibbern, 2004)	
"Production costs comprise the costs in terms of time, effort, and money spent that arise for performing the actual activities necessary to complete the tasks associated with the production of content modules and/or bundles."	
Pc1	Our editors work more cost efficiently, if they have access to content that is stored centrally rather than decentrally.
Pc2	Our editors work faster, if they have access to content that is stored centrally rather than decentrally.
Pc3	Media products can be produced at a lower cost, if our editors have access to content that is stored centrally rather than decentrally.
Transaction Cost Advantage (Tc): reflective (Dibbern, 2004)	
"Transaction costs comprise all frictional costs in terms of time, effort, and money spent, that arise when content is exchanged between and among editorial units."	
Tc1	Search costs incurred are lower if our editors have access to content that is stored centrally rather than decentrally.
Tc2	Coordination problems encountered (e.g. redundant work) occur less, if our editors have access to content that is stored centrally rather than decentrally.
Tc3	Management costs (e.g. version or meta-data management) incurred are lower, if our editors have access to content that is stored centrally rather than decentrally.
Tc4	Frictional costs incurred in the form of waiting time or time delays during the search and exchange of content are lower, if our editors have access to content that is stored centrally rather than decentrally.

Table 4.2.2-1: Measures of comparative cost advantages

There is a long history in the discussion of the implications of technology on organizations. Numerous conceptual contributions on the strategic and operational role of IS/IT in organizations have been put forth. Most basically, the functions and ramifications of IT in firms can be boiled down to either improving existing processes to enhance flexibility, agility, and time-to-market (e.g., Sambamurthy/ Bharadwaj/ Grover, 2003; Ross, 2003) or opening up completely new kinds of business opportunities by increasing long-term business value and firm performance (e.g., Melville/ Kraemer/ Gurbaxani, 2004; Santhanam/ Hartono, 2003; Ragu-Nathan/ Ragu-Nathan/ Tu, 1999). Accordingly, IT can either be viewed as 'lubricant' in day-to-day business operations or as 'enabling driver' for the competition against competitors. For the operationalization process at hand, these two notions of IT were used to distinguish strategic and operational advantages, which arise due to the allocation of content that can be conceived of as one form of information technology.

Strategic contribution advantage:

Although a host of conceptual papers exists on the strategic role of information technology, only few studies have operationalized the concept and applied it in quantitative empirical studies. In most of the empirical papers, the strategic role of IS has been assessed by asking for the extent to which IS contributes to achieve various types of strategic objectives, of which a company's self-assertion in the competition against rival organizations or the realization of synergy effects are the most cited ones. Drawing on BARNEY's definition of sustained competitive advantage (Barney, 1991, p. 102), DIBBERN developed three items that reflect the degree to which the contribution of an IS function to generate a sustained competitive advantage can better be achieved in-house rather than through outsourcing (Dibbern, 2004, p. 152). Following DIBBERN's way of measuring the strategic contribution advantage construct, three items were adapted to the context of this study. Accordingly, respondents had to compare centralized and decentralized content allocation on the basis of its strategic constribution to the achievement of strategic goals (Strat1), the successful competition against rival firms (Strat2), and the realization of synergy effects (Strat3).

Table 4.2.2-2 provides a definition of strategic contribution advantage and also shows how the construct is measured.

Item #	Constructs, definitions, and indicators
Strategic Contribution Advantage (Strat): reflective (Dibbern, 2004)	
"Strategic contribution advantage is defined as the degree to which the allocation of content contributes to generate a sustained competitive advantage (e.g., through reducing costs, adding new features to differentiate existing products or services, or improving customer service)."	
Strat1	The achievement of our strategic goals is better strengthened, if our editors have access to content that is stored centrally rather than decentrally.
Strat2	The ability of our organization to compete successfully against our competitors is better supported, if our editors have access to content that is stored centrally rather than decentrally.
Strat3	The realization of synergy effects (e.g. by the reutilization of content) is better furthered, if our editors have access to content that is stored centrally rather than decentrally.

Table 4.2.2-2: Measures of comparative strategic advantages

Operational contribution advantage:

Drawing on the empirical study from RAGU-NATHAN ET AL. (Ragu-Nathan/ Ragu-Nathan/ Tu, 1999, pp. 349ff.), who developed indicators to validate operational measures for the dimensions of MCFARLAN AND MCKENNEY's strategic grid framework (McFarlan/ McKenney, 1983), four items have been adopted (Opera1-Opera4). The measures reflect the degree to which the operational contribution of content allocation to an organization's day-to-day business operations (i.e., the efficiency of content workflows) is strengthened, if content is deployed centrally rather than decentrally.

Item #	Constructs, definitions, and indicators
Operational Contribution Advantage (Opera): reflective (Ragu-Nathan/ Ragu-Nathan/ Tu, 1999) *"Operational contribution advantage is defined as the degree to which a publishing organization's day-to-day business operations critically depend on the efficient allocation of media content."*	
Opera1	The efficiency of our organization's content workflow in our day-to-day business activities is better strengthened, if our editors have access to content that is stored centrally rather than decentrally.
Opera2	The production of content in our day-to-day business operations is more efficient, if our editors access content that is stored centrally rather than decentrally.
Opera3	With regard to a possible reuse of content, the editorial production of content in our day-to-day business activities is faster, if our editors ccess content that is stored centrally rather than decentrally.
Opera4	The frictionless operation of our daily business activities is better supported, if our editors access content that is stored centrally rather than decentrally.

Table 4.2.2-3: Measures of comparative operational advantages

4.2.3 Content-, production process-, and market-related characteristics

4.2.3.1 Content characteristics from TCT theory

Similar to the content allocation indicators, items for content specificity were developed by the author. The scale development process was inspired by theoretical pre-studies at the ISNM. In particular, the works of SCHULZE (Schulze, 2005), ANDING (Anding, 2004), and RAWOLLE (Rawolle, 2002) provided a conceptual foundation for the item generation process. Pairs of opposing attributes were deduced from a content analysis of state-of-the-art literature, capturing different aspects of content specificity. After several evaluation cycles, content specificity was finally conceptualized as a second-order construct (e.g., Chin/ Marcolin/ Newsted, 1996, p. 39) formed by the following three dimensions: (1) specificity of topic, (2) specificity of structure, and (3) specificity of layout. Each of the three constructs has been measured reflectively, using a 7-point semantic differential-type format, where each response was located on an evaluative bipolar rating scale (from specific to unspecific). Since content specificity could not be assessed on the level of individual content modules or bundles due to the constraints of the data collection method, publishing companies were asked to give an estimation of the specificity of their content portfolio on an average basis. Table 4.2.3-1 illustrates the structure of the semantic differential in detail.

Item #	Constructs, definitions, and indicators
Topical Specificity (TopSpec): reflective (developed by author)	
"Topical specificity denotes the extent to which the topic or genre of content is tailored or suited to specific media output channels."	
TopSpec1	With regard to the topic, content that is typically integrated into our media products, can best be described as (...) *"targeting a very narrow – very broad customer group".*
TopSpec2	(...) *"topically specific – topically unspecific".*
TopSpec3	(...) *"badly – easily reutilizable".*
TopSpec4	(...) *"rapidly devalued (highly current) – slowly devalued (timeless)".*
Structure Specificity (StrucSpec): reflective (developed by author)	
"Structural specificity denotes the extent to which the structure or organization of content is recurrent or systematic in kind and therefore adjusted to specific media output channels."	
StrucSpec1	With regard to the structure, content that is typically integrated into our media products, can best be described as (...) *"monolithic – modular".*
StrucSpec2	(...) *"badly – easily structurable".*
StrucSpec3	(...) *"complex – simple structure".*
Layout Specificity (LaySpec): reflective (developed by author)	
"Layout specificity denotes the extent to which the layout or design of content is tailored or adjusted to specific media output channels."	
LaySpec1	With regard to the layout, content that is typically integrated into our media products, can best be described as (...) *"badly – easily convertible".*
LaycSpec2	(...) *"individualized/customized – standardized".*
LaySpec3	(...) *"layout dependent – layout independent".*

Table 4.2.3-1: Measures of content specificity

Content transaction frequency was assessed by drawing on the indicators of VAN DE

VEN AND FERRY, which measured the work flow interdependence between departmental units in organizations (Van de Ven/ Ferry, 1980, pp. 166ff.). Analogous to workflows in organizations, which represent the exchange of materials, objects, or clients between people within organizational units, content workflows or transactions were assessed by the direction and degree of content work interdependence. In this regard, independent, sequential, reciprocal, and team-oriented content workflows were distinguished (see Table 4.2.3-2). On the assumption that the types of workflows, which are represented by the four questionnaire items ConTran1-4, exhibit the characteristics of a Guttman scale (as argued by Thompson, 1967), answers to these items were weighted by multiplying the response to independent flows by zero, sequential flows by .33, reciprocal flows by .66, and team flow by one. Then, all the products were added up to obtain the overall content transaction frequency score.

Item #	Constructs, definitions, and indicators
Content Transaction Frequency (ConTrans): reflective (Van de Ven/ Ferry, 1980) *"Content transaction frequency refers to the degree of content workflow interdependence among and between editorial units."*	
ConTrans1	Individual editorial units in your company … … work independently of one another (independent workflows).
ConTrans2	… cooperate with other editorial units in one-directional input-/output-relationships (sequential workflow).
ConTrans3	… cooperate with other editorial units in reciprocal exchange relationships (reciprocal workflow).
ConTrans4	.. cooperate with other editorial units in projects.

Table 4.2.3-2: Measures of content transaction frequency

4.2.3.2 Content characteristics from RBV theory

The relatedness constructs were measured drawing on items used and validated in a study by TANRIVERDI AND VENKATRAMAN (Tanriverdi/ Venkatraman, 2005, p. 108). Existing measures were adapted and accordingly worded to capture the respondents' perspective on their firms' content, production process, and market relatedness (see Table 4.2.3-3). While the items for content relatedness referred to the basic characteristics of content, namely the genre, structure, and layout of content, measures for the production process and market relatedness represented reflective indicators for individual constitutents of applied production processes and targeted customer segments. Respondents were asked whether a given relatedness factor was unique and specific to each editorial unit or common and applicable to multiple units. The 5-point response scale spanned categories from "unique in all or almost all of the editorial units" to "common across all or almost all of editorial units". By emphasizing the degree to which publishing firms use common resources, production processes, and market know-how rather than the potential applicability of these factors across editorial units, the response scale is designed to capture the actual, realized relatedness of a given content, production process, and market know-how portfolio rather than a potential relatedness.

Item #	Constructs, definitions, and indicators
Content Relatedness (ConRel): reflective (Tanriverdi/ Venkatraman, 2005) *"Content relatedness refers to the similarity of media content among editorial units in publishing companies."*	
ConRel1	Regarding the genre, our content (e.g. articles, pictures, photos, etc.) is ... (1) unique in all or almost all of the editorial units (2) unique in a majority of the editorial units (3) unique in about half of the editorial units, common across the other half (4) common across a majority of the editorial units (5) common across all or almost all of editorial units
ConRel2	The structure and organization of our content is (...)
ConRel3	The layout and design of our content is (...)
Production Process Relatedness (ProRel): reflective (Tanriverdi/ Venkatraman, 2005) *"Production process relatedness refers to the similarity of production operations among editorial units in publishing companies regarding processes, skills, and applied technologies."*	
ProRel1	The complexity of our content production process steps is (...)
ProRel2	The time for and number of content production cycles is (...)
ProRel3	The technical skills to produce our content are (...)
ProRel4	The applied technologies and systems to produce our content are (...)
Market Relatedness (MarkRel): reflective (Tanriverdi/ Venkatraman, 2005) *"Market relatedness refers to the similarity of customer demands and preferences among editorial units in publishing companies."*	
MarkRel1	The preferences, demands, and buying behavior of our customer groups are (...)
MarkRel2	The characteristics of our customers are (...)
MarkRel3	The market environment surrounding our products is (...)

Table 4.2.3-3: Measures of relatedness

The interdepartmental synergy effects (or complementarities) between these three first-order factors, which is defined as the extent to which a publishing organization uses a complementary set of common content and knowledge resources across its editorial units (Tanriverdi/ Venkatraman, 2005, p. 103), were measured by introducing a second-order construct, which is reflected by three relatedness factors. This second-order factor models the complementarity of the first-order factors by accounting for their multilateral interactions and covariance. The directions of the structural links are from the second-order factor to the first-order factors, indicating that a publishing house that is in pursuit of interdepartmental synergy effects seeks to achieve relatedness in a complementary set of relatedness domains simultaneously (Tanriverdi/ Venkatraman, 2005, p. 111).

To measure the strategic value of content, items were adopted from empirical studies in MIS research (Grandon/ Pearson, 2003; Subramanian/ Nosek, 2001, pp. 65ff), mainly capturing strategic characteristics of content in RBV research (e.g. Eisenhardt/ Martin, 2000). As the strategic value of content could not be measured on an objective scale, perceptual measures were used. Each respondent was asked to rate the extent of uniqueness, non-substitutability, inimitability, and reutilization potential of their respective organization's content portfolio. Three items have been worded in accordance to the construct definition (see Table 4.2.3-4).

Item #	Constructs, definitions, and indicators
\multicolumn{2}{l}{**Perceived Strategic Content Value (ConVal): reflective (Grandon/ Pearson, 2003)**}
\multicolumn{2}{l}{*"Perceived strategic content value denotes the extent to which content bears a potential strategic value as indicated by its uniqueness, inimitability, non-substitutability and reutilization potential on a perceptual basis."*}
ConVal1	Our content stands out against the content of other competitors due to its uniqueness.
ConVal2	Vis-à-vis our competitors, we have the strategic advantage to possess content that is hardly imitable and substitutable.
ConVal3	Our content holds a greater reutilization potential than the content of our competitors.

Table 4.2.3-4: Measures of perceived strategic content value

4.2.4 Contingency variables

The 'business strategy' construct, which concerns the way a firm aligns actions and approaches to produce successful performance in order to build a long-term competitive advantage (Porter, 1985), was measured by drawing on items from studies in management (e.g. Miller, 1988) and MIS research (e.g. Brown/ Magill, 1994, pp. 395ff.; Floyd/ Wooldridge, 1990, pp. 52f.). For the sake of space constraints, each generic type of strategy was assessed just by one item taking into account the limited content validity and item reliability. While item BusStrat1 referred to the strategy of cost leadership by asking publishers whether they would outperform competitors with respect to cost efficiency in content production processes, item BusStrat2 addressed the strategy of differentiation by posing the question whether the responding publishers would differentiate their product offering from rivals' products. Last but not least, publishers should indicate whether they would strive to serve the entire market for their product or just a narrow market segment (BusStrat3). For all three items, respondents should assess on a 5-point Likert scale to what extent they would agree with the statements. Table 4.2.4-1 depicts the operationalizations of the three generic types of business strategy.

Item #	Constructs, definitions, and indicators
Business Strategy: individual constructs (Brown/ Magill, 1994)	
"Business strategy concerns the actions and the approaches to produce successful performance in order to build a strong long-term competitive position."	
LowCost	Our publishing organization employs a strategy of low-cost, i.e. we strive to produce more cost-efficiently than our competitors do.
Differ	Our publishing organization employs a strategy of differentiation, i.e. we seek to differentiate our product offering from rivals' products.
Focus	Our publishing organization utilizes a focus strategy, i.e. we don't strive to serve the entire, but a narrow portion of the market.

Table 4.2.4-1: Measures of business strategy

Organizational structure was operationalized using three sub-scales introduced into the contingency literature by the empirical works of AIKEN AND HAGE (Aiken/ Hage, 1968; Hage/ Aiken, 1967) and further reassessed and validated by DEWAR ET AL. (Dewar/ Whetten/ Boje, 1980, p. 122). The degree of organizational centralization in publishing companies (1) should capture the distribution of decision-making rights and responsibilities between the management and editorial units of publishers. In this vein, the level of editorial units' (operational) autonomy should be assessed. The degree of organizational formalization (2) refers to the level of systematization and structuring in publishing companies. More specifically, it captures the extent to which rules, procedures, and/or operational guidelines are predetermined in the production and bundling of content. Finally, in order to capture the degree of the division of labor, the level of specialization in publishing companies (3) should reflect the scope of tasks editors cover in day-to-day production and bundling operations.

The relationships between the three first-order variables (organizational centralization, formalization, and specialization) and the second-order factor "organizational structure" are modeled in the *reflective* mode (Eggert/ Fassott, 2005, p. 36; Jarvis et al., 2003, p. 201). That is, the structure of an organization is manifested in different structural outcomes that relate to each other.

Item #	Constructs, definitions, and indicators
Degree of Centralization in Organizations (OrgCent): reflective (Dewar/ Whetten/ Boje, 1980) *"The degree of centralization in organizations refers to the extent to which decision-making and directive power is distributed between top management and organizational units in publishing comapnies."*	
OrgCent1	Any decision editors have to make needs the approval of a central organizational unit.
OrgCent2	All decisions within our editorial units are strictly made from a central position.
OrgCent3	Our single editorial units enjoy extensive decision autonomy in day-to-day business operations.
Degree of Formalization in Organizations (OrgForm): reflective (Dewar/ Whetten/ Boje, 1980) *"The degree of formalization in organizations refers to the extent to which rules are used for the production and bundling activities in publishing organizations."*	
OrgForm1	The production and bundling of our content is precisely described in rules, procedures, and workflows.
OrgForm2	For every incident in the production and bundling of content, we have specific rules and guidelines to follow.
OrgFomr3	Every step in the production and bundling of content is documented in detail.
Degree of Specialization in Organizations (OrgSpec): reflective (Dewar/ Whetten/ Boje, 1980) *"The degree of specialization in organizations refers to the extent to which editors are capable of covering a broader or narrower spectrum of tasks in the production or bundling of content."*	
OrgSpec1	Every editor has a specific job to do.
OrgSpec2	Our editors are specialized in a specific step in the production and bundling of content.
OrgSpec3	Every editor has to cover several process steps in the production and bundling of content.

Table 4.2.4-2: Measures of organizational structure

Researchers have expressed concern that size has previously been defined too globally and is more likely a multidimensional construct (e.g., Gupta, 1980). Accordingly, as suggested in a host of previous studies in strategic management (e.g., Tanriverdi/ Venkatraman, 2005; Yasai-Ardekani, 1989; Beyer/ Trice, 1979) and MIS research (e.g., Raymond, 1990; Gremillion, 1984; Ein-Dor/ Segev, 1982), organization size was computed as natural logarithm of both the number of editorial units and the number of employees (i.e., the number full-time employees were weighted by multiplying the responses by one, the number of part-time employees by .5). The log transformation[15] was considered necessary, because several studies have suggested a curvilinear relationship between size and other organizational variables (Kimberly, 1976; Child, 1973). Additionally, the circulation size of a publisher's best-selling product was included as organizational size criterion in order to compare publishers within their respective sub-industry (Carter, 1984, pp. 257f.).

Item #	Constructs, definitions, and indicators
Organization Size (OrgSize): reflective (Ein-Dor/ Segev, 1982; Brown/ Magill, 1994) *"The size of an organization is defined as being reflected by the number of editorial units, the number of full- and part-time working employees, and the circulation size of the best-selling media product of a publishing organization."*	
OrgSize1	Total number of editorial units (log)
OrgSize2	Total number of full- and part-time workers (log)
OrgSize3	Circulation of best-selling media product (log)

Table 4.2.4-3: Measures of organizational size

In addition to the structure and size of the organization, the responding publishers were classified either as book, magazine, or newspaper publishing company (Pub-Type) on the basis of the type of product, which accounted for the biggest share of revenue in the content portfolio. This was implemented by letting respondents tick off[16] and rank media products in descending order according to the level of their contribution to turnover. Furthermore, the number of media channels, which were provided by publishers, was computed, serving as a proxy for the degree of media diversification (NumMedChan)[17].

Three items for the measurement of IT governance were adopted from an empirical study by RAGU-NATHAN ET AL. (Ragu-Nathan et al., 2004, p. 469), which captured the extent to which the management of IT-related tasks (ITGov1), database control (ITGov2), and workflow activities (ITGov3) are supported by a central IT unit (e.g. department).

The structural organization of the IS function was operationalized polytomously (ITOrg). As an appropriate classification scheme, the six organizational models for designing information technology activities of MERTENS AND KNOLMAYER were

---

[15] The usual reasoning is that a logarithmic size measure provides a better empirical fit between size and structural variables.

[16] Boxes with media products next to them had to be checkmarked by respondents, if covered by the publishing organization.

[17] Both the measurement items for publisher type and the number of provided media channels are not further specified in Table 4.2.4-3, as the simple measurement mode doesn't need further explication.

selected (Mertens/ Knolmayer, 1998[18]). According to this typology, the IS function can be organized in-house as staff function, IT department, cross-departmental function, or line function. Alternatively, the IS function can be outsourced to an IT service provider either inside or outside the corporate (publishing) group.

Item #	Constructs, definitions, and indicators
IT Governance (ITGov): reflective (Ragu-Nathan et al., 2004)	
"IT governance refers to a set of responsibilities and practices exercised by senior management of the organization designed to establish and communicate strategic direction, ensure realization of goals and objectives, mitigate risk, and verify that assigned resources are used in an effective and efficient manner."	
ITGov1	The management of all IT-related tasks is performed by a central IT department.
ITGov 2	Content databases are administered by a central IT department.
ITGov 3	Content production and bundling activities are supported and controlled by a central IT department.
IT Organization (ITOrg): polytomous (Mertens/ Knolmayer, 1998)	
"The organization of the IT function refers to how IT-related activities are formally institutionalized in publishing companies."	
ITOrg	Our IT function is organized as …
	(1) staff function (just a consulting function without authority).
	(2) IT department in its own right next to other departments (e.g., marketing, sales or editorial units).
	(3) cross-departmental function (i.e. centralized IT department and decentralized IT units embedded into one or more editorial units).
	(4) line function (i.e. just decentralized IT units embedded into one or more editorial units).
	(5) external IT service provider inside the corporate publishing group.
	(6) external IT service provider outside the corporate publishing group.

Table 4.2.4-4: Measures of IT governance and IT organization

Due to the lack of validated measures in previous studies, indicators on technological path dependence were developed by the author. Drawing on the seminal theoretical papers in the field of technological path dependence (Barnes/ Gartland/ Stack, 2004; Arthur, 1989; David, 1985), three items for IT investment-related and IT usage-based path dependencies have been worded respectively, basically referring to the importance of past IT investments and prior IT usage habits for current and future content allocation decisions.

---

[18] The typology by MERTENS AND KNOLMAYER closely relates to other approaches to structure the IT function in organizations (see for example Agarwal/ Sambamurthy, 2002 or Zmud, 1984).

Item #	Constructs, definitions, and indicators
IT Investment-related Path Dependencies (ITInvestPath): reflective	
"IT investment-related path dependencies refer to IT investments in the past that potentially constrain the latitude of a content allocation decision in the presence."	
ITInvestPath1	The present and future storage location for our content is mainly dependent on prior IT-investments in hardware and software.
ITInvestPath 2	The existing IT-infrastructure primarily predetermines the current and future location of our content.
ITInvestPath 3	A rearrangement of the current content allocation configuration would entail high switching costs for hardware, software, and personnel.
IT Usage-based Path Dependencies (ITUsagePath): reflective	
"IT usage-based path dependencies refer to habituation effects in the usage of IT that potentially constrain the latitude of a content allocation decision in the presence."	
ITUsagePath1	The current distribution and integration of content is the result of historically grown working structures of our employees.
ITUsagePath2	For our employees, the costs to adjust to new ways in the allocation of content would be too high.
ITUsagePath3	Historically or culturally grown working structures within our organization are not considered when decisions are made on the distribution and integration of content.

Table 4.2.4-5: Measures of technological path dependencies

Indicators for infrastructural IT-imperatives (see Table 4.2.4-6; see also Figure 3.3.3.3-4 for the theoretical constructs) were adopted from several studies in MIS research (Ravichandran/ Lertwongsatien, 2005, p. 270; Jain et al., 1998, p. 27; Tractinsky/ Jarvenpaa, 1995, p. 516), and wording was modified to fit the content allocation context to be studied. For the sake of simplicity, all items were worded in the direction of the advantageousness of central content allocation, which pilot testing indicated was easier to understand. A written notice above the block of items pointed out that no general tendency in favor of central content allocation should be suggested. Respondents should rather critically judge the extent to which they agree with the statements (on a 5-point Likert scale).

System reliability was measured by referring to the availability of content and robustness of content provisioning during the production and bundling phases (ITImp1 and ITImp2). System performance was captured by asking respondents for the access speed to content, indirectly referring to the latency time of content repositories (ITImp3). The operationalization of system security was performed through item ITImp5, which addressed concrete security measures like backup and content access rights management. System scalability and extensibility were measured by directly addressing the scalability of content processing and the ease of the integration of additional content resources (ITImp4 and ITImp7). Emerging from pilot testing, indicators ITImp6 and ITImp8 were included into the item battery as complementary indicators, referring to the ease of content management (i.e., metadata, version, and access rights management) on the one hand, and to the level of content consistency on the other. As all of the indicators represent constituent elements rather than equivalent representatives of infrastructural IT-imperatives, the *formative* measurement mode was chosen (Eggert/ Fassott, 2005, pp. 38f.; Jarvis et al., 2003, p. 201).

Item #	Constructs, definitions, and indicators
Infrastructural IT-imperatives (ITImp): formative (Jain et al., 1998) *"IT-related imperatives refer to infrastructural characteristics of IT systems that constrain or enable the feasibility of task fulfillment."*	
ITImp1	The access to centralized as opposed to decentralized content is advantageous, because ... ... the availability of our entire content stock during production and bundling phases is more optimal.
ITImp2	... the error-proneness of content delivery during production and bundling phases is lower.
ITImp3	... the access speed to content for our editors is more optimal during production and bundling phases.
ITImp4	... the scalability of content processing is more optimal during production and bundling phases.
ITImp5	... the management and execution of security measures (e.g. content access rights, daily backups, etc.) can be realized more consistently.
ITImp6	... content can be organized (e.g. content management), archived (e.g. versioning), and maintained (e.g. access rights management) more optimally.
ITImp7	... the integration of another editorial unit with additional content is realizable more easily.
ITImp8	... our editors have always access to the most current versions of our content during production and bundling phases (i.e. less version inconsistencies).

Table 4.2.4-6: Measures of infrastructural IT-imperatives

4.2.5 Overview of formative and reflective measurement constructs

To reiterate the construct-to-item relationships (i.e. the correspondence rules between the theoretical and empirical world) applied in this study, the following table recapitulates constructs, sub-constructs (in the case of second-order constructs), and respective measurement modes.

Construct	Measurement mode (# of items)	Sub-construct	Measurement mode (# of items)
Content distribution	Reflective (3)		
Content integration	Reflective (4)		
Production cost advantage	Reflective (3)		
Transaction cost advantage	Reflective (4)		
Strategic contribution adv.	Reflective (3)		
Operational contribution adv.	Reflective (4)		
Content specificity	Formative (3), second order	Topic specificity	Reflective (4)
		Structural specificity	Reflective (3)
		Layout specificity	Reflective (3)
Content transaction frequency	Formative (4), weighted index		
Interdepartmental comple-mentarities	Reflective (3), second order	Content relatedness	Reflective (3)
		Pro. process relatedness	Reflective (3)
		Market relatedness	Reflective (3)
Perceived strategic content value	Reflective (3)		
Strategy of low cost	Single item		
Strategy of differentiation	Single item		
Strategy of focus	Single item		
Organizational structure	Reflective (3), second order	Degree of centralization	Reflective (3)
		Degree of formalization	Reflective (3)
		Degree of specialization	Reflective (3)
Organizational size	Reflective (3)		
IT governance	Reflective (3)		
IT organization	Single item		
IT investment-related path dependencies	Reflective (3)		
IT usage-based path dependencies	Reflective (3)		
Infrastruct. IT-imperatives	Formative (8)		

Table 4.2.5-1: Measurement modes of research constructs

4.3 Data collection

Due to the variance-based character of this research study (see Figure 2.2-2), the collection of empirical data followed a cross-sectional approach, in which a given population of publishing organizations is composed into one large sample at only one single point in time. A questionnaire was developed and sent to book, magazine, and newspaper publishers in Germany in order to test the previously developed model on content allocation.

In the following, background information will be provided on the design of the questionnaire (see chapter 4.3.1), the sample selection (see chapter 4.3.2), and the mailing procedure (see chapter 4.3.3). Finally, the chapter concludes with the presentation of the survey response data (see chapter 4.3.4), which resulted from the mailing procedures.

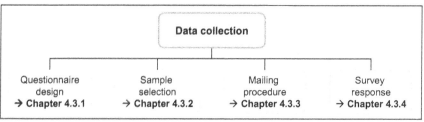

Figure 4.3-1: Data collection issues

4.3.1 Questionnaire design

In designing the questionnaire, two partially opposing objectives had to be brought in line. On the one hand, the questionnaire had to match the theoretical objectives of the study. On the other hand, it had to be assured that the questionnaire is respondent-friendly, which is critical for achieving a high response rate (Dillman/ Sinclair/ Clark, 1993, p. 300). One of the preconditions to achieve both objectives is the researcher's familiarity with the survey method, as well as with the language and the main terminology used in practice. Therefore, two pre-studies on the determinants of content allocation have been conducted.

The objective of the first pre-test, which was conducted by telephone and mail with CIOs of 12 publishing companies[19], was twofold. On the one hand, the relevance of major decision criteria for the allocation of content should thus be evaluated. Given decision criteria, which were derived by a literature analysis, should be rated accord-

---

[19] In each publishing sector (i.e. books, magazines, and newspapers) four companies helped the author to reflect on survey items and finally improve the entire measurement instrument. All of the pre-testing companies also confirmed the importance of the content allocation topic in the publishing sector.

ing to their relative importance. Additionally, open questions gave the respondents the opportunity to add further aspects. On the other hand, the dependent research variable, i.e. content allocation, was tested methodologically in order to improve the content adequacy of the survey items measuring content distribution and content integration (see chapter 4.2.1). Finally, the variance in the research variable was examined in dependence of common contingency variables.

After having incorporated the major findings of the first pre-test stage into the measurement instrument, the survey items of the independent variables were integrated taking into account conventional recommendations in the formulation of attitudinal questions (Sudman/ Bradburn, 1982, p. 121). The preliminary version of the entire survey was reviewed by a faculty member and fellow researchers from the ISNM, conversant with either the topic of content integration or the research methodology.

In a second face-to-face pre-test round with four CIOs of different publishing companies, all the survey items of the questionnaire were discussed intensively and reworded according to the feedback of the respondents. Some of the initial survey questions were even deleted in this iterative feedback process, because they were perceived to be redundant, i.e., too similar in wording. This pre-test cycle allowed assessing the face and content validity of items and ensured that the target persons understood the instructions, questions, and response scales of the instrument as intended. Table 4.3.1-1 once again summarizes the pre-test steps in the questionnaire development process, including the initial scale construction of the dependent research variable mentioned in chapter 4.2.1.

Pre-test stage	Activities in questionnaire development process	Pre-test sample
1.	Scale development and evaluation of dependent variable regarding convergent and discriminant validity	122 students and fellow researchers
2.	Test of relative importance of decision criteria and of face and content validity of dependent research variable	12 CIOs of publishing companies
3.	Intensive discussion of entire questionnaire regarding face and content validity of all items	4 CIOs of publishing companies

Table 4.3.1-1: Pre-test stages in questionnaire development and design

After a final round of slight adjustments, based on comments from fellow researchers, the questionnaire was discussed with undergraduate students[20] in a course on empirical methods at the Institute for Information Systems and New Media at the University of Munich. Additional insights for the wording and design of the question-

---

[20] All of the five students had gained valuable experiences either with survey designs or with the particularities of the book, magazine or newspaper publishing sector prior to this course. One of the students, majoring in book science, even worked at a book publishing firm on part-time basis in parallel to this course and was of great help in formulating the survey questions.

naire were finally integrated into the measurement instrument. The resulting product of this recursive pre-test procedure is the finalized version of the questionnaire, as presented in Appendix C (see C1 for the German and C2 for the English version).

4.3.2 Sample selection

In accordance with prior studies on the allocation of IT-related resources (e.g., Kahai/ Snyder/ Carr, 2002; Ahituv/ Neumann/ Zviran, 1989; Tavakolian, 1989), the IS executives[21] of publishing firms were chosen as the target group to answer the questionnaire. Due to the challenges entailed in achieving sufficient response rates and common practice in comparable empirical research studies, a single informant per firm were addressed during the data collection phase (Bagozzi/ Phillips, 1982, p. 469; Seidler, 1974, pp. 816ff.). In order to minimize any potential measurement error that may result from the use of a single informant, the methodological suggestions by HUBER AND POWER were followed (see Huber/ Power, 1985, pp. 172ff.).

In order to explore publisher-type specific differences in content allocation, a stratified sample of publishing organizations was drawn from the three biggest German associations of book, magazine, and newspaper publishers: Börsenverein des Deutschen Buchhandels[22] (German Association of Book Publishers), Verband Deutscher Zeitschriftenverleger[23] (German Association of Magazine Publishers) and Bundesverband Deutscher Zeitungsverleger[24] (German Association of Newspaper Publishers). As elaborated in chapter 2.2, legally independent publishing companies[25] represent the unit of analysis. Accordingly, the questionnaire was explicitly not addressed to corporate publishing houses, but to publishing firms with independently operating editorial units. At the outset of the data collection phase, it was intended to mail the questionnaire to all the members of the German associations of publishing companies, approximately representing the characteristics of the overall population.

As the membership lists just occasionally provided the full contact information of the respective IS executive, publishers were contacted by telephone to ask f the missing contact information. In the majority of cases, the names and contact information of IS executives were disclosed without any hassle. Additionally, if IS executives could be reached in person, they were pre-notified of the upcoming survey (Duncan, 1979, pp. 42f.). However, a small fraction of contacted publishers ruled out a participation right

---

[21] If there did not exist an IS executive, the CEO of the publishing organization was asked to answer the questionnaire in consultation with a production editor.

[22] BVDB: http://www.boersenverein.de

[23] VDZ: http://www.vdz.de

[24] BDVZ: http://www.bdzv.de

[25] Those publishing companies are included that have a minimum of editorial independence. For instance, publishing firms that adopt the cover of a national newspaper, but additionally include local news are considered as editorially independent.

from the start. This resulted in the deletion of a number of firms from the list. The final list of contacted companies included 450 firms in the book publishing sector, 250 firms in the newspaper publishing sector, and 400 companies in the magazine publishing sector, totaling to 1100 publishing firms (see Table 2.1.1-1).

4.3.3 Mailing procedure

The initial survey package included a 5-page questionnaire, a personally addressed cover letter, explaining the purpose of the study and a postage-paid reply envelope. Serving as an incentive to fill out the questionnaire, five Apple iPods 'Shuffle' (with 512 MB storage capacity) and one Apple iPod (20 GB) were announced to be raffled off among the participants of the survey. In addition, respondents were offered an executive summary of the research results to encourage their participation.

While the questionnaire was sent to the members of BDZV and VDZ by mail and simultaneously by e-mail, it was dispatched to the BVDB members only by e-mail[26]. This was due to the fact that the partnering organization on the side of the BVDB, AKEP[27], operates a mailing list with 450 book publishers particularly interested in technology-related topics. As AKEP argued that these members regularly show a high involvement with respect to answering technology-related surveys, a mail-order by post was omitted. Book publishers of BVDB[28] other than the AKEP members were not included into the survey, as it was argued that the response rate of this residual group would be rather low.

Approximately three weeks after the initial mailing, a follow-up electronic mailing was initiated. This e-mail included a reminder cover letter and the questionnaire as attachment. The initial and follow-up cover letters in German are presented in Appendix B. After another two weeks, it was attempted to personally contact the IS executives of those companies that did not return a questionnaire. A group of students were given instructions on how to contact this residual group of respondents. In particular, they were instructed to remind the IS executives of the purpose of the study and the importance of their participation.

---

[26] Both in the cover letter and the e-mail, it was additionally pointed out that the questionnaire could also be downloaded in diverse output formats from the Internet website http://www.wi.bwl.uni-muenchen.de/query/mehrfachnutzung.asp. A user name and password were included for an exclusive survey access.

[27] AKEP (Arbeitskreis Elektronisches Publizieren) is a working group within the BVDB that deals with new developments in the field of electronic publishing (http://www.akep.de). As previous empirical studies were carried out together (e.g., Benlian, et al., 2005), this follow-up research project was also supported by AKEP.

[28] BVDB is the association of German book publishers in Germany and comprises about 6.386 members (BVDB, 2004, S. 13).

4.3.4 Survey response

Overall, 115 usable questionnaires[29] were returned from the total contacted sample of 1100 companies (see Table 4.3.4-1).

Type of publisher	Population		Contacted sample		Survey response	
	n	Pct.	n	Pct.	n	Pct.
Books[30] (BVDB)	1.827[31]	70%	450	40.9%	32	27.8%
Magazines[32] (VDZ)	450[33]	17%	400	36.4%	47	40.9%
Newspapers[34] (BDZV)	347[35]	13%	250	22.7%	36	31.3%
Σ Sum	2.624	100%	1.100	100%	115	100%

Table 4.3.4-1: Characteristics of population, contacted sample, and survey response

This equals a response rate of 10.5%, representing a satisfactory response rate relative to comparable empirical studies[36] and given the length and complexity of the questionnaire[37]. Computing the response rate for each publisher sub-type, 7.1% for

---

[29] As the majority of the received surveys could be traced back to the respective publishing house, initially missing values could most frequently be completed by asking the respondents once more to fill out the entire questionnaire.

[30] In the context of this study, book publishing houses are defined as organizations that exclusively or primarily publish books that represent collections of leaves of paper, affixed in some manner to one another, with or without a case or cover. Publishing organizations like universities, clubs or firms of other industries are excluded. Book-trading companies are also completely excluded. In contrast to periodicals like magazines or newspapers, books are not published periodically.

[31] 1.827 book publishing firms ("Herstellender Buchhandel") are members of the BVDB (BVDB, 2004, S. 13), which is also assumed to be the underlying population size of this research study.

[32] Magazine publishing firms are defined as organizations that publish periodicals at least on a weekly basis. In this study, companies that publish journals and other periodicals different from newspapers are subsumed under magazine publishers in this research study.

[33] This data originates from BDZV, 2004, p. 396 and Reitze, 2004, p. 41. A statistical overview on the structure of the German newspaper industry is given in Schütz, 2001, 2005.

[34] Newspaper publishing firms ("Verlage als Herausgeber") are defined as organizations that publish periodicals issued at frequent intervals (e.g. daily, weekly, semi-weekly), containing news, opinions, advertisements, and other items of current, often local, interest. Advertising papers are also included in this category.

[35] The members of the VDZ represent about 90% of the overall number of magazines in Germany (Michalk, 2004, p. 2). This statistic was also used to extrapolate the population size.

[36] The empirical study of DIBBERN on the selective outsourcing of IT functions, for instance, reported a response rate of 8.4% (Dibbern, 2004, p. 165). A similar study by POPPO AND ZENGER achieved a response rate of 5% (152 of 3000) in a mail survey on the outsourcing of IS function (Poppo/ Zenger, 1998, p. 862).

[37] The literature on survey response rates is very inconsistent in evaluating the impact of the length of questionnaires on the survey response (Dillman/ Sinclair/ Clark, 1993, p. 290; Childers/ Ferrell, 1979, p. 430). On the one hand, the length of the questionnaire is taken as a signal for its importance. On the other hand, it increases the respondent's cost perceptions in comparison to the expected benefits from participation.

book publishers, 11.8% for magazine publishers, and 14.4% for newspaper publishers could be achieved.

Due to the restrictive mailing policy of AKEP, book publishers were underrepresented in the response sample, while magazine and newspaper publishers were overrepresented. Consequently, comparing the expected and observed group sizes, a chi-square test revealed a significant deviation ($\chi^2_{df=2} = 9.229$; p<0.01), leading to the fact that statements inferred from the response sample should be transferred carefully to the underlying population. Nevertheless, as the main goal of this research study is to develop a structural equation model that maximizes the explained variance in content allocation, this deviation is not considered as severe. Furthermore, the validity of hypotheses generated in this study may have a validity in a setting different from the one presented here. That is, discovered relationships between explanatory factors and the allocation of content may also be useful and applicable to other contexts, despite of the potential non-existence of statistical, sampling-based generalizability (Lee/ Baskerville, 2003, pp. 228ff.; von der Lippe/ Kladropa, 2002, pp. 141ff.).

On the one hand, survey non-response was evaluated in pre-notification and follow-up telephone interviews with publishing firms (Donald, 1967). A lot of CIOs in book, magazine, and newspaper publishing companies complained about being overloaded with questionnaires from all kinds of institutions and expressed their disbelief in the value that they can achieve from survey participation[38]. A few number of non-respondents even indicated that they couldn't cope with the length and complexity of the questionnaire or that the questionnaire would distract and prevent them from fulfilling their job.

On the other hand, a non-parametrical Mann-Whitney-U-tests was carried out to compare early with late respondents (Mann/ Whitney, 1947). This procedure is based on the assumption that late respondents are more similar to non-respondents (Armstrong/ Overton, 1977, pp. 60f.). No structural differences between early and late respondents could be detected with regard to organizational size, structure, and content integration. However, significant differences on the sub-type of publishing organization and content distribution behavior could be observed. Analyzing the descriptives from explorative data analysis revealed that book publishers represented the majority group among late, and the minority group among early respondents. This indicated once more, that the actual response sample was distorted, because of too few responses of book publishers relative to the responses of magazine and newspaper publishers.

There is one note of caution that needs to be addressed before providing an overview over sample characteristics. Due to the distorted response sample, in particular

---

[38] For exploring reasons for non-response, see also Baruch, 1999.

the book publisher group, the descriptives may not be representative for a larger population. For that reason, the main purpose of their presentation is to give the reader background information on the sample, that will be used for model testing subsequently.

4.4 Sample characteristics

For the sake of clarity and guiding the process of the empirical analysis, the response sample of this study can be subdivided into different sub-samples, of which the allocation dimension, the content type, the time perspective of content allocation, and the publisher type play the most relevant discriminating factors. Figure 4.4-2 illustrates how the entire sample can be broken down to the corresponding sub-samples with respective sample sizes.

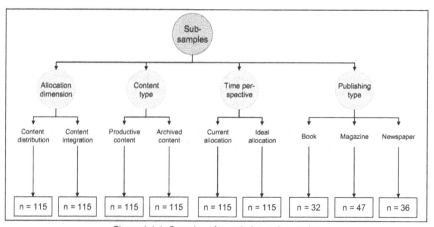

Figure 4.4-1: Grouping of sample into sub-samples

Before starting to test the sub-samples on content allocation across allocation dimensions and content types in chapter 4.5, though, it is worth to present a number of statistics that describe the average characteristics of the responding organizations[39]. Together, they provide more detailed information on the demographics of the respondents (see chapter 4.4.1), the content allocation practices of publishers (see chapter 4.4.2), and structural differences and commonalities between publisher subtypes (see chapter 4.4.3). Figure 4.4-2 depicts the organization of the following chapters.

---

[39] While the comparison of current and ideal content allocation practices and other structural characteristics of the different types of publishers will be taken up next when major sample descriptives are presented, the SEM-based analysis will focus on variances caused by different allocation dimensions and content types.

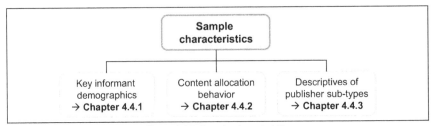

Figure 4.4-2: Sample characteristics

4.4.1 Key informant demographics

To check whether the key informants were sufficiently qualified to answer the questionnaire, their functions (or position) within the publishing company was evaluated[40]. Figure 4.4.1-1 makes clear that the majority of the respondents can be assigned to the desired target group, namely IS executives .

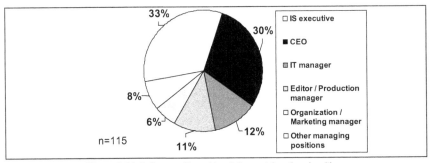

Figure 4.4.1-1: Composition of key informant functions/positions

As CEOs of rather small- or mid-sized publishing firms are often thoroughly informed about IT systems, it is not astonishing, either, that they represent the second biggest group of respondents. Although 14% of the respondents do not reside at the very heart of the desired target group (e.g. organization, marketing, and other managers), it can be assumed though that they are qualified enough to answer the questions appropriately. An indicator of this assumption is that this residual group of respondents has accumulated working experiences for about 6.5 years on average in their publishing firm. Overall, the respondents that answered the questionnaire had on average 9 years working experience (book publishers: 9.25 years; magazine publishers: 8.72 years; newspaper publishers: 9.79 years) with their company (see Table

---

[40] The majority of the names of the respondents on the reply envelopes matched the original addressees. This, together with our personal telephone contacts, increases the confidence that the questionnaires where actually answered by the target group of the research study.

4.4.1-1), indicating that the key informants of the research sample were highly knowledgeable about the questions asked in this study.

Company Membership	Mean (of years)	St.Dev.
Book publisher	9.25	7.33
Magazine publisher	8.72	5.82
Newspaper publisher	9.79	7.89
Average across total sample	*9.20*	*6.89*

Table 4.4.1-1: Company membership of key informants

4.4.2 Content allocation behavior

Subsequently, the content allocation behavior of publishing companies should be analyzed first on an aggregate level, then on the level of the individual publisher sub-type. Finally, a brief gap analysis should be performed shedding light on current and desired content allocation.

Overall, content distribution and integration are significantly and positively related to one another in publishing firms (Spearman-rho r=0.65, p<0.01). That means, if content is allocated centrally, the access to content for editors is rather integrated than isolated. The other way round, if content is allocated decentrally, the scope of access to content is rather low. The conceptual typology illustrated in chapter 2.1.2 (see Figure 2.1.2-2), where four types of content allocation were conceptually deduced, also reflects this strong association (see Chi^2-test in Table 4.4.2-1).

Content distribution

		Centralized	Decentralized
Content integration	Integrated	(1) **Amalgamation** 40,7%	(2) **Connectedness** 12,0%
	Isolated	(3) **Disconnectedness** 18,5%	(4) **Separation** 28,7%

$\chi^2_{df=1} = 16.080$, p<0.001 (based on a Chi^2-test)

Table 4.4.2-1: Aggregated content allocation behavior

The amalgamation of content turns out to be the most frequent content allocation sub-type, whilst connectedness the least frequent. Altogether, the content allocation behavior of publishing companies draws a rather bi-polar picture with almost 70% of publishing companies allocating content either centrally or decentrally. On the level of the individual types of publishing firms, however, a more heterogeneous picture can be painted. While magazine publishers almost perfectly match the relative distribution between different content allocation sub-types as illustrated at the crosstab above, newspaper and book publishers show almost diametrically opposing allocation characteristics, offsetting each other's extreme behavior. With about only 50% of centralized and 40% of integrated productive content, book publishing companies exhibit the most decentralized and isolated content allocation behavior compared to the others. By contrast, newspaper publishing companies store about 80% of their productive and archived content stock at a central location, while letting editors have access to about 80% (85%) to their productive (archived) content portfolio (see Table 4.4.2-2).

Type of publisher	Content distribution		Content integration	
	Productive	*Archived*	*Productive*	*Archived*
Book publishers	50.6%	54.4%	39.4%	41.4%
Magazine publishers	65.7%	65.5%	62.3%	66.8%
Newspaper publishers	80.1%	79.0%	79.9%	85.2%
Differences between groups	$\chi^2_{df=2} = 15.01^*$	$\chi^2_{df=2} = 11.73^*$	$\chi^2_{df=2} = 18.79^{**}$	$\chi^2_{df=2} = 25.91^{**}$

* $p<0.05$, ** $p<0.005$ (based on a Kruskal-Wallis H-Test)

Table 4.4.2-2: Share of centrally stored content in book, magazine, and newspaper publishing firms

So far, only the *current* content allocation behavior has been investigated. Juxtaposing the current and ideal distribution of productive and archived media content, it could be found that publishing companies desire to centralize their productive and archived content to an even greater extent (see Figure 4.4.2-1).

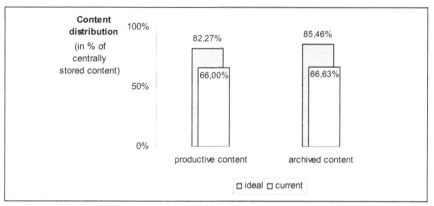

Figure 4.4.2-1: Current and ideal distribution of productive and archived content

While between productive and archived content distribution only minor, but no significant differences could be identified for current and ideal allocation arrangements[41], a
significant difference could be observed when evaluating the transition from current
to ideal content distribution. Publishing companies stated that they centralize on average 66% of their entire productive content portfolio, indicating that in an ideal content distribution arrangement, they would even centralize 82.27% (p<0.001). With
regard to archived content, a similar picture can be painted: on average, 66.63% of
the entire archived content stock is currently centralized, while publishing companies
consider ideal to centralize their archived content at a level of 85.46% (p<0.001).

Statements of publishing companies about the current and ideal integration of productive and archived content yielded similar, even more extreme differences (i.e.
wider gaps) between current and ideal content integration behavior (see Figure
4.4.2-2). An ideal degree of content integration was indicated as having publishing
companies providing access to on average 84.42% of the entire productive content
stock and to around 89.33% of the entire archived content stock. By contrast, the
current allocation situation for productive and archived content respectively remains
at a lower integration degree, leveling off at 60.48% and 65.50% on average.

---

[41] This result may be an indication that no big distinctions are made between productive and archived
content regarding allocation decisions.

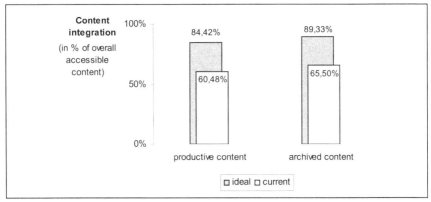

Figure 4.4.2-2: Current and ideal content integration of productive and archived content

Having provided an overview of content allocation differences and commonalities between the different sub-types of publishing companies, further relevant discriminating factors will be investigated to characterize the research sub-samples.

4.4.3 Descriptives about publisher sub-types

In order to check for the typical structural differentiators between book, magazine, and newspaper companies, the three publisher sub-types were compared on the basis of (1) the number of editorial units and employees, (2) content transaction frequency (or the intensity of interdepartmental content exchange), (3) content reutilization, and (4) content devaluation speed.

(1) Sample composition

In the response sample on hand, magazine publishers represented the smallest firm size class with on average 10.68 editorial units and 155.75 employees, whereas newspaper publishers were the biggest with on average 13.11 editorial units and 398.67 employees (see Table 4.4.3-1).

	Editorial units		Full- and part-time empl.	
Type of publisher	Mean of #	St.Dev. of #	Mean of #	St.Dev. of #
Book publisher	11.18	24.09	223.06	564.29
Magazine publisher	10.68	22.14	155.75	232.24
Newspaper publisher	13.11	17.51	398.67	1008.54
Total sample	11.30	20.66	250.53	656.87

Table 4.4.3-1: Organizational size of book, magazine, and newspaper publishers

As mean values and standard deviations give only a rough idea about the relative distribution of organizational size, publishers were assigned to three sub-groups with different value ranges for editorial units and employees respectively (see Figure 4.4.3-1 and Figure 4.4.3-2).

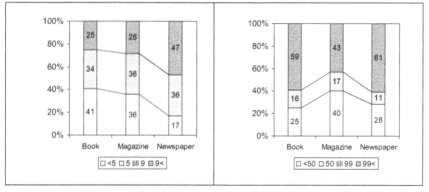

Figure 4.4.3-1: Size composition of editorial   Figure 4.4.3-2: Size composition of employees
        units in publishing companies   in publishing companies

The analysis of the size composition of the sample revealed that book-publishing companies had the largest share of companies with less than five editorial units. By contrast, almost half of the newspaper publishers, which participated at the study, comprised more than nine editorial units. When looking at the size breakdown of employees in publishing companies, magazine companies turned out to have the biggest share (40%) of firms with less than 50 employees, while about 60% of book and newspaper companies respectively employed at least 100 employees. Moreover, both book and newspaper companies exhibited very similar size compositions.

(2) Content transaction frequency

With regard to the differences between publisher sub-types on the basis of content transaction frequency (CTF)[42], a tendency towards an increasing intensity of content exchange across editorial units can be observed from book (median $m_{CTF\_Books}=5.12$) over magazine ($m_{CTF\_Magazine}=5.97$) to newspaper publishers ($m_{CTF\_Magazine}=6.96$). As theoretically outlined in chapter 2.2, the empirical sample confirms that newspaper publishers show the highest degree of intra-organizational content exchange, while book publishers exchange content the least intensively. This may primarily be attributed to the functional differentiation in the value chains of book, magazine, and newspaper publishers. While magazine and newspaper organizations most frequently produce media content on their own in the respective editorial units, content (e.g. book manuscripts and proposals) is for the most part just edited and layouted by

---

[42] Content transaction frequency represents a weighted index of four questionnaire items scaled from 0 to 10 with increasing levels of transaction frequency (see Table 4.2.3-2).

editors in book organizations. Hence, the probability is far lower in book than in newspaper publishing companies to search for additional pieces of content in content repositories of other editorial units during the production and bundling process. In Figure 4.4-3, boxplots illustrate the relationship between the type of publishing organization and the content transaction frequency.

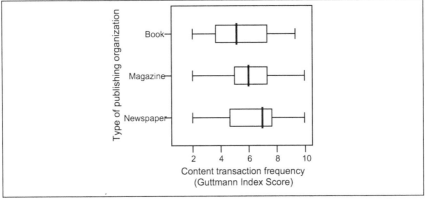

Figure 4.4-3: Content transaction frequency in book, magazine, and newpaper publishing firms

(3) Content reutilization bevahior

Closely interwined with content transaction frequency are content reutilization practices of publishers. As content is more frequently exchanged among editorial units, the level of content repurposing usually increases as well. Regarding Figure 4.4-4, this intuitive notion is confirmed, at least for the research study's sample. With a median of 22.5%, book publishing companies reutilize productive content the least. By contrast, magazine and newspaper publishers repurpose content on a 30% and 42.5% level respectively, indicating a clear rise in the intensity of content reutilization from book to newspaper publishers. However, this result seems to stand in stark contrast to the findings made concerning the number of media channels maintained by publishers. A significant difference between the different types of publishers could be observed (Kruskal-Wallis-F-Test $\chi^2_{df=2} = 29.573$, p<0.01), with book publishers having on average 4.84, magazine publishers on average 3.64, and newspaper publishers on average 2.28 media channels in their respective content portfolio. Apparently, although book publishers maintain more media channels compared to the other publishing types, they usually do not share and deploy the content across media channels. This may also be due to the lower devaluation speed of book content which will be examined next.

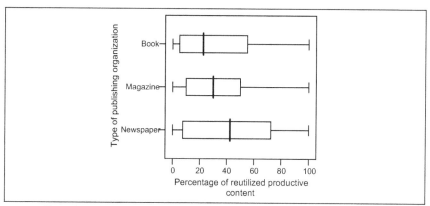

Figure 4.4-4: Content reutilization in book, magazine, and newpaper publishing firms

(4) Content devaluation speed

Last but not least, all of the three sub-types of publishing organizations were also compared on the basis of their statements vis-à-vis the devaluation speed of their respective content portfolios. A non-parametrical Kruskal-Wallis-F-Test revealed a significant difference ($\chi^2_{df=2} = 8.073$, p<0.05). While book and magazine companies rated their content as devaluating at an average speed rate, newspaper companies indicated a rather high degree of devaluation speed. These empirical results mostly support the theoretical conceptions in state-of-the-art literature (e.g., Schulze, 2005, pp. 93-104), although one would have assumed a clearer difference in content devaluation speed between book and magazine companies as observed in this empirical sample.

Having laid out major descriptives about the content allocation behavior of publishing companies and provided first insights into discriminating factors between publisher sub-types, the ground is prepared for the estimation and evaluation of the mid-range theoretical framework illustrated in Figure 3.5-1.

4.5   Model estimation and evaluation

Before delving into the analysis and evaluation of the causal model illustrated in Figure 3.5-1, the estimation procedure used in assessing the structural equation model has to be explicated, as different methodological and statistical assumptions as well as objectives are attached to its application. For that reason, a brief introduction into the two main procedures in SEM (see chapter 4.5.1) precedes the final selection of the more appropriate estimation technique (see chapter 4.5.2). A brief overview on the evaluative criteria to be analyzed in the course of the model estimation process finally sets the stage for the assessment of the measurement (see chapter 4.5.3) and structural model (see chapter 4.5.4). Figure 4.5-1 summarizes the steps for the model estimation and evaluation.

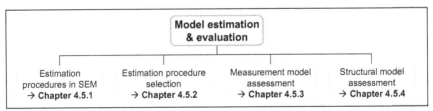

Figure 4.5-1: Overview on model estimation and evaluation

4.5.1 Estimation procedures in structural equation modeling

Structural Equation Modeling (SEM) techniques are second generation data analysis techniques (Bagozzi/ Fornell, 1982, p. 5) that are increasingly being used in behavioral science research for the causal modeling of complex, multivariate data sets in which the researcher gathers multiple measures of proposed constructs. This capability for simultaneous analysis differs greatly from most first generation regression models such as linear regression or MANOVA, which can analyze only one layer of linkages between independent and dependent variables at a time. Thus, SEM permits complicated variable relationships to be expressed through hierarchical or non-hierarchical structural equations, in order to present a more complete picture of the entire model (Bullock/ Harlow/ Mulaik, 1994, pp. 253ff.).

In general, two alternative estimation techniques can be distinguished for evaluating structural equation models, namely that of *covariance-based* SEM and of *component-based* SEM, also referred to as partial least squares (PLS). Both modeling approaches can be characterized and compared with each other on several criteria, which are shown in Table 4.5.1-1 (based on Chin/ Newsted, 1999, p. 314).

The covariance-based SEM approach and PLS differ in the way (i.e. algorithm) the main parameters of the model are estimated. Two basic types of parameters may be distinguished. First, the path coefficients reflect the strength of the relationships of the structural model. Second, the item loadings indicate the strength of the link between constructs and measures.

Basically, the covariance-based SEM approach *"[...] attempts to minimize the difference between the sample covariances and those predicted by the theoretical model [...]. Therefore, the parameter estimation process attempts to reproduce the covariance matrix of the observed measures"* (Chin/ Newsted, 1999, p. 309). In fitting the data with the specified model, it takes into account the covariances between all indicators of the model. In addition to the main parameters of the model, i.e., the factor loadings and path coefficients, it also estimates the error terms of all observed variables and all dependent latent variables. That is, covariance-based procedures *"[...]*

always seek to recover the full correlation matrix of observed variables" (Fornell, 1989, p. 166). Moreover, the covariance-based estimation procedure is based on the assumption that the data points for each indicator follow a multivariate (most often normal) distribution, and that the observations are independent from each other (Chin/ Newsted, 1999, p. 309). To be consistent with the statistical algorithm that assumes that the correlations among indicators for a particular latent variable are caused by that latent variable, covariance-based SEM requires a construct to be measured by reflective indicators (Chin, 1998a, p. IX).

Criterion	SEM with PLS	Covariance-based SEM
Objective:	Prediction oriented	Parameter oriented
Approach:	Variance based	Covariance based
Assumptions:	Predictor specification (non-parametric, bootstrapping)	Typically multivariate normal distribution and independent observations (parametric)
Parameter estimates:	Consistent as indicators and sample size increase (i.e., consistency at large)	Consistent
Latent variable scores:	Explicitly estimated	Indeterminate
Epistemic relationship between a latent variable and its measures:	Can be modeled in either formative or reflective mode	Typically only with reflective indicators
Implications:	Optimal for prediction accuracy	Optimal for parameter accuracy
Model complexity:	Large complexity (e.g., 100 constructs and 1.000 indicators)	Small to moderate complexity (e.g., less than 100 indicators)
Sample size:	Power analysis based on the portion of the model with the largest number of predictors; minimal recommendations range from 30 to 100 cases	Ideally based on power analysis of specific model; minimal recommendations range from 200 to 800

Table 4.5.1-1: Procedure comparison between PLS- and Covariance-based SEM

In contrast to the parameter oriented covariance-based approach, the component-based PLS method is prediction oriented (Chin, 1998b, p. 352). It seeks to predict the variations in all the dependent variables of the model. More specifically, it uses an iterative algorithm of ordinary least square regressions that seeks to minimize the residual variances of the dependent latent variables and all the reflective indicators (Wold, 1989a, p. XXVI). Consequently, it has also been called "variance-structure" approach (Fornell, 1989, p. 166). Within the iterative test procedure, three categories of parameters may be distinguished. They are estimated in a step wise manner[43]. The first step includes the estimation of the indicator weights for each latent variable. The weights enable the calculation of component scores for each latent variable. The second stage includes the calculation of the path coefficients and the item loadings.

---

[43] For a detailed explanation of the PLS algorithm see Betzin/ Henseler, 2005.

The third step finally refers to the estimation of the means and location parameters for indicators and latent variables. Since PLS does not account for the covariances of all indicators, but only for those variances that have been specified in the model, it is closer to the actual data than the covariance-based procedure. Consequently, it is less likely that the theory "overrides" the data (Fornell, 1989, p. 165), i.e., that the analysis goes "beyond the data" (Fornell, 1989, p. 167).

In the last couple of years, partial least squares (PLS) modeling has emerged as a complement to the more widespread covariance-based modeling techniques. In particular, PLS modeling has prompted widespread and international methodological discussion about its applicability very recently (e.g., Henseler, 2005; Tenenhaus et al., 2005; Götz/ Liehr-Gobbers, 2004; Ringle, 2004; Zinnbauer/ Eberl, 2004). In the context of economics and business administration, PLS techniques have already been applied in marketing[44], strategic management[45], and MIS research[46].

Having provided an overview on the two most widespread SEM modeling techniques, a selection of the more appropriate estimation and evaluation procedure has to be performed, which will be taken up next.

4.5.2 Selection of appropriate estimation and evaluation procedure

According to CHIN AND NEWSTED, PLS modeling should be preferred to covariance-based SEM in those cases, where one or more of the following conditions apply (Chin/ Newsted, 1999, p. 336):

(a) Predictions should be made about the relationship between independent and dependent variables.

(b) The causal model is complex and has many indicators.

(c) The phenomenon under investigation has not been examined comprehensively yet from an empirical point-of-view.

(d) Empirical observations are mutually independent.

(e) Multivariate normal distribution of empirical data is not provided.

(f) The sample size is comparatively low: The covariance-based procedure critically depends on sample size (usually >200) to achieve consistent parameter

---

[44] Examples for marketing research papers using PLS are Smith/ Barclay, 1997 and Fornell, 1982.

[45] An overview on four recent studies in strategic management drawing on the PLS technique is provided by Hulland, 1999.

[46] In MIS research, PLS modeling techniques are primarily applied in IT adoption or acceptance research (see e.g., Ravichandran/ Rai, 2000; Mathieson/ Peacock/ Chin, 2001; Chwelos/ Benbasat/ Dexter, 2001; Karahanna/ Straub, 1999). A complete literature overview of the application of PLS in different research disciplines is given in Fassott, 2005, S. 22-24.

estimates. PLS is much less dependent on sample size which should be ten times greater than the number of indicators of the most complex formative measurement model (Chin, 1998b, p. 311; Barclay/ Thompson/ Christopher, 1995, pp. 285ff.). Although a small sample size can produce inconsistent construct scores in PLS models, this problem does not really impede the estimation procedure, because it can be alleviated by increasing the number of indicators.

(g) The causal model includes latent variables that are operationalized in a formative measurement mode.

Against the background of these decision criteria (a-g) for either choosing covariance-based or PLS-based SEM, a selection of a modeling technique pertintent to the research study at hand is performed in the following paragraphs.

The purpose of this research project is to explain why publishing organizations behave differently in the allocation of media content. A theoretical framework has been developed that seeks to explain the variations in the current and ideal degree of productive and archived content allocation. Accordingly, it is of interest to know the amount of variance, which is explained by the predictors. This objective is satisfied best by the PLS approach, since it is prediction oriented.

At the same time, a complex net of theoretical relationships, that explain the content allocation behavior, has been developed. Accordingly, as PLS can handle a greater model complexity without losing consistency, PLS represents the more suitable estimation procedure. Moreover, PLS is simpler and faster in calculating the parameter estimates and therefore has also procedural advantages over the covariance-based method.

With regard to the maturity of the research problem, an extensive body of state-of-the-art literature could be identified. However, most of the research papers investigated the allocation problem using a conceptual or exploratory methodology (see Table Appendix-A1). Only few research papers really tried to merge different theoretical streams into one coherent whole applying sound confirmatory analysis. Hence, as not all of the paths in the specified causal model were previously tested and therefore are not based on a well-grounded and strong theory, PLS seems the more appropriate estimation technique, since it both accounts for confirmatory analysis and potential exploratory extensions (Chin/ Newsted, 1999, p. 314).

Although the empirical observations on the variables of this study are independent in the sense that the sampling of one observation does not affect the choice of a second observation, normal distribution of the study's empirical data could not be provided. Hence, parametric statistical analysis, as advocated by the parameter-oriented covariance-based approach, is not adequate for the estimation and evaluation of the theoretical model developed in this study. By contrast, PLS does not require the data to follow a certain distribution and therefore is distribution free. This fact also speaks in favor of the application of PLS as estimation procedure.

Additionally, the size of the overall sample, as presented in Figure 4.4-1, falls below the minimum recommendation of 200 cases for covariance-based SEM. By contrast, the minimum threshold for PLS modeling is met by a sample size of 115 publishing firms. Finally, in the course of the operationalization phase, the measures of one construct (infrastructural IT-imperatives) have been specified in the formative mode. As this mode is only supported by PLS, covariance-based approaches have to be ruled out as estimation techniques for this study's research model.

All in all, as the PLS approach has clear advantages in specification flexibility (modeling of both formative and reflective indicators), and is facing considerably lower constraints in the requirements for data distribution, independence of observations, and sample size, the PLS estimation procedure is selected for the evaluation of the study's SEM.

To provide an aggregate view on the assessment of PLS-based models, the structural model is evaluated by looking at the percentage of the variance explained (R^2) of all dependent latent variables. To complement the overall (structural) model estimation, the effect magnitude provides insights about the impacts of particular exogenous variables on R^2 when they are introduced into the model (f^2). By examining the size and stability[47] of the coefficients associated to the paths between latent variables, hypotheses, which were proposed during the model specification process, are finally analyzed for their significance.

However, before describing and explaining the evaluative criteria for measurement and structural models of PLS-based SEM at a greater depth, Table 4.5.2-1 first provides an overview on what kinds of evaluative criteria the subsequent analysis will focus on. Furthermore, recommended thresholds for the evaluative criteria are presented, serving as a guideline for the interpretation of estimation results.

---

[47] The stability of the estimates is examined by using the t-statistics obtained from bootstrapping resampling (Venaik/ Midgley/ Devinney, 2001, p. 20). Bootstrapping is a non-parametric resampling procedure that is used to assess the quality of PLS-based model estimations without assuming certain distributions of the underlying data. In the course of bootstrapping, N sample sets are created by randomly selecting N cases from the given sample, which finally produces N estimates of a standard error value, and hence a t-statistic. For more thorough accounts of bootstrapping procedures, the interested reader is directed to Nevitt/ Hancock, 2001 and Bollen/ Stine, 1993.

Part of causal model to be evaluated	Evaluative criteria	Recommended value thresholds
Reflective measurement model → Chapter 4.5.3.1	IR: Indicator Reliability CR: Composite Reliability AVE: Average Variance Extracted	IR ≥ 0.4 - 0.6 (Chin, 1998a) CR ≥ 0.6 (Chin, 1998b) AVE ≥ 0.5 (Bagozzi/ Yi, 1988)
Formative measurement model → Chapter 4.5.3.2	Pc: Path coefficients or weights	Pc ≥ 0.1 (Lohmöller, 1989b) Pc ≥ 0.2 (Chin, 1998b)
Structural model: Overall model estimation → Chapter 4.5.4.1	R²: Squared multiple correlation or coefficient of determination f²: Effect magnitude	R² ≥ 0.4 (Homburg/ Baumgartner, 1985) $0.02 \leq f^2 \leq 0.35$
Structural model: Hypotheses testing → Chapter 4.5.4.2	Hypotheses testing: based on bootstrapping Pc: Path coefficients or weights	t-value ≥ 1.96; p<0.05 Pc ≥ 0.1 (Lohmöller, 1989b) Pc ≥ 0.2 (Chin, 1998b)

Table 4.5.2-1: Evaluative criteria for PLS-based models

4.5.3 Measurement model assessment

In the context of assessing the measurement models of this study's causal model, reflective and formative measurement models have to be distinguished, since they are based on different correspondence rules (see chapter 4.1). While classical evaluative criteria (i.e. factor analytical) apply for the evaluation of reflective measurement models, they cannot be simply transferred to formative measurement models (Diamantopoulos, 1999, p. 453). In lieu of traditional evaluative criteria, other criteria have to be considered that take into account the specific nature of formative correspondence rules.

4.5.3.1 Reflective measurement models

The reflective measurement models of this study (see Table 4.2.5-1, p. 114) were validated using the standard procedures recommended in state-of-the-art literature (e.g., Straub, 1989; Churchill, 1979; Campbell/ Fiske, 1959). Items of scales in a related domain were pooled and factor analyzed to assess their convergent[48] and dis-

---

[48] A reflective scale is said to possess adequate convergent validity when all of its items load highly on one factor. As each item reflects the same latent variable, the construct is unidimensional, and therefore the items should be correlated, making measures of internal consistency appropriate.

criminant validity[49]. While convergent validity (or internal consistency) should be determined both at the individual indicator level and at the specified construct level (Homburg/ Baumgartner, 1985), discriminant validity was assessed by analyzing the average variance extracted and the cross-loadings (see Figure 4.5.3-1).

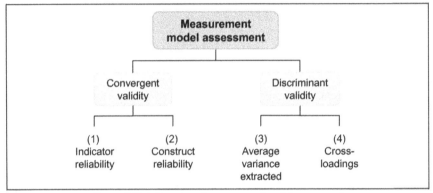

Figure 4.5.3-1: Overview of measurement model assessment

Before presenting the results of the reflective measurement model assessment, the evaluative criteria are briefly described next.

(1) Indicator reliability:

Indicator reliability (IR) represents a measure, which expresses the share of an indicator's variance that can be explained by the underlying latent variable, rather than by its measurement error (Peter/ Churchill, 1986, p. 4). In the reflective mode of measurement, the individual item reliability can be examined by looking at the item loadings of each construct. As a rule of thumb, the item loadings should be higher than at least 0.6, indicating that each measure is approximately accounting for more than 50 percent of the variance of the latent variable (Bagozzi/ Yi, 1988). In addition to the item loadings, PLS provides the weights with which the indicators are related to a construct. In the reflective mode of measurement, the weights should be distributed about equally across the indicators of a given construct, indicating that each item is approximately accounting for the same amount of variance of the underlying construct (Götz/ Liehr-Gobbers, 2004, p. 727).

---

[49] If all scale items pertaining to one construct have low cross-loadings on other factors, the scale is deemed to exhibit adequate discriminant validity. An iterative process of dropping items with high loadings on multiple factors and reassessing the factor loadings is a common convention for refining measurement scales.

(2) Construct reliability:

Construct reliability (CR) indicates the consistency of the measurement of a block of indicators for a given construct. It captures the extent to which the variation in a construct is explained by the combined variation of its indicators, rather than by measurement error. It is calculated by using the following formula (Götz/ Liehr-Gobbers, 2004, p. 728):

$$CR = \frac{\left(\sum \lambda_i\right)^2}{\left(\sum \lambda_i\right)^2 + \sum_i \text{var}(\varepsilon_i)}$$

where λ_i are the parameter estimates for the indicator loadings of a construct and $\text{var}(\varepsilon_i) = 1 - \lambda_i$ represents the measurement error (Chin, 1998b, pp. 320f.). CR can take on values between 0 and 1, with values greater than 0.6 being acceptable (Bagozzi/ Yi, 1988). Indicators exhibiting a low correlation with other reflective measurement items of the same construct should be eliminated (Eggert/ Fassott, 2005, p. 38).

(3) Average variance extracted:

Discriminant validity (DR) captures the extent to which items appear to measure the construct of interest and not relate to any other construct (Bagozzi/ Phillips, 1982, p. 469). In PLS the discriminant validity can be assured by examining if the average variances extracted (AVEs) are greater than the square of the correlations among the latent variable scores (Fornell/ Larcker, 1981, p. 46). AVE is calculated as follows:

$$AVE = \frac{\sum \lambda_i^2}{\sum \lambda_i^2 + \sum_i \text{var}(\varepsilon_i)}$$

where an AVE of less than 0.5 is considered as insufficient, because in that case more than half of the variance would be attributed to the measurement error (Rodgers/ Pavlou, 2003, p. 25).

(4) Cross-loadings:

An alternative way of investigating the discriminant validity is to examine the cross loadings, which are obtained by correlating the component scores of each latent variable with both their respective block of indicators and all other items that are included in the model (Chin, 1998b, p. 321).

In order to determine convergent and discriminant validity for the reflective measurement models of this study, a principal components factor analysis was conducted in PLS using z-standardized items of the study's reflective constructs, with no relationships specified between the constructs[50]. In correspondence to the order followed above, the item reliabilities of all constructs measured in a reflective mode are presented next (1). Then, both CR and AVE values are shown for each factor (2+3). To complete the assessment of all reflective measurement models, cross-loadings are briefly analyzed (4).

(1) Analysis of item reliabilities of reflective constructs:

With regard to the content allocation construct, the two sub-constructs, i.e. content distribution and content integration, were submitted to a factor analysis for both productive and archived content. Although items 1 and 2 of both sub-constructs loaded highly on one factor, items 3 of both constructs and item 4 of content integration just loaded poorly on the first factor, while loading highly on a second factor. Since the survey feedback from publishers indicated that the number of employees managing data distribution and integration as well as content reutilization efforts were just poor proxies for content allocation, items 3 and 4 were removed from the scale (see rows highlighted in light grey) and the item loadings were reassessed once more (see the second columns next to content distribution and integration below factor loadings and weights in Table 4.5.3.1-1). All in all, the high and significant loadings of items 1 and 2 of both sub-constructs on one factor may be interpreted that content distribution and integration are actually part of a higher order factor[51], namely content allocation, confirming the conceptualizations made when presenting the foundations of this research study (see also Figure 2.1.2-1). For the purpose of this study and with regard to the structural model, both sub-constructs of content allocation will be analyzed separately though.

With regard to the comparative advantage constructs (production and transaction costs as well as strategic and operational contribution advantages), all of the measures have loadings above the suggested threshold and are significant at the 0.01 level across all sub-samples and were therefore kept in the individual scales (see Table 4.5.3.1-1).

Item reliability measures for content allocation and comparative advantage constructs are presented in Table 4.5.3.1-1 for both productive and archived content types.

---

[50] The software application SmartPLS (Version 1.01) of the University of Hamburg was used to estimate the parameters of the measurement and structural model (Ringle/ Wende/ Will, 2005). Additional computations were performed manually.

[51] A Cronbach's Alpha of 0.91 also points at a sufficient reliability. Furthermore, loadings were way above the recommended values at a significance level of p<0.001.

Variable and indicators		Productive content		Archived content	
		Load	*Weight*	*Load*	*Weight*
Dist	Dist1	0.95 0.98	0.49 0.51	0.97 0.98	0.51 0.52
	Dist2	0.96 0.98	0.49 0.51	0.97 0.98	0.49 0.50
	Dist3	-0.32 --	-0.21 --	-0.23 --	-0.14 --
Int	Int1	0.95 0.98	0.46 0.51	0.94 0.98	0.43 0.50
	Int2	0.95 0.98	0.44 0.51	0.94 0.98	0.45 0.52
	Int3	0.06 --	0.07 --	0.08 --	0.04 --
	Int4	-0.55 --	-0.26 --	-0.56 --	-0.30 --
Pc	Pc1	0.94	0.41	0.94	0.43
	Pc2	0.89	0.34	0.90	0.30
	Pc3	0.88	0.36	0.89	0.37
Tc	Tc1	0.81	0.32	0.83	0.33
	Tc2	0.82	0.28	0.85	0.26
	Tc3	0.89	0.31	0.90	0.30
	Tc4	0.82	0.29	0.86	0.27
Strat	Strat1	0.94	0.45	0.88	0.39
	Strat2	0.89	0.29	0.85	0.36
	Strat3	0.91	0.36	0.88	0.40
Opera	Opera1	0.92	0.27	0.91	0.27
	Opera2	0.91	0.30	0.93	0.28
	Opera3	0.90	0.27	0.93	0.28
	Opera4	0.92	0.26	0.90	0.26

Table 4.5.3.1-1: Item reliability of content allocation and comparative advantage constructs

A more differentiated picture had to be drawn for the constructs measuring content-, production process-, and market-related characteristics. Except for content transaction frequency, all of them were operationalized in a reflective measurement mode. As opposed to content specificity[52], the relatedness factors were not only measured reflectively on a first-order, but also on a second-order level. For that reason, the assessment of the second-order construct 'interdepartmental complementarities (Int-Compl)' was also included here. In this regard, the three first-order factors (i.e. the relatedness constructs) served as reflective indicators themselves, aggregated to component scores by factor analysis.

Two items of the specificity sub-constructs had to be dropped due to low factor loadings. First, the item capturing the devaluation speed (TopSpec4) had to be removed,

---

[52] Content specificity as second-order construct was suggested to be operationalized in a formative manner. That's why the assessment of this measurement model will be taken up in the following chapter.

as it showed very low and even a negative loading. This finding points to the fact that devaluation speed doesn't reflect the breadth or narrowness regarding the topic of media content. Interestingly enough, content reutilization potential (TopSpec3) revealed to be the most significant indicator for topic specificity. While all of the items of structural specificity exhibited sufficient factor loadings, item 2 of layout specificity (LaySpec2) had to be deleted. Neither the factor loading nor the significance of the item's impact on layout specificity was sufficient enough to keep the item in the scale. The remaining items of the specificity constructs had loadings above the recommended threshold at a significance level of 0.01 and were used for calculating the component scores which entered the stage of formative measurement model assessment (see chapter 4.5.3.2).

A reliability problem could neither be observed with regard to the loadings of the individual reflective items of the first-order relatedness factors nor with the loadings of the component scores, which served in turn as reflective indicators for 'interdepartmental complementarities'. All factor loadings were significant at a 0.01 significance level. The same results for the item reliability assessment could be observed for perceived strategic content value (ConVal). No item had to be dropped, because of too low item loadings or insignificance.

The loadings and weights of constructs representing content-, production-, and market-related characteristics for productive content[53] are illustrated in Table 4.5.3.1-2.

---

[53] As there are only minor deviations from the loadings and weights for the *archived* content subsample, they will not be presented here and in the following tables. The item's loadings, which are more relevant for reflective measurement modes, can be looked up in the cross-loadings tables in Appendix D.

Variable and indicators		Productive content				Variable and indicators		Productive content	
		Load		Weight				Load	Weight
TopSpec	1	0.77	0.75	0.24	0.24	ProRel	1	0.85	0.23
	2	0.80	0.80	0.36	0.36		2	0.82	0.30
	3	0.83	0.85	0.63	0.63		3	0.84	0.34
	4	-0.04*	--	-0.11	--		4	0.84	0.32
StrucSpec	1	0.74		0.57		ConRel	1	0.61	0.27
	2	0.79		0.52			2	0.93	0.49
	3	0.57		0.29			3	0.89	0.42
LaySpec	1	0.89	0.93	0.75	0.82	MarkRel	1	0.95	0.44
	2	0.46*	--	0.28	--		2	0.92	0.25
	3	0.63	0.63	0.34	0.37		3	0.92	0.39
ConVal	1	0.99		0.89		IntCompl	ProRel	0.83	0.44
	2	0.71		0.00			ConRel	0.89	0.45
	3	0.73		0.17			MarkRel	0.70	0.34

* not significant

Table 4.5.3.1-2: Item reliability of content-, production-, and market-related characteristics

Business strategy constructs were measured using individual items for Porter's three generic types of business strategy. As just one item was used, neither convergent nor discriminant validity could be assessed, which was conceived of as operational disadvantage. However, as the strategy constructs did not respresent crucial constructs, the potentially error-prone measurement models were accepted.

With regard to organizational structure, which was measured reflectively by three first-order constructs, item 2 of organizational centralization and item 1 of organizational specialization had to be removed from the scales, because they showed too low factor loadings. All other measurement items of the first-order constructs exhibited sufficient and significant factor loadings. After the remaining indicators of the first-order constructs had been aggregated to component scores, the second-order construct "organizational structure" was tested for reliability (see 'OrgStruc' in Table 4.5.3.1-3). Interestingly, while organizational centralization loaded negatively on organizational structure, organizational formalization and specialization were positively associated with organizational structure. Due to this major difference in the impact on organizational structure, the second-order construct was reduced and split up again to three separate first-order constructs (see cross annotated at OrgStruc). This time, the three constructs were measured without the removed indicators. All three first-order constructs had loadings above the recommended threshold with a significance at a 0.01 level (see the second columns next to OrgCent and OrgSpec in Table 4.5.3.1-3).

Variable and indicators		Productive content		Variable and indicators		Productive content	
		Load	Weight			Load	Weight
LowCost	1	1.00	1.00		1	0.82	0.69
Differ	1	1.00	1.00	OrgSize	2	0.96	0.24
Focus	1	1.00	1.00		3	0.67	0.21
	1	0.57 0.72	0.68 0.59		1	0.87	0.35
OrgCent	2	0.06* --	-0.49 --	ITGov	2	0.94	0.52
	3	0.79 0.81	0.81 0.71		3	0.75	0.29
	1	0.87	0.46		1	0.71	0.44
OrgForm	2	0.83	0.33	ITInvestPath	2	0.51	-0.15
	3	0.82	0.39		3	0.94	0.81
	1	0.36* --	0.07 --		1	0.76 0.83	0.61 0.69
OrgSpec	2	0.76 0.76	0.53 0.54	ITUsagePath	2	0.64 0.74	0.50 0.57
	3	0.85 0.86	0.67 0.68		3	0.47* --	0.46 --
	OrgCent	-0.46	-0.41	ITOrg	1	1.00	1.00
(OrgStruc)[†]	OrgForm	0.80	0.83				
	OrgSpec	0.37	0.41				

* not significant; [†] second-order construct was split up due to the lack of item reliability

Table 4.5.3.1-3: Item reliability of reflective contingency variables

After the indicators of organizational size had been log-transformed and z-standardized, they showed high loadings and significant impact on a 0.01 level, so that all of them could be kept in the measurement scale. Similar significant statistical results were produced for IT governance and IT investment-related path dependencies. For IT usage-based path dependencies, item 3 was dropped, because it showed only an average loading (Kim/ Young-Soo, 2003, pp. 86ff.). After reassessing the construct's factor loadings, improved results could be observed for the item reliability measures (see the second columns next to ITUsagePath in Table 4.5.3.1-3). Similar to the foregoing constructs, factor loadings were significant at a 0.01 level.

(2+3) Analysis of construct reliability and average variance extracted:

After the reflective measurement models' item reliabilities had been assessed, the remaining factor loadings of each construct were submitted to the computation of CR's and AVE's in order to evaluate construct reliability and discriminant validity. With respect to the content allocation and comparative advantage variables, all reflective constructs displayed adequate internal consistency and discriminant validity across both sub-samples (see Table 4.5.3.1-4).

Variable	Productive content		Archived content	
	CR	AVE	CR	AVE
Dist	0.97	0.95	0.98	0.96
Int	0.98	0.95	0.98	0.96
Pc	0.93	0.81	0.94	0.83
Tc	0.90	0.69	0.92	0.74
Strat	0.93	0.82	0.90	0.76
Opera	0.95	0.82	0.96	0.84

Table 4.5.3.1-4: Composite reliability and average variance extracted (Part I)

After the item purification process presented before, all other constructs exhibited satisfactory composite reliability and discriminant validity (see Table 4.5.3.1-5). Only the AVE-value of structural specificity just about achieved the recommended threshold value of 0.50, meaning that exactly half of the variance of the construct can be attributed to the measurement items and half to measurement error. For the scope of the research study at hand, this value was not considered critical. Thus, structural specificity was kept unmodified.

Variable	Productive content		Variable	Productive content	
	CR	AVE		CR	AVE
TopSpec	0.84	0.63	LowCost	1.00	1.00
StrucSpec	0.75	0.50	Differ	1.00	1.00
LaySpec	0.77	0.63	Focus	1.00	1.00
ConTrans	1.00	1.00	OrgCent	0.73	0.58
ConRel	0.86	0.67	OrgForm	0.88	0.70
ProRel	0.90	0.70	OrgSpec	0.79	0.65
MarkRel	0.95	0.87	OrgSize	0.86	0.68
IntCompl	0.85	0.65	ITGov	0.89	0.73
ConVal	0.86	0.67	ITInvestPath	0.77	0.55
ITOrg	1.00	1.00	ITUsagePath	0.77	0.62

Table 4.5.3.1-5: Composite reliability and average variance extracted (Part II)

(4) Analysis of cross-loadings:

The discriminant validity of the construct items was also assured by looking at the cross-loadings for each sub-sample (see Tables Appendix-D2 till Appendix-D7). The loadings of the construct items on their respective constructs are highlighted. Moving across the rows reveals that each item loads higher on its respective construct than on any other construct, additionally confirming discriminant validity in each sub-sample.

Having examined convergent and discriminant validity, the first part of the assessment of measurement models has been accomplished. In the following chapter, the
second part will be tackled by investigating formative measurement models.

4.5.3.2 Formative measurement models

In contrast to reflective measurement models, formative constructs reverse the direction of causality in that the indicators form or cause the latent variable. Thus, the latent variable is a summative index of the items. This reversion of causality requires a
significant difference in the interpretation of the measurement model. In particular,
convergent, discriminant validity, and unidimensionality cannot be used to judge the
quality of the measurement model. Thus, for formative indicators, one examines item
weights, which can be interpreted as a beta coefficient in a standard regression, ex-
pressing the strength with which each indicator forms a given construct (e.g.,
Sambamurthy/ Chin, 1994). As the formative measurement model is based on the
principle of multiple regression, the weights provide information about the predictive
power of each indicator in relation to the dependent variable(s) that is (are) associated with the construct. Frequently, weights will normally have smaller absolute values than item loadings (Chin, 1998b, p. 307), because PLS-based models, those
weights are optimized to maximize the magnitude of the explained variance in the
dependent variable (Götz/ Liehr-Gobbers, 2004, p. 729).

The purification process of formative measurement items follows several steps. First,
indicators with a weight sign other than the hypothesized one are eliminated. Second, indicators that have weights with values smaller than 0.2, are removed, since
their contribution to the formation of the construct are negligible. Finally, those items
are excluded from further analyses that do not have a significant impact on the overall latent construct.

In the study on hand, three formative constructs were applied with two first-order (i.e.
ConTrans and ITImp) and one second-order constructs (i.e. ConSpec). As content
transaction frequency was computed as weighted index of its four indicators and has
been validated several times in recent studies, it won't be considered in the measurement assessment any further. However, since infrastructural IT-imperatives form a
construct in this study, which has not previously been applied in this constellation, it
will be investigated here. After having assessed the single weights of each indicator,
item 5 ("system security measures") and 7 ("ease of integration of additional content
resources") showed rather low values. As these technical aspects appeared to be
crucial for content allocation processes though and should therefore better not be
skipped, exploratory reanalysis brought to light that those two items loaded highly on
a second factor. Based on these new findings, both factors were reassessed once
again. This time, item 6 ("ease of content management") and 8 ("content consistency") bore no significant impact on the first factor, leaving item 1 till 4 alone with
their significant impact on factor one. After the third reassessment cycle, separate

factors for item 6 and item 8 were set up, as weights on one and the same factor had not been significant. The step-wise reanalysis finally resulted in four factors, which were retagged more distinctively according to their basic meaning:

- "Infrastructural IT imperatives (InflTImp)": item 1 till 4

- "Strategic IT imperatives (StratlTImp)": item 5 and 7

- "Administrative IT imperatives (AdminITImp)": item 6

- "Consistency IT imperatives (ConITImp)": item 8

After the reassessment, all of the indicators displayed significant weights (at least at the 0.05 level) conforming to the recommendations in the literature. Factors InflTImp and StratlTImp were additionally examined for the existence of multi-collinearity, which can cause serious interpretation problems, because of instable regression co-efficients and the difficulty to ascribe explained variance to a single item. Variance Inflation Factors (VIF) and Tolerance (Tol) values were computed for each item. Both for the original and refined formative measurement models, no multicollinearity could be observed. The VIF- and Tol-values of each item were all far away from critical threshold values. Table 4.5.3.2-1 shows the weights and loadings of original and re-fined scales for IT imperatives which were all estimated with a formative measurement model[54].

Variable and indicators	Productive content		Variable and indicators	Productive content	
	Load	*Weight*		*Load*	*Weight*
IT-Imp 1	0.70	0.44	InflTImp 1	0.76	0.41
2	0.75	0.39	2	0.80	0.40
3	0.24	0.29	3	0.25	0.29
4	0.79	0.29	4	0.83	0.54
5	0.46	0.09*	StratlTImp 5	0.78	0.62
6	0.38	0.32	7	0.80	0.64
7	0.47	0.21*	AdminITImp 6	1.00	1.00
8	0.65	0.35	ConITImp 8	1.00	1.00

* not significant

Table 4.5.3.2-1: Loads and weights of IT-imperative constructs

After having evaluated the reflective correspondence between the first-order con-structs of content specificity and its respective indicators in chapter 4.5.3.1, compo-nent scores were computed on the basis of the remaining measurement items. The component scores in turn served as formative indicators for content specificity, as it

---

[54] As the results for the archived content sub-sample are very similar, they are not presented here.

was supposed that they individually form content specificity without influencing each other necessarily (see Table 4.5.3.2-2).

Variable and indicators		Productive content	
		Load	Weight
	TopSpec	0.49	0.37*
(ConSpec)[†]	StrucSpec	0.93	0.84
	LaySpec	0.55	0.05*

* not significant;
[†] second-order construct was split up due to lack of item reliability

Table 4.5.3.2-2: Loads and weights of content specificity in formative measurement mode

However, the results of the second-order factor assessment were discouraging for both sub-samples. Only structure-related specificity showed a significant impact on the second-order construct content specificity, indicating that no real second-order construct existed. As a result, content specificity was split up again into three first-order constructs, each operationalized in a reflective measurement mode. The reassessment of the refined measurement scales of the specificity constructs has already proved to produce more encouraging results with all measurement items displaying loadings above the recommended threshold values and significances at least at a 0.05 level (see Table 4.5.3.1-2).

With the last measurement model being satisfactorily assessed, the item purification process was brought to a close. To summarize the results, Table Appendix-D1 gives an overview of all the constructs and associated items that were included into the estimation of the structural model, which will be investigated in the following chapter.

4.5.4 Structural model assessment

The preceding sections provided confidence that the constructs are measured appropriately. The item purification process ensured that sufficient convergent and discriminant validity is provided by all measurement models. The next step is to test the explanatory and predictive power of the model on content allocation. More specifically, the strength of the overall model and the validity of the particular hypotheses will be examined next.

As opposed to covariance-based SEM, PLS does not generate an overall goodness-of-fit index. That's why PLS-based models are primarily assessed by examining R^2, the coefficient of determination[55], and the structural paths (i.e., the parameter coefficients of the inner model), as one would with a regression model. R^2 provides evidence about the percentage of variance that is explained by one or more independ-

---

[55] R^2 measures the proportion of the total variation in the dependent variable that is explained by all independent variables (Mirer, 1995, p. 93).

ent variables (i.e. predictors) that are hypothesized to impact the respective dependent variable. Within the scope of this study, the explained variance of all endogenous variables will be presented together with the effect magnitude of each latent exogenous construct on content allocation (see chapter 4.5.4.1).

Beside the global measures of the explanatory and predictive power of the model, the parameter values provide insights into the strength of the particular parameter estimates. In this realm, it is important to test whether the parameter estimates are statistically significant, i.e., to determine the level of probability with which the hypotheses, that the parameter estimates are not different from zero (Null-hypothesis), can be rejected[56].

In this study, hypothesis testing is performed in three consecutive steps. First, the strength of the predictors' direct impact on content allocation will be assessed (see chapter 4.5.4.2.1). Second, the hypothesized indirect impacts on the degree of content allocation together with additionally posited working hypotheses will be examined (see chapter 4.5.4.2.2). Third, moderator effects on the relationship between IT governance and content allocation will be analyzed (see chapter 4.5.4.2.3).

Figure 4.5.4-1 provides an overview of the different steps in the structural model assessment process in subsequent chapters.

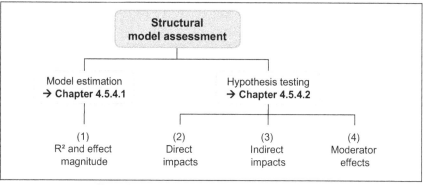

Figure 4.5.4-1: Overview of structural model assessment

4.5.4.1 Overall model estimation

The goal of the estimation of the overall model is to find regularities or invariations that characterize publishing companies with regard to their content allocation behavior. To this end, the R^2 of each dependent variable of the model will be examined.

---

[56] This probability is also called confidence level which is usually indicated at a 99%, 95%, or 90% level. The other way round, one may also speak of the probability that null-hypotheses are true. In this case, one speaks of critical distances. They should be limited to probability levels of 1% (p=0.01), 5% (p=0.05), or 10% (p=0.1) (e.g., Bortz/ Döring, 2002, pp. 30f.).

The R^2 provides evidence about the percentage of variance that is explained by one or more independent variables (i.e. predictors) that are hypothesized to impact the respective dependent variable. The causal model developed in this study has two central dependent variables: (1) the degree of content distribution and (2) the degree of content integration. It is intended to explain as much of the variance of these two variables as possible.

In covariance-based SEM it is suggested that the R^2 of the central dependent variables of a model should approximately reach values of 0.4 or higher, indicating that approximately 40% of their variation can be accounted for (Homburg/ Baumgartner, 1985, p. 364). For a showcase R^2 assessment of three latent endogenous variables, CHIN refers to values of 0.67, 0.33, and 0.19 as being "substantial", "moderate", and "rather weak" (Chin, 1998b, p. 323). For all other dependent variables that the researcher is interested in, without being of central concern, it is suggested to take note of the R^2, but not to consider them as critical for the predictive merit of the model (Homburg and Baumgartner, 1985, p. 364).

As shown in Table 4.5.4.1-1, the R^2 of the degree of content distribution (Dist) and integration (Int) meet the threshold values across all sub-samples. For the productive (archived) sub-sample, approximately 57% (56%) of the variance in content distribution and about 45% (49%) of the variance in content integration are accounted for by the independent constructs in the model, which can be interpreted as reasonably high.

Variable		Productive content R^2	Archived content R^2
Content allocation	Dist	**0.57**	**0.56**
	Int	**0.45**	**0.49**
Comparative advantage constructs	Pc	0.10	0.12
	Tc	0.06	0.04
	Strat	0.06	0.08
	Opera	0.04	0.04

Table 4.5.4.1-1: Squared multiple correlations of dependent variables

Further valuable insights into the explanatory power of individual predictors can be gained, when the effect magnitude is analyzed. The effect magnitude f^2 is an indicator for the change in R^2 when one latent exogenous variable at a time is excluded from the analysis (Cohen, 1988, pp. 410-413). That is, the change in R^2 is yielded by calculating R^2 with and without the observed independent variable:

$$f^2 = \frac{R^2_{included} - R^2_{excluded}}{1 - R^2_{included}}$$

f^2-values of 0.02, 0.15, and 0.35 indicate whether an exogenous latent variable has a weak, moderate (or medium), or substantial effect on the endogenous latent variable it is associated with (Chin, 1998b). Table 4.5.4.1-2 provides an overview of the effect magnitudes of latent exogenous variables that are directly related to the content allocation sub-constructs. In order to enable a quick access to the most important predictors, values above 0.04 are boldened and highlighted.

Exogenous latent variable	Prod. content $R^2_{excluded}$		Prod. content f^2		Arch. content $R^2_{excluded}$		Arch. content f^2	
	Dist	Int	Dist	Int	Dist	Int	Dist	Int
Pc	0.53	0.44	**0.093**	0.018	0.53	0.49	**0.068**	0.000
Tc	0.56	0.44	0.023	0.018	0.55	0.48	0.023	0.020
Strat	0.57	0.37	0.000	**0.145**	0.54	0.42	**0.045**	**0.137**
Opera	0.52	0.41	**0.116**	**0.073**	0.53	0.48	**0.068**	0.020
LowCost	0.57	0.44	0.000	0.018	0.55	0.48	0.023	0.020
Differ	0.56	0.45	0.023	0.000	0.56	0.49	0.000	0.000
Focus	0.56	0.44	0.023	0.018	0.56	0.49	0.000	0.000
OrgCent	0.56	0.45	0.023	0.000	0.53	0.49	**0.068**	0.000
OrgForm	0.57	0.45	0.000	0.000	0.56	0.49	0.000	0.000
OrgSpec	0.55	0.41	**0.047**	**0.073**	0.56	0.47	0.000	0.039
OrgSize	0.57	0.44	0.000	0.018	0.55	0.46	0.023	**0.059**
ITGov	0.55	0.43	**0.047**	0.036	0.54	0.49	**0.045**	0.000
InflTImp	0.54	0.41	**0.070**	**0.073**	0.55	0.49	0.023	0.000
StratITImp	0.57	0.45	0.000	0.000	0.56	0.49	0.000	0.000
AdminITImp	0.53	0.44	**0.093**	0.018	0.54	0.46	**0.045**	**0.059**
ConITImp	0.56	0.44	0.023	0.018	0.56	0.49	0.000	0.000
ITGov x ITInvest-Path	0.57	0.44	0.000	0.018	0.55	0.49	0.023	0.000
ITGov x ITUsagePath	0.54	0.42	**0.070**	**0.055**	0.52	0.44	**0.091**	**0.098**

Table 4.5.4.1-2: Effect magnitude of exogenous latent variables

A closer examination of the effect magnitudes reveals that, across sub-samples, comparative production cost advantages and particularly comparative operational advantages have a moderate impact on content distribution, while the main predictor of content integration are comparative strategic advantages. Comparative transaction cost advantages, same as business strategy constructs, have only negligible effects on both content distribution and integration.

Organizational variables have, generally speaking, a minor leverage on content allocation. While in the productive content sub-sample just the degree of specialization has an effect on content allocation, in the archived content sub-sample, content distribution is influenced by the degree of organizational centralization and content inte-

gration by organizational size, respectively. It is interesting to note that technical constructs taken together exert a stronger effect on content distribution than on content
integration. In particular, IT governance and IT imperatives that come along with content management tasks (AdminITImp) influence the content distribution decision significantly.

The moderating impacts of IT investment-related and IT usage-based path dependencies on the relationship between IT governance and content allocation were assessed analogously. Compared to the path model without moderating effects, only IT
usage-based path dependencies could enhance the explanatory power of IT governance on content allocation, while IT investment-related had almost no bearing. It is
interesting to note that the moderating effect of IT usage-based path dependencies
on the association between IT governance and content distribution had even the
strongest effect magnitude in the archived content sub-sample.

While the effect magnitude can only give hints about the explanatory power of an
independent on a dependent variable, it does not directly convey whether the observed relationships arose by chance or not. That's why procedures for hypothesis
testing will be taken up next.

4.5.4.2 Hypotheses testing

A first impression about the strength of the relationships between independent and
dependent variables can be obtained by looking at the magnitude of the standardized
parameter estimates between constructs. These path coefficients can be interpreted
similar to regression coefficients. They indicate the extent to which a marginal increase in the independent variable is followed by a positive or negative variation in
the dependent variable. In order to gain confidence in the robustness of the strength
of the theoretical relationships, tests of significance were conducted. In accordance
with the assessment of the significance of the item loadings and weights, the levels
of significance of the structural paths were obtained using the bootstrap routine (see
footnote number 47).

With reference to the structure of the inner model on content allocation (see Figure
3.5-1), three types of relationships can be distinguished. First, the strength of the direct impact of the predictors on content allocation will be assessed (see chapter
4.5.4.2.1). Afterwards, the indirect impacts on the degree of content allocation as well
as proposed working hypotheses will be examined (see chapter 4.5.4.2.2). Finally,
the significance of the moderating effects discussed in this path model will be analyzed (see chapter 4.5.4.2.3). Although all three types of relationships were tested
simultaneously, the results of the parameter estimation and evaluation are presented
subsequently.

4.5.4.2.1 Test of direct impacts on content allocation

An overview of the path coefficients[57] and the respective levels of significance for the direct impacts on the content allocation decision is presented in Table 4.5.4.2.1-1[58]. Significant paths are again boldened and highlighted.

Exogenous latent variable	Hypothesis	Productive content		Archived content	
		Dist	Int	Dist	Int
Pc	H2b(-)	**-0.270******	0.083	**-0.258******	-0.053
Tc	H2a(-)	0.123	0.126	**0.158***	0.135
Strat	H4a(-)	-0.058	**-0.352******	**-0.210*****	**-0.352******
Opera	H4b(-)	**-0.325******	**-0.303****	**-0.291****	**-0.226***
LowCost	H5ai(-)	-0.056	-0.082	**-0.127***	**-0.113***
Differ	H5aii(+)	0.101	0.050	0.058	0.095
OrgCent	H5bi(-)	0.095	-0.015	**0.193****	0.070
OrgForm	H5bii(-)	-0.063	0.014	-0.013	-0.045
OrgSpec	H5biii(-)	**0.139***	**0.215*****	0.063	**0.186****
OrgSize	H5c(-)	-0.008	0.119	-0.100	-0.187
ITGov	H5d(-)	**-0.192*****	**-0.177****	**-0.197*****	-0.070
InflTImp	H5fi(-)	**-0.223****	**-0.266****	**-0.175***	-0.127
StratITImp	H5fii(-)	-0.093	0.079	-0.058	-0.096
AdminITImp	H5fiii(-)	**-0.313******	**-0.162***	**-0.224****	**-0.268****
ConITImp	H5fiv(-)	-0.133	-0.085	-0.059	-0.080

* p<0.1, ** p<0.05, *** p<0.01, **** p<0.005

Table 4.5.4.2.1-1: Hypothesis tests of direct impacts on content allocation

The first two constructs, comparative advantages of centrally-deployed content in transaction and in production costs, were derived from transaction cost theory. They were hypothesized to be negatively related to both the degree of content distribution and the degree of content integration. Consistent across both sub-samples, no support could be found for the negative impact of central content allocation advantages in transaction costs, contradicting H2a. An exception represents the relationship between Tc and content distribution in the archived content sub-sample, where a weak

---

[57] Because the path model was run using standardized construct values, the beta values can be interpreted directly. For instance, a one standard deviation increase in comparative operational advantages of centralizing content results in, ceteris paribus, a 0.325 standard deviation increase in the centralization of content.

[58] There is one note of caution that needs to be addressed once more concerning the direction of the posited hypotheses. An increase in the degree of content distribution and integration indicates a movement towards decentralization. That's why, for instance, the relationship between comparative production costs advantages of centralizing as opposed to decentralizing content (PC) is associated negatively with content allocation constructs, as it is hypothesized that content decentralization decreases with a rise in Pc.

significance could be ascertained. Unlike the posited direction of H2a, a high magnitude of perceived transaction cost advantages was even found to be positively rather
than negatively related to the extent to which content is allocated. More encouraging
are the findings for the hypothesized impacts of comparative advantages in production costs (H2b). While the relationship with content distribution is highly significant,
no significance could be observed for the association with content integration. These
results apply both for productive and archived content.

The next set of predictor variables includes constructs derived from resource-based
theory. They comprise comparative strategic and operational advantages of centralizing as opposed to decentralizing content within publishing firms. These two independent variables are proposed to negatively impact both the extent to which (productive and archived) content is distributed and integrated. Except for the relationship
between perceived differences in stragegic benefits and productive content distribution, all other proposed hypotheses proved to be highly significant. While comparative strategic advantages in centralizing content exhibited stronger linkages to content integration though, comparative operational advantages were more strongly related to content distribution. Overall, the findings from the analysis of these relationships are more consistent across the sub-samples than those from the impacts of
perceived cost differences.

The remaining antecedent variables, which were drawn from a strategy, organization,
and technology contexts, were derived from contingency literature. The empirical
analysis revealed no support for hypotheses H5ai and H5aii in the productive content
sample, while the association between the strategy of cost leadership and content
allocation was slightly significant. By and large, the different business strategies suggested by Porter did not exhibit constant and invariable links to content allocation
configurations though. Some unexpected findings emerged from the analysis of an
organizational structure's impact on content allocation. While organizational centralization is significantly related to archived content distribution and organizational specialization to productive and archived content integration, organizational formalization
showed no substantial linkages at all. It is interesting to note, however, that contrary
to H5bi(-) and H5biii(-), a positive rather than negative association of organizational
variables and sub-constructs of content allocation could be discovered. With respect
to organizational size, only insignificant relationships could be ascertained for all sub-
samples of the research study.

More significant findings were discovered for the scope of influence in the governance of IT of a central IT department. Except for one sub-sample (i.e. archived con-
ten integration), all hypotheses could be confirmed. It is also noteworthy that the
strength of the impact of IT governance on content distribution was bigger than on
content integration, in both sub-samples. Last but not least, the analysis revealed
somewhat inconsistent findings with regard to the different sub-forms of IT imperatives. Surprisingly, publishing companies did not recognize security or content consistency issues as systematically related to content allocation constructs. With re-

spect to infrastructural (H5fi(-)) and administrative IT imperatives (H5fiii(-)), however, strong support of the suggested hypotheses could be found in the majority of cases.

Having examined the direct effects on the degree of content allocation, the next step is to analyze the indirect impacts.

4.5.4.2.2 Test of indirect impacts and working hypotheses

Indirect relationships seek to explain the variation in those dimensions that directly impact the content allocation decision. In particular, they help to understand and explain why comparative advantage variables, like production costs or the strategic contribution of content allocation, appear to differ between the centralized and decentralized provision of productive and archived content.

Table 4.5.4.2.2-1 provides an overview of the strength and significance of the path coefficients in the structural models for productive and archived content.

Exog. latent variable	Dep. variable	Hy-pothesis	*Prod. content*	Result of hyp. test	*Arch. content*	Result of hyp. test
TopSpec	Pc	H1ai(-)	-0.12	Rejected	0.06	Rejected
	Tc	H1bi(-)	-0.07	Rejected	0.10	Rejected
StrucSpec	Pc	H1aii(-)	**-0.25****	Supported	**-0.21***	Supported
	Tc	H1bii(-)	-0.11	Rejected	0.07	Rejected
LaySpec	Pc	H1aiii(-)	-0.01	Rejected	0.02	Rejected
	Tc	H1biii(-)	-0.02	Rejected	-0.04	Rejected
ConTrans	Pc	H1c(+)	0.03	Rejected	**0.17****	Supported
	Tc	H1d(+)	**0.14***	Supported	0.10	Rejected
ConVal	Strat	H3a(+)	0.11	Rejected	0.06	Rejected
IntCompl	Strat	H3b(+)	**0.21****	Supported	**0.27******	Supported
	Opera	H3c(+)	**0.21***	Supported	**0.21***	Supported

* p<0.1, ** p<0.05, *** p<0.01, **** p<0.005

Table 4.5.4.2.2-1: Hypothesis tests of indirect impacts on content allocation

Derived from TCT-analysis, content specificity, and content transaction frequency were proposed to have an impact on both comparative production and transaction cost advantages. As the content specificity construct as such couldn't be confirmed as a second-order variable (see chapter 4.5.3.2), it was split up into three first-order factors, namely topic, structural, and layout specificity. With one exception, the impact of these constructs on comparative production and transaction cost advantages, however, proved to be almost non-existent. Just structural specificity exhibited a weak, but significant association to comparative production cost advantages across both samples and in line with the posited negative direction of hypthesis. The findings concerning the relationship between content transaction frequency (ConTrans) and comparative cost advantages appeared to be more encouraging, albeit their inconsistency across both sub-samples. In the productive content sample, ConTrans was significantly related with comparative transaction cost advantages, whereas it was significantly connectd to comparative production cost advantages in the archived content sample.

With respect to the variables, which were drawn from resource-based theoretical thinking, it could not be shown that a publishing company's perception on the strategic value of its content portfolio influences content allocation significantly. Neither could a consistent relationship to content reutilization behavior be observed, which was tested in the course of evaluating the proposed working hypothesis (see Table 4.5.4.2.2-2). Although a weak, but significant correlation between perceived strategic content value and content reutilization could be discovered for productive content (Spearman-r=0.24), this finding could not be found for the archived content sub-sample (r=0.18). It is insightful to note, however, that a systematic linkage between content reutilization and content allocation could be observed across all sub-samples, with non-parametric correlation coefficients ranging from r=-0.22 to r=-0.41, which were all significant at a 0.01-level. Thus, it may be said that increased endeavors in content reutilization activities are associated with an increasing level of content centralization as well as integration and vice versa.

Relationship between	Working hypothesis	Productive content	Archived content
Perceived strategic content value and content reutilization	Working hypothesis I	r = 0.24*	r = 0.18
Content relatedness and production process relatedness	Working hypothesis II	r = 0.51***	
Content relatedness and market relatedness	Working hypothesis II	r = 0.47***	

* p<0.05, *** p<0.001, r = Spearman-rho correlation coefficient

Table 4.5.4.2.2-2: Test of working hypotheses

Overall, solid support could be found for the notion that interdepartmental complementarities in content, production process, and market relatedness explain a significant part of the differences in comparative strategic (Strat) and operational (Opera) advantages between content centralization and content decentralization. Moreover, it is instructive to note that the links to "Strat" constantly showed a stronger level of significance than the links to "Opera", indicating that the impact of relatedness and complementarity constructs is more substantial on strategic variables than on operational ones. The evaluation of the correlation between content, production process, and market relatedness also yielded significant results (see Table 4.5.4.2.2-2), corroborating that all three constructs capture significant portions of common variance of third variables, such as of "Strat" or "Opera".

4.5.4.2.3 Test of moderator effects

In order to analyze moderating (or interaction) effects[59] in PLS, the direction and magnitude of a moderator variable's impact on a relationship between another exogenous variable and an endogenous variable are evaluated. To account for interaction effects between the moderating and exogenous variable, interaction terms (i.e., the pairwise multiplication of standardized indicators of moderator and exogenous variable) are calculated and integrated into the path model as indicators for an additional independent variable[60].

In this research study, moderating effects of two kinds of path dependencies on the relationship between IT governance and content allocation were evaluated[61]. With respect to the effect magnitudes of the moderators, it has already been discovered that IT usage-based path dependencies exert a substantial effect on the relationship between IT governance and content allocation, while IT investment-related path dependencies appeared to have no effect at all.

When looking at the path coefficients of the moderated relationship between IT governance and content allocation constructs (see Table 4.5.4.2.3-1), it becomes obvious that the moderating effect of IT usage-based path dependencies (ITUsagePath) at least stabilizes, at most bolsters the relationship between IT governance (ITGov) and content allocation.

Exogenous latent variable	Hypothesis	Productive content		Archived content	
		Dist	*Int*	*Dist*	*Int*
ITGov	H5d(-)	**-0.192***	**-0.177**	**-0.197***	-0.070
ITGov x ITInvestPath	H5ei(-)	-0.080	-0.093	-0.12	-0.04
ITGov x ITUsagePath	H5eii(-)	**-0.182**	**-0.187***	**-0.233***	**-0.246***

* p<0.1, ** p<0.05, *** p<0.01

Table 4.5.4.2.3-1: Hypothesis tests of moderating effects on content allocation

In particular in the archived content sample, the link between ITGov and content integration doesn't get significant until ITUsagePath is introduced into the path model.

---

[59] Recent research has suggested that moderator effects may be more prevalent in IS research than empirical findings have been able to demonstrate yet (Chin/ Marcolin/ Newsted, 1996, p. 23; Bharadwaj/ Bharadwaj/ Konsynski, 1995, p. 183).

[60] The details of how moderator effects are calculated for reflective and formative measurement models are provided in Götz/ Liehr-Gobbers, 2004, p. 725. For more information on moderating effects in PLS models see Eggert/ Fassott/ Helm, 2005 and Chin/ Marcolin/ Newsted, 1996. Basic instructions on the correct interpretation of moderator effects are also given in Carte/ Russell, 2003.

[61] Regarding the evaluation of moderating effects, it is desirable that exogenous and moderating variable do not correlate highly (Baron/ Kenny, 1986, p. 1174). This prerequisite was met in this study, as coefficients exhibited only slight correlations between 0.05 and 0.27.

By contrast, IT investment-related path dependencies not only fail to show any significant impact on the association between ITGov and content allocation (i.e., H5ei is rejected), but also turns out to mitigate it consistently across sub-samples. It is also interesting to note, that the main effect of IT governance on content allocation is reinforced to a great extent when the moderating variables are introduced to the overall model. The absolute values of inner path coefficients for the relationship between IT governance and productive content distribution rise from 0.16 ($p<0.05$) to 0.19 ($p<0.025$), while they even increase from 0.14 ($p<0.1$) to 0.18 ($p<0.05$) for productive content integration, as soon as path dependency constructs are integrated into the causal model. Similar findings can also be observed for the archived content subsample.

4.6 Recapitulation

In this chapter, the mid-range theoretical model on content allocation, which was developed in chapter 3, was transformed into a structural equation model and tested using the Partial Least Squares (PLS) approach. To empirically test the model, information was gathered from altogether 115 book, magazine, and newspaper organizations in Germany. By and large, the empirical findings provided solid support for the proposed model. The explained variances for the two dependent variables are encouraging. They exceed the threshold of 40% in all sub-samples. Closer examinations of the path coefficients revealed strong support for some hypotheses across all sub-samples, whereas for few hypotheses mixed support could be ascertained across productive and archived content samples.

The distribution of productive content is primarily influenced by operational and production cost-oriented thinking (see Figure 4.6-1). Comparative production costs, in turn, are significantly affected by structural content specificity, whereas the variance in comparative transaction costs is explained to a lesser extent by the frequency of content transactions. Interdepartmental complementarities have a significant impact on both relative operational and strategic benefits. A big deal of explained variance is also attributed to technological variables with administrative IT imperatives exhibiting the relatively highest explanatory power. Astonishingly, organizational variables only play a minor role in the prediction of productive content distribution.

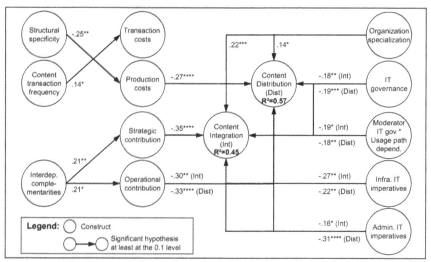

Figure 4.6-1: Significant path coefficients for productive content allocation

On the other hand, the decision of how to integrate productive content is both affected by strategic and operational considerations emphasizing the resulting benefits of content deployment. While organizational specialization is a more significant predictor of content integration than of content distribution, the overall impact of organizational variables is comparably low on content integration. Analogous to content distribution, IT-related variables explain a significant share of the overall variance of content integration.

Similar findings can be presented for the archived content sub-sample (see Figure 4.6-2). Comparative advantages in production costs[62] and operational benefits represented once again those antecedents which displayed the highest predictive power. This time, however, comparative strategic benefits and, to a minor extent, transaction costs additionally influenced archived content distribution significantly, rendering the causes for content distribution behavior more multidimensional. Moreover, the business strategy of cost-leadership and organizational centralization were not related to content distribution purely by chance either. Instead, they showed significant, albeit weak impacts. Only with slight deviations, a parallel between the productive and archived content sub-samples could be drawn with regard to the findings for the impact of IT-related variables on content distribution. It is conspicuous, however, that the influence of administrative IT imperatives is weaker, while the impact of the two-way

---

[62] Comparative advantages in production costs, in turn, are significantly affected by structural content specificity and the number of content transactions within the publishing company. Interdepartmental complementarities were once more a good predictor for both relative operational and strategic benefits.

interaction of IT governance and IT usage-based path dependencies is stronger compared to the productive content sample.

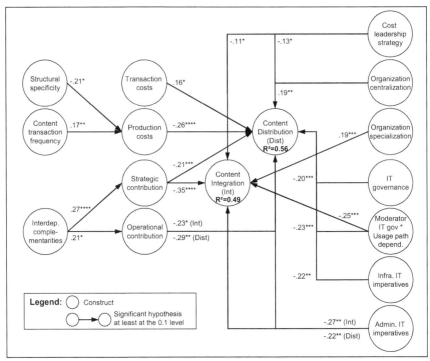

Figure 4.6-2: Significant path coefficients for archived content allocation

The explanation of archived content integration gets a boost especially by administrative IT imperatives and the moderating effect between IT governance and content integration, while losing explained variance from IT governance practices and infrastructural IT imperatives. Apart from these differences, content integration is still primarily influenced by comparative advantages in strategic and operational benefits. In contrast to content distribution, not organizational centralization, but organizational specialization exerts a significant impact on content integration. As with archived content distribution, the cost-leadership strategy was also revealed to have a weak effect on content integration.

All in all, the results indicate that there is a core pattern of relationships that explains the content allocation behavior of organizations, which is complemented by a set of distinctive context-dependent relationships. The context itself comprises both content characteristics as well as strategic, organizational, and technological factors. Depending on the particular constellation of content allocation dimension, content type and publisher sub-type, this core pattern changes to a greater or lesser extent.

So far, mere statistical results about the content allocation behavior in publishing companies have been presented without placing them into a greater context. In order to fully understand the implications of the results though, they have to be put into a "big picture" context, where they are brought together, linked to each other, and interpreted as a whole. By shedding light on theoretical and practical implications of the study's findings in the following chapter, an attempt is made to develop such a big picture view on content allocation.

5 Discussion of model findings

Having presented the findings of the model testing, the next step is to interpret the findings. First, major theoretical implications will be summarized by dovetailing the study's findings into the particular theoretical contexts where constructs were drawn from (see chapter 5.1). To this end, the concepts and relationships developed in the course of the causal model specification (see Figure 3.5-1) will be reviewed against the backdrop of the empirical findings. Second, practical implications from the study results will be presented from a perspective of publishing companies that strive to enhance their content infrastructure (see chapter 5.2). Third, the theoretical and methodological limitations of this study will be identified (see chapter 5.3) and, finally, avenues for future research will be suggested (see chapter 5.4). Figure 5-1 illustrates the organization of the discussion of model findings in the following chapters.

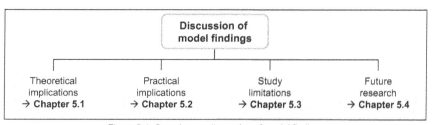

Figure 5-1: Overview on discussion of model findings

5.1 Theoretical implications

To give order to the discussion of theoretical implications, the following sections are organized in accordance to Figure 4.2-1, where different clusters of variables were picked up as structuring elements. Beginning with the major findings regarding the content allocation behavior of publishing companies, commonalities and differences between the different dimensions of content allocation, the different types of content, and the different publisher sub-types will be examined (see chapter 5.1.1). In a next step, the contributions of comparative advantage constructs and their corresponding determinant factors to the content allocation decision will be inspected (see chapter 5.1.2). Finally, the impacts of the contingency variables investigated in this study are reviewed and meshed with the existing body of literature (see chapter 5.1.3).

5.1.1 Content allocation behavior of publishing firms

Depending on the angle, from which content allocation is viewed (see Figure 4.4-1 for different sub-sample groupings), implications for different research communities can be inferred. In the study on hand, three major juxtapositions have been put forward which are once again illustrated in Figure 5.1.1-1.

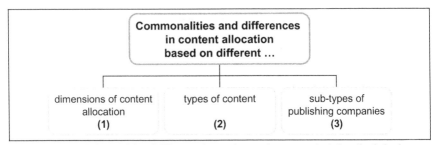

Figure 5.1.1-1: Comparision of different sub-sample groupings on content allocation behavior

These juxtapositions will be taken up next one after another.

(1) Commonalities and differences between different dimensions of content allocation

Drafted as theoretical sub-concepts at the outset of this study, content integration and distribution were conceived of as being two sides of a coin, each stressing a slightly different aspect of "content allocation". The results discovered in this study turned out to be very encouraging. Both concepts share a big deal of explained variance from comparative advantages in operational benefits as well as technological variables, which account for a major portion of the total variance explained. In particular, administrative IT imperatives as well as IT governance moderated by IT usage-based path dependencies, consistently impact content distribution and integration across all sub-samples. In addition, productive content distribution and integration have in common that they are also significantly influenced by infrastructural IT imperatives, IT governance, and organizational specialization at the same time.

Despite being strongly interrelated, both sub-constructs exhibited also different patterns of explanation. While content integration was more strongly and more consistently influenced by strategic considerations and organizational specialization, content distribution was rather predicted by comparative operational benefits and production cost oriented aspects. By the same token, most of the technological variables examined in this study were found to be consistent sources of systematic variance in the content distribution behavior of publishing companies, whereas technological variables played an important role for content integration only in the productive content sub-sample. Accordingly, content integration seems to be judged more in terms of strategic reasoning with a long-term timeframe, whereas content distribution is assessed more in operational and technological terms. With regard to the magnitude of explained variance, content distribution exceeds content integration considerably. This can mainly be attributed to the fact that all significant paths to content distribution exhibit, on average, stronger correlations with content distribution than do significant paths to content integration. Again, especially IT-related variables prevail in the prediction of content distribution, also indicating that fewer variables were taken into consideration to explain content integration.

All in all, these findings are consistent with existing findings in the MIS literature and current market reports, in which 'integration' and 'IT infrastructure' consistently represent topics that are listed among the top five issues on the information technology agenda of German and U.S. organizations (e.g., Capgemini, 2005, p. 6; Benjamin/ Blunt, 1992; Boynton/ Zmud, 1987, p. 63). The extent of content access to editors is obviously perceived by IS executives as contributing more strongly to the long-term success of centralizing content. This may be due to the fact that an increasing scope of access to content may heighten the probability to come up with more adequate content bundles (Anding/ Hess, 2004, p. 10) and to expand the stock of content assets more cost efficiently (Markides/ Williamson, 1994, p. 150), which can generate further revenue streams. By contrast, content distribution is perceived as being rather a matter of productivity enhancement, predicted by operational and technical variables. This finding also substantiates related MIS research, which basically could discover that the provision of data should be aligned with the allocation of other IT-related artifacts such as hardware, software, and networks (Kahai/ Snyder/ Carr, 2002, pp. 48ff.). In addition, although it may be argued that content concentration and integration support organization-wide coordination and production cost savings, the findings also suggest that losses in local autonomy and flexibility are incurred, if integration and centralization are pushed to the extreme. This finding also backs up previous research studies in the MIS field (e.g. Goodhue/ Wybo/ Kirsch, 1992, p. 293). It thus can be concluded that a maximum in content centralization and integration endeavors is rather seen as harm- than fruitful to the processing of content, so that the degree of centralization and integration settles down at values between the two extremes (proportions of content centralization to decentralization are for instance 50% to 50% at book publishers, 66% to 33% at magazine publishers, and 80% to 20% at newspaper publishers; see Table 4.4.2-2).

Boiled down to the essence it may be concluded that despite the differences in the explanatory power of particular kinds of independent variables (see chapters 5.1.2 and 5.1.3), content distribution is explained to a greater extent than content integration by the research model at hand.

(2) Commonalities and differences between different types of content

At the outset of this study, productive and archived content was distinguished through the discriminating characteristic of a content module's age (see Table 2.1.1-1). While archived content was defined as content that was produced in past content workflow cycles and is kept in long-term storages for future retrieval, productive content was referred to as content being pushed through the content workflow for the first time. Although no explicit hypotheses were formulated to examine potential variations in productive versus archived content allocation behavior, one can evaluate commonalities and differences by comparing the findings (i.e. the path coefficients and R²) in the productive and archived content samples as provided in Figure 4.6-1 and Figure 4.6-2. The objective of a comparison of such a kind may be to deduce common or/and different strategies of treating productive and archived content. This may be information which can turn out to be invaluable not only for publishing companies, but also for future research endeavors in the field of media asset management.

When juxtaposing both path models next to each other, especially one thing strikes at first sight. The gap between the total variance explained of content distribution and content integration decreases when shifting from productive to archived content. Content integration gains ground on content distribution mainly due to stronger explanatory power of administrative IT imperatives and moderated IT governance. Moreover, this relative shift between the explained variations of the dependent variables indicates, that for archived content, the access to content can be better predicted relative to content distribution than for produtive content.

Another quite obvious finding is that archived content is consistently stored more centrally than productive content. As archived content is not up-to-date any more, it is usually stored in central locations, so-called archives, where it is kept for later retrieval. As per definition, productive content modules are produced and bundled for the first time, so they are bound to move around more frequently, leading to more decentralized content allocation settings. This research study corroborates these obvious structural differences.

It is also interesting to note that, in contrast to the productive content sub-sample, archived content allocation is associated to the cost leadership strategy, additionally backing up the fact that archived content allocation is recognized as being a more strategic issue than productive content allocation. In addition, this result can be interpreted as being in line with the finding that transaction costs do play a significant, albeit weak role with regard to content distribution, when shifting from the productive to the archived sub-sample. According to the respondents, less transaction costs are incurred, if archived content is placed at a central location than if productive content is place centrally. Thus, transaction costs are a more important and significant factor in the decision on the deployment of archived content. On the other hand, productive content allocation is more significantly related to comparative operational advantages stemming from the distribution and, in particular, from the integration of content. As productive content has to be moved and accessed more frequently while it is created, bundled, and pumped through the content workflow, the findings of this research study make sense.

Overall, it may be deduced from the empirical findings of this study that the topic of content allocation, that is the placement and retrieval of content, is perceived as looming larger in the context of archived than of productive content. This claim finds evidence in the greater number of significant path coefficients and a higher total variance explained.

(3) Commonalities and differences between different types of publishing companies

With respect to the content allocation behavior in each sub-sector in the publishing industry, clear differences could be found. While book publishers tend to decentralize both productive and archived content, magazine and, even more, newspaper companies rather place their content stock at central locations. The same pattern could be observed among the three types of publishers concerning content integration. Newspaper companies let their editors have access to about four fifth of their entire productive and archived content portfolio, whereas book publishers' editorial units share only 40% of the entire content base.

These variations in content allocation behavior between different types of publishers can mainly be attributed to structural differences as described when laying the theoretical foundations of this study (see chapter 2.2). In book publishing companies, different editorial units are basically more loosley coupled than in other publishing companies. This is particularly reflected in the magnitude of content transaction frequency and the level of content reutilization, where significant differences could be discovered. It is interesting to note, however, that the variance in cross-industry content allocation behavior does not stem from different levels of content relatedness, production process relatedness, and market relatedness across editorial units. Minor differences in these criteria turned out to occur just by chance. This result may be valuable insofar as it demonstrates that a potential for cross-unit exploitation of content resources definitely exists also in book publishing firms.

The findings of the comparison of content devaluation speed between publishing types also indicate that the daily pressure to publish content especially spurs newspaper companies to concentrate resources around locations where the strongest technical expertise resides. Consequently, coordination mechanisms are much more pronounced and prevalent compared to book publishing firms. Once more, the increasing degrees of content transaction frequency and content reutilization from book to newspaper publishing firms are excellent indicators to shore up this line of argumentation.

5.1.2 Comparative advantage criteria and related characteristics

The theoretical implications of findings referring to comparative advantage criteria and corresponding determinant factors can best be demonstrated when discussing the contributions of each theoretical lens. While the implications of the empirical findings from the test of transaction cost theory and from the resource-based view will be presented in this chapter, further illuminating insights can be uncovered from the dis-

cussion of empirical findings ascribed to the influence of contingency-based variables, which will be taken up in the subsequent chapter.

(1) Transaction Cost Theory:

This research study is one of the rare examples that directly tested the efficiency argument of TCT by incorporating both transaction costs and production costs in the
analysis of IT-related resource allocation configurations (see also Nault, 1998;
Gurbaxani/ Whang, 1991). This approach is in line with WILLIAMSON's original contributions. He emphasized that beside transaction costs, production cost would have
to be considered in the governance choice. Moreover, he argued that both types of
costs would partially be influenced by the same contextual factors (Williamson, 1981,
p. 560).

Based on this conceptualization, a noteworthy finding of this study is that a lack of
correlation between comparative advantages in transaction costs and the allocation
of content could be observed across all sub-samples[184]. This supports the findings of
former empirical studies which discovered that organizations rarely recognize transaction costs when evaluating and comparing make-or-buy options (Dibbern/ Heinzl/
Leibbrandt, 2003, p. 534; Barthélemy, 2001, pp. 67ff.). Obviously, the same holds
true when IS executives weigh up different modes of content allocation within the
boundaries of their company. Rather than comparative transaction costs, comparative production costs figure large and are factored in when deciding upon productive
and archived content distribution.

Moreover, this research enhances the knowledge about the impact of indirect factors
on the content governance choice. Previous research has mostly examined the direct
impact of factors like asset specificity or transaction frequency on allocation decisions. Although, the empirical support for these impacts was quite encouraging, the
actual economic reasoning for these influences, that is whether differences in asset
specificity or transaction frequency translated into cost- or benefit-related factors, remained untested. In trying to overcome these explanatory limitations, this research
has treated comparative transaction and production cost advantages as mediators
that link content characteristics with content allocation. By testing these mediator effects, it soon became apparent that the initially conceptualized construct "content
specificity" couldn't be formed as second-order construct, which resulted in its split-up
into three sub-constructs representing topic, structure, and layout specificity of content. Investigating each sub-construct for its impact on differences in production costs
between centrally- and decentrally-deployed content, only structural specificity was
found to have a consistent and significant effect in the direction as suggested in this
research study (see chapter 3.3.1.3). With regard to topic or layout specificity,

---

[184] One exception is the weak interaction of comparative transaction costs with archived content distribution.

though, no discriminating effects could be stated on any of the comparative cost variables. Consequently, variations in content allocation behavior and associated production cost differences can partially be traced back to the question as to how easily
content can be dismantled into modules, but are independent of layout restrictions or
the degree of topical breadth. Apparently, the topic of publishers' content is too detached from content infrastructure management to be a determinant factor. More astonishing is the fact, however, that the degree of layout standardization did not play a
significant role. As layout issues in publishing firms are – despite the increasing diffusion of mark-up languages in the print sector (Benlian et al., 2005, pp. 219f.) – still
most often inextricably entangled with the content itself, it would have made sense if
a rise in the standardization of layout entailed a rise in the centralization of content.
Nevertheless, these conceptualizations of types of content-related specificity may
serve as a spring board for future research that seeks to vigorously examine the effects not only on content allocation, but also on content production and bundling related themes. Moreover, the knowledge that modularization has an effect on the efficiency of content provisioning may further the understanding of production and cost
functions in publishing firms.

When evaluating the impact of content transaction frequency (ConTrans) on content
allocation, it is remarkable that ConTrans' impact is dependent upon the type of content. While ConTrans is related to transaction cost differences with regard to productive content, it exhibits an impact on production cost differences with regard to archived content. As the quick and purposeful provision of productive content is more
contingent upon the seamless coordination between editorial units (i.e., without causing significant frictions and delays between two consecutive tasks) in the content
workflow, the minimization of relative transaction costs might be of major concern in
the decision upon the placement and access scope of content. On the other hand, as
archived content is usually not only stored more centrally, but also retrieved more
seldomly, comparative production costs (e.g. costs for equipment or archivists) seem
to be more prevalent as decisive factor for content allocation, whereas costs for the
transmission of content reside to the background.

To recapitulate, the TCT seems to be fruitfully applicable to the content allocation
problem, as the logic of TCT enables a comparative as well as a trade-off analysis of
two opposing content allocation arrangements. It provides answers to the organizational questions of specialization (as conceptualized by the kind and magnitude of
content specificity) and coordination (as conceptualized by the degree of content
transaction frequency). Viewed in this vein, content allocation may best be understood as an organizational design decision that can be broken down into the basic
process elements of decision making (see Figure 3.2.4-2). When transferring this
view of decision making into a variance theoretical perspective as was yet suggested
in chapter 2.2, an organization's current content allocation behavior may be seen as
a decision outcome derived from evaluating, weighting, and aggregating a number of
decision criteria. These decision criteria may then be interpreted as cost drivers that

manipulate the allocation of content in a cost-economizing way. Especially in situations, in which objective evaluative criteria of different content allocation arrangements (e.g. based on an ROI-analysis) are just hardly available, such a comparative analytic approach may seem to be a good proxy for mirroring decision-making in practice (e.g., Ailawadi/ Dant/ Grewal, 2004).

(2) Resource-based View

The resource-based view, a theoretical approach which complemented transaction cost-based thinking in theorizing about the allocation of content by introducing benefit-based evaluative criteria, also offered valuable empirical findings. The construct validity of the recently suggested second-order construct "interdepartmental complementarities" (Tanriverdi/ Venkatraman, 2005, p. 108), comprising three relatedness factors concerning the content, production process, and market knowledge across editorial units, could be confirmed in this study. This not only advanced theory development in relatedness research, but also provided a parsimonious model of the phenomenon under investigation, as first-order factors could be condensed into a second-order construct[185].

The approach of structural equation modeling has allowed the examination of individual subconstructs within the constructs under investigation, providing insight as to what aspects of these constructs are particularly salient in the context of content allocation. The combination of subconstruct weights and loadings indicates that both content relatedness and production process relatedness across editorial units exhibited a stronger contribution to the exploitation of interdepartmental complementarities for predicting content allocation than market relatedness. One reason might be that similarities of customer needs and characteristics across editorial units are more loosely connected to the actual content infrastructure than similarities in content production processes and content characteristics, which more directly contribute to harnessing synergy benefits strategically as well as in day-to-day business operations.

Nevertheless, all three sub-factors exhibited sufficient construct validity to form interdepartmental complementarities, which in turn had significant impacts on comparative advantages of centralized as opposed to decentralized content allocation in strategic and operational benefits across all sub-samples. Consequently, the study at hand informs us about the fact that the coexistence and interactions of different forms of relatedness spur content centralization, since major strategic and operational cross-unit advantages can be exploited. Unlike most prior studies, which focused only on synergy effects from economies of scale and scope emanating from an efficient allocation of IT-related resources (e.g., Brown/ Magill, 1998; von Simson, 1990), this study recognizes that the complementarity of different resources can also serve as an important source of synergy. With its second-order, multidimensional concep-

---

[185] The second-order model led to fewer parameters estimates and mere degrees of freedom.

tualization of cross-editorial complementarities, this study captures both the sub-additive production cost synergies arising from the relatedness of content, product processes, and market knowledge domains (i.e. traditional economies of scope), and the super-additive value synergies arising from the complementarity of different types of synergy sources (see Figure 3.3.2.3-3). On the one hand, this result confirms the prevalent findings in diversification literature by ascertaining that a centralized deployment of resources more efficiently supports the sharing, reconfiguration, and transfer of related resources for achieving superior value (see Eisenhardt/ Martin, 2000). On the other hand, the existing body of synergy literature in media management can also avail itself of the research study's findings, because the sole existence of content relatedness is not always a 'carte blanche' to realize cross-unit synergies. Most frequently, other sources of relatedness have to coincide in order to achieve super-additive value synergies (Tanriverdi/ Venkatraman, 2005, p. 115).

This is also the first empirical study that has examined the linkage between perceived strategic content value and the level of comparative advantages in the strategic and operational contribution of centrally- as opposed to decentrally-deployed media content. As was proposed during the model specification phase, perceived content value was suggested to have an impact on content allocation due to a hypothesized conceptual intersection with content reutilization. However, as could be discovered by the empirical analysis, consistent significant links could be ascertained neither to content reutilization nor to comparative advantage constructs, whereas it could be shown indeed that content reutilization correlates with content allocation significantly. Despite the fuzziness of a construct that is bound to capture only an aggregate strategic content value[186], the findings still allude to the fact that perceived strategic characteristics of content are not reflected in the rather operational content infrastructure. Consequently, the study reveals that it is not possible to infer from a specific level of strategic content value to a content allocation mode which can be deemed optimal.

Overall, the study's combination of transaction cost reasoning with the resource-based view suggests that while conflicts between the two theories certainly do exist, strong complementarities between them should not be ignored. Consequently, another contribution of this study refers to a more advanced understanding of those factors that explain cost and benefit differences between centralizing and decentralizing content in publishing firms. This research study was one of the first to come up with constructs that have not yet been investigated empirically using a large-sample method. In order to encourage and advance a theory of media management, it is thus crucial to further comprehend and clearify the nomological relationships between constructs such as content reutilization, specificity, relatedness, and modularization.

---

[186] As the content portfolio in publishing companies most frequently consists of heterogeneous types of content, an aggregate assessment of the perceived strategic value inevitably entails distortions.

5.1.3 Contingency factors

Drawing on the structural framework used in Figure 3.3.3.3-1, the theoretical implications of the relationships between content allocation and selected contingency factors are presented in a top-down fashion, starting with types of competitive strategy and ending with IT-imperatives.

The findings with regard to the linkages between content allocation and the types of organizational competitive strategy are rather inconsistent. Just the competitive strategy of cost leadership showed a weak significant association with archived content allocation, while the strategy of differentiation was not found to covary with content allocation practices of any kind. Prior findings that suggested and also discovered alignment between strategy and IT structure (e.g., Brown/ Magill, 1998; Tavakolian, 1989) can therefore not be confirmed. One explanation for the inconsistent findings may be that the causal link from strategy to content allocation is too long and that important organizational and technological factors exist that mediate the relationship between strategy and the content allocation structure. This may particularly apply to publishing companies that most often implement and extend their content infrastructure in an ad-hoc manner irrespective of the underlying business strategy.

As opposed to the suggestion by DEWAR ET AL. (Dewar/ Whetten/ Boje, 1980), organizational structure could not be modeled as a second-order construct in this study. Instead, the impact of organizational centralization, formalization, and specialization on content allocation were evaluated separately. Contradicting to the posited hypotheses and findings discovered in previous research studies (e.g., Kahai/ Snyder/ Carr, 2002), organizational centralization was found to only exhibit conflicting and not reinforcing contingencies on archived content distribution. It could rather be observed that the more organizational decision-making is centralized, the more content is decentralized. This may be due to the fact that stronger control from a central point spreads more discipline among decentralized storage locations and therefore allows overseeing the dispersal of content to multiple locations more easily. In most cases, however, organizational centralization was not found to be associated with the degree of content allocation, contradicting the findings made by EIN-DOR AND SEGEV, who could discover a consistent link between organizational and MIS structure (Ein-Dor/ Segev, 1982). Consequently, it cannot generally be concluded that different content allocation structures in publishing organizations fit different organizational contexts. Only in the case of archived content distribution, a link could be observed. In order to be able to yield more thorough and convincing statements about this relationship, more research has to be performed in this interesting research area.

More unequivocal albeit contradicting observations could be made concerning the relationship between organizational specialization and content allocation. It was hypothesized that growing levels of division of labor go hand in hand with increasing bureaucratic structures and hence a tendency towards content centralization. Instead, the opposite could be observed. The more organizational tasks performed by editors are specialized and are limited to only some few steps in the content work-flow, the more content tends to be decentralized. Usually, a consequence of growing specialization would be higher organizational differentiation, which, according to classical organizational literature (e.g., Kosiol, 1962, pp. 76-79), would be encountered through the increasing use of integrating mechanisms. However, as this tendency could not be ascertained in this research study, one can assume that publishing companies, which traditionally foster a culture of autonomy and independence among its editorial units, grants wide latitude to managers of editorial or production units to make decisions about their respective work practices, including task specialization and content allocation.

Although size has been identified as a factor for determining IS structures and IS success in prior studies (e.g., Ein-Dor/ Segev, 1982), no significant relationship could be observed in this study. This result backs up findings in empirical studies by GREMILLION (Gremillion, 1984) or RAYMOND (Raymond, 1985) who couldn't discover a direct link between size and IS-related constructs. In particular, empirical results about the relationship between organizational size and IS sophistication have also been somewhat mixed (Lehman, 1986, pp. 82ff.), since significant associations were not found for many sophistication criteria. The lack of a consistent relationship between organizational size and content allocation may be attributed to two opposing explanatory approaches probably offsetting each other's impact on content allocation. On the one hand, one may argue that with increasing size, the publishing organization also increases its division of labor and level of differentiation, which results in the dissemination and isolation of content. On the other hand, it may be assumed that larger firms tend to recentralize content to overcome the structural inefficiencies encountered in prior lifecycle phases. These opposing explanatory approaches are reflected by the empirical data observed in this research study. It can't be ruled out, however, that the insignificant impact of organizational size on content allocation in the hotchpotch of all publishing companies superposes individual effects in sub-types of publishing organizations.

Except for one exception, IT governance as indicated by the scope of influence of a central IT department was found to be attuned to content integration, and particularly to content distribution in publishing companies. The more a central IT department sets guidelines and controls IT-related tasks concerning the content workflow and its associated information systems, the more content will be allocated centrally. This adds to the findings of a large body of MIS literature that agree upon the importance of sophisticated IT governance practices for the efficient allocation of IT-related resources (e.g., Kahai/ Carr/ Snyder, 2003; Kahai/ Snyder/ Carr, 2002; Sambamurthy/ Zmud, 1999). In particular, it is regularly found that the allocation of data resources should be managed according to its MIS context. This claim can also be corroborated by the findings of this study. At first sight, these results clash with the findings gained above when investigating the contingencies between the locus of organizational decision-making and content allocation. Most apparently, it is crucial to distinguish between decision-making that centers on the distribution of responsibilities between the corporate department and editorial units and decisions that are related to managing IT resources. Particularly with regard to archived content, simultaneously conflicting and reinforcing contingencies of organizational and IT-related decision-making seems to be a feasible and sustainable solution for publishing companies.

This study contributes to the IS literature by introducing and highlighting IT-related path dependencies as critical moderators between IT governance and content allocation. The effect of the two-way interaction of IT-related path dependencies and IT governance on content allocation exhibited mixed findings. While the effect of IT governance on content allocation appears to be independent of prior IT investements, the existing IT usage patterns of employees, in particular of editors, seem to have a substantial bearing on the final outcome. These findings are partially consistent with results reported in IT acceptance and adoption literature (e.g., Premkumar/ Ramamurthy, 1994, pp. 175). Prior IT investments in publishing firms (i.e. hardware, software and networks) seem to be already flexible enough to be adjusted to new modes of content allocation. It can, for instance, be argued that complexities arising from distributed systems are mitigated or even thwarted by technical abstraction mechanisms enabling the access to and placement of content regardless of any change in the allocation of content. Hence, the technological burden of the past apparently doesn't hamper the transition from one to another mode of content allocation and therefore doesn't affect the relationship between IT governance and content allocation in a significant way. However, a different interpretation of the findings applies to IT-usage based path dependencies as a moderating factor.

The more employees balk at switching to a new content infrastructure, the more susceptible and responsive IT governance activities must be to account for the habits and desires of IT users. Changing a content infrastructure without the support of editors may otherwise lead to less effective IT governance (e.g. battles between IT department and editors) and productivity. A publishing company still striving after realizing a new content allocation structure may either ease the transition by adjusting the perceived usefulness and ease of use of the new content infrastructure (Davis, 1989, pp. 320ff.) or may attempt to leave employees unaffected by hiding the changes beneath technical abstraction layers. All in all, the findings suggest that a more social perspective provides an important paradigm for understanding and explaining effective designs for IT structures. This respresents a finding, which is continuously reiterated in MIS literature (e.g., Peterson/ O'Callaghan/ Ribbers, 2000, p. 445).

Furthermore, the study revealed that IT imperatives need to be treated as a multidimensional construct. It was found that different types of IT imperatives have different impacts on content allocation. Content security and consistency issues, for example, did not play a major role with regard to content allocation practices in publishing companies. These findings partially contradict the findings in related literature (e.g. Loch/ Carr/ Warkentin, 1992), which emphasize the operational and strategic importance of taking precautions against unauthorized access to, disclosure, or even destruction of IS resources. Since content is not only used as input factor, but constitutes the main outcome of content production processes, one could have assumed that the allocation of content is a matter of security and consistency. Once more, it cannot be ruled out that the impacts of these factors vary between individual types of publishing companies and blur when being aggregated.

Infrastructural and administrative IT imperatives, however, which are rather operational aspects, exhibited a substantial impact on content allocation, indicating that content availability, content access speed, and the scalability of content processing are of major concern to IS executives when deciding upon the allocation of content. In addition, the ease of content management, a rather administrative matter, turned out to highly correlate with the content allocation constructs suggesting that tasks usually provided by content management systems (i.e. the organizing, versioning, and archiving of documents) should be in line with the underlying content allocation structure. This result further bolsters the findings reported in MIS literature that not only IT management or governance issues, but also more operational IT requirements play a vital role in the design of content infrastructures. JAIN ET AL., for instance, found that data centralization is often the preferred option for companies that require a tighter grip on IT resources, because data concentration goes along with ensuring compatibility, reducing redundancy, and maintaining integrity (e.g. Jain et al., 1998).

In this research study, the selection view of fit was used to investigate the interrelationships between selected contingency variables and the content allocation variable (see chapter 3.3.3.2). It was presumed that the more contextual and structural variables co-align and are congruent with each other, the higher the efficiency and performance impacts will be. This implicit link to performance effects was taken as evaluative logic for the manifestation of certain content structures. Overall, the application of the concept of fit in the selective mode revealed to be an adequate complement to the more rational evaluative criteria of comparative costs and benefits. It enabled to capture additional strategic, organizational, and technological reasoning with regard to content allocation within the overall framework of Comparative Institutional Performance (see Figure 3.2.4-1).

The findings indicate that, particularly for technological contingencies, there is no one way to structure an efficient content allocation infrastructure. In this context, the concept of fit is therefore particularly useful. Given a vector of variables that define the structure of content allocation, as in this research study, successful allocation depends on the extent to which the particular values fit the organizational and technological environment. Especially on the basis of technological contingency variables, which were mostly revealed as good predictors, this contextual anticipation of the corresponding content allocation structure turns out to be fruitful. That is, the concept of fit can explain in these situations why a content allocation structure that is appropriate in one situation may be inappropriate in another.

5.2 Practical implications

As the management of information systems (MIS) is not just a research field but also a profession, the applicability of an IS theory to different settings is important not only for purposes of applied research, but also for purposes of managing and solving problems that corporations and other organizations experience in every day business operations. In order to further a tight interplay between practice and research and, what is still pending, to pick up and answer the research question focusing prescriptive research (see Table 1.2-1), practical implications of this study's research findings will be deduced in this chapter. But before starting to dig deeper into the practical implications of this research study, it appears useful to provide some background information on why and how research of this kind provides fruitful insights for practitioners. According to LEE, practical relevance deduced from IS research, which is based on the positivist-functionalist research paradigm, can be achieved as follows:

"A researcher formulates, tests, and validates a theory that specifies independent variables, dependent variables, and the relationships among them. In doing this, the researcher is careful to make sure that, first, the dependent variables represent the outcomes the practitioner is interested in achieving and, second, the independent variables represent factors that not only indeed influence the outcome but also can be manipulated or changed by the practitioner. A practitioner could then apply the theory by manipulating the independent variables in order to achieve the desired level in the dependent variable" (Lee, 1999, p. 31).

Following this instrumental model of practice, it appears to be fruitful to step into the shoes of an IS executive of a publishing firm who has to decide upon a content infrastructure that should optimally fit the company. Thereby, potential avenues for improving organizational practices can be pointed out. Pursuing a top-down approach, general advantages of rationalizing content allocation decisions compared to ad-hoc decision-making is compared first (1). Then, based on the empirical findings of this study, concrete suggestions for which independent variables may be manipulated to influence content allocation structures will be deduced (2).

(1) General practical implications of rationalized content allocation

Based on the experiences made during pre-test interviews and on the empirical findings of this study, the majority of IS executives of publishing firms either have not recognized the necessity yet to distribute media content efficiently at all or have played a hunch so far to decide upon content allocation. The latter aspect is also frequently superposed by decisions made in the course of content architecture management, which is more extensive and far-reaching in scope, but also more abstract.

As a result, emerging content allocation infrastructures have most often evolved in ad-hoc ways leading to ineffective content delivery during the production and bundling of content. However, knowing the context affecting a content infrastructure that fits with a publishing company, may contribute a lot to a more robust understanding of IT contexts and management planning approaches (Boynton/ Zmud, 1987, p. 69). It thus allows injecting more rationality and reason into the infrastructure planning process, which appears to be imperative for publishing companies in the face of emerging technologies that support new and more efficient ways of distributing and integrating content. In recognition of such a lack in rationalizing on appropriate content allocation forms, this study attempted to develop a framework for understanding the proper alignment between content allocation structures and emerging determinant factors based upon the linking framework of institutional performance.

The findings of this study basically emphasize the need to design publishing organizations that follow certain patterns of congruency and consistency in order to realize greater effectiveness. These observed patterns or invariabilities, which can be considered this study's most valuable outcomes for practitioners, may provide IS managers with a *benchmark* against which they can reassess the design of their own content allocation configuration (e.g. in order to adjust current or prioritize future content allocation endeavors). Aligned content infrastructures can be considered to dramatically increase the smoothness of content flows and to enhance production and bundling capabilities. A major reason for the enhanced efficiency can be attributed to higher network externalities (i.e. network-based economies of scale), as editors are able to search, find, and redeploy content more quickly for production and bundling processes. In this regard, content interactions that tend to cluster around just a few editorial units can be supported by the development of so-called content network hubs, while editorial units that work independently can store their content at different places. In strategic terms, publishing companies that are in pursuit of reacting flexibly to new trends in their respective markets, for instance to take advantage of content reutilization or to realize seamless business process redesign projects, have to be able to adjust their content infrastructure in a seamless way. Sensible publishing companies that want to harness the benefits of greater content infrastructure flexibility should therefore think several steps ahead and work back from the outcome that bests fit to the publisher. Otherwise, potential opportunities may be foregone. Starting points for rationalizing the content allocation decision are the patterns or invariabilities identified in this study, which will be exploited more thoroughly for the practical context in the following subsection.

(2) Practical implications of empirical findings

What could not only be learned from this study, but also from numerous prior related studies, is the fact that there is no one best way to allocate media content. The findings suggest to IS executives that they ought not to adopt a standardized, uniform approach to managing their content infrastructure. They rather need to adopt a selective approach depending on the individual contingencies they might want to adjust to those identified in this study. Basically, all factors that were found to have a significant impact on content allocation in this research study lend themselves to be examined and thoroughly weighed against each other in the decision on the optimal content allocation structure. Thus, IT executives must endeavor to accurately gauge the salience and implications (regarding both the mode of content allocation and the costs and benefits attributed to particular allocation modes) of individual contingency forces impacting their firm at any given point in time. They not only may give hints about which triggers and levers to pull to influence the content allocation structure, but also may provide insights which areas in the company to focus on.

First of all, practitioners in the publishing industry can avail themselves of the study's findings that content distribution is mainly contingent on operational benefits and production cost savings. Time, productivity, and process improvements are the major drivers that count in the decision for or against an optimal content allocation structure. Furthermore, a publishing company's content allocation structure should be designed in sync with the prevailing form of IT decision-making and responsive to infrastructural and administrative IT imperatives. For example, publishing companies that concede great autonomy to editorial units but nonetheless want to reap the benefits of sharing content effectively can foster a centralized content allocation structure by establishing centralized IT governance practices. However, as indicated by the significant moderator effects of IT usage path dependencies, a firm culture should be in place that takes into account the usage behavior of editors before switching to a new content allocation arrangement or existing disincentives will probably thwart using a new content infrastructure. The research study could show that such a constellation of different contingencies is not only workable but also seems to be sustainable.

Moreover, practitioners may also take advantage of the finding that the decision on the provisioning of content access rights to editors (i.e. content integration) is more dependent on long-term and strategic than on short-term and cost-based decision factors. The recognition of these invariabilities may be exploited to create thumb rules for organizing content in order to facilitate an executive's decision-making about positioning content as a strategic differentiator. This result also foreshadows that the level of content integration is perceived as having an impact on product innovation in the form of content reutilization. All the more it is crucial to handle content integration decisions carefully and informed.

Additionally, the research study provides insights into the situations where operational and especially strategic benefit advantages of centralizing media content can be reapt more easily. For instance, some editorial units with a high level of content, production process, and market relatedness among each other should be integrated based on a centralized content database and far-reaching content access, while others can rather be kept separately, because of missing synergy potentials. Thus, cross-functional and related business activities call for more content integration between editorial units and such increased need for mutual cooperation can be met by integrating dispersed IS including data and networks. The implications of interdepartmental complementarities also indicate that the relatedness of a content portfolio across editorial business units is defined by a complementary set of different valuable resources. Publishing firms seeking to get a grip on their content infrastructure should not only explore whether their individual content-, production process-, and market-related resources are related, but also whether the complementarity of different resources is an absolute prerequisite for concentrating media resources. The findings of this study suggest that sporadic or isolated attention to the relatedness of an individual resource may not suffice to implement a centralized content infrastructure. Rather a combination and alignment of individual resources may prove more appropriate to decide upon the allocation of content.

The results at hand also show that the alignment between strategy and IT structure has not sufficiently been tackled so far, most probably due to a lack of consciousness. All the more it is crucial that IS practitioners get their content infrastructures attuned to the overall business strategy, as misalignments between strategy and IT structure could hamper the pursuit and seamless realization of strategic projects. Numerous case studies have proven that a misfit between strategy and IT structure can lead to poor economic performance (see for example Avison et al., 2004; Henderson/ Venkatraman, 1993). For that reason, practitioners are certainly better off to muse more thoroughly about how content infrastructures can leverage the overall business strategy.

Practitioners are also well advised to be aware of the conjunction between organizational specialization and content integration. Publishing firms that exhibit higher levels of division of labor were found to keep productive and archived content more disintegrated. As IT becomes deeply entrenched within the business fabric of publishing firms, these results may help IS executives how to tackle both differentiation and integration. Traditionally, organizations have resorted to the oversimplified "pendulum swing" of centralization and decentralization. However, this "centralization vs. decentralization" panacea obscures the real organizational issues that should be managed. Uncovered contingencies between organizational centralization and archived content distribution as well as between organizational specialization and content integration may thus deliver more revealing and instructive information for potential areas of horizontal design mechanisms in publishing companies. Anyway, practitioners with an organizational and/or technical background (i.e. infrastructure architects) should know the risks they run if they attempt to challenge these relationships with organizationally inconsistent content allocation structures. In this regard, well-informed decisions on the allocation of content may enable publishing organizations to circumvent crises by flexibly adjusting the organizational design to unpredictable environmental changes (see for example Breyer-Mayländer/ Seeger, 2004).

On the technological side, practitioners can learn from this study that IT governance plays a crucial role in the positioning of media content. It could be shown that a centralization of decision-making on IT governance tends to foster a centralization of content, as a central IT department most probably attempts to get a grip on a publishing company's most valuable resource. Before deciding on the placement of content, though, publishing companies are recommended to take usage habits of their editors into consideration, because a rash transition in the allocation of content may prompt displeasure or even refusal. A striking result of this study was that data security and consistency issues are not taken into account as much as infrastructural and administrative IT imperatives. As security concerns are more and more moving to the strategic front burner of companies (e.g. Capgemini, 2005, S. 6), practitioners should ponder about the proper alignment of their content infrastructure with security-enforcing measurements as well.

Finally, this study can also help practitioners develop new functionalities for the design of content logistics support systems as part of upcoming content management systems. As the orchestration of content distribution and integration represents an important pillar of content architecture management, in particular for companies whose major resources and outputs consist of digital content, routing content to the spots where it is needed in a timely manner may improve production and bundling processes. In addition, the tracking of content retrieval and access may unveil regular usage patterns of editors which could be analyzed and availed of by IS executives for the future optimization of content allocation. Usage patterns may, for example, provide information about what content modules lend themselves for increased content reutilization practices. This increased information transparency may indeed turn out to be invaluable not only for content allocation endeavors, but also for content portfolio management decisions as a whole.

To summarize the major practical implications, this study has provided patterns of alternative modes of content allocation and the contingency conditions associated with their adoption. Table 5.2-1 and Table 5.2-2 illustrate the major contingencies of content distribution and content integration identified in this research study in the form of a contingency plan. With such contingency plans at hand, practitioners can benchmark the interaction effects between contingency factors and content infrastructures found in this study against their company's particular situation. Although it is not recommended to blindly follow the proposed relationships, as conflicting contingencies might occur within the same company, contingency plans may serve as a basis for further discussion and provide rules of thumb that could help practitioners to make more grounded decisions.

There is one note of caution, however, that should be kept in mind. Publishing organizations should not rely on any single structural relationship identified in this study, when evaluating and comparing alternative content allocation options. They should rather pursue a multidimensional approach that recognizes the interdepend-

ence between existing contingencies. They should especially develop a good understanding of the cost and benefit drivers, organizational and social impacts, technical
requirements, and particular characteristics of their content portfolio before starting to
compare their current content allocation arrangement with alternative ones .

Contingencies	Content distribution mode	
	Productive content	*Archived content*
Production cost advantages of content centralization (Pc)	High centralization	High centralization
Transaction cost advantages of content centralization (Tc)	---	High centralization
Strategic benefit advantages of content centralization (Strat)	---	High centralization
Operational benefit advantages of content centralization (Opera)	High centralization	High centralization
Greater emphasis on low cost strategy (LowCost)	---	High centralization
High organizational centralization within organization (OrgCent)	---	High decentralization
High task specialization within organization (OrgSpec)	High decentralization	---
High concentration of IT decision-making within organization (ITGov)	High centralization	High centralization
High infrastructural IT-requirements for centralization within organization (InflTImp)	High centralization	High centralization
High administrative IT-requirements for centralization within organization (AdminITImp)	High centralization	High centralization

Table 5.2-1: Contingency plan for content distribution

| Contingencies | Content integration mode | |
	Productive content	Archived content
Strategic benefit advantages of content centralization (Strat)	Higher integration scope	Higher integration scope
Operational benefit advantages of content centralization (Opera)	Higher integration scope	Higher integration scope
Greater emphasis on low cost strategy (LowCost)	---	Lower integration scope
High task specialization within organization (OrgSpec)	Lower integration scope	Lower integration scope
High concentration of IT decision-making within organization (ITGov)	Higher integration scope	---
High infrastructural IT-requirements for centralization within organization (InfITImp)	Higher integration scope	---
High administrative IT-requirements for centralization within organization (AdminITImp)	Higher integration scope	Higher integration scope

Table 5.2-2: Contingency plan for content integration

5.3 Study limitations

Although the findings of this study have emerged from a well grounded research procedure, there are several things that should be kept in mind. Besides methodological
limitations, especially the theoretical boundaries of this research study should be
pointed out.

First, in order to keep the complexity of this study's research variables at the same
time low, but non-trivial, the dimensions of content allocation considered in this study
were confined to two aspects: content distribution and content integration. Both sub-
constructs were operationalized by tapping into complementary content domains.
Content integration, however, could have also captured the extent to which disseminated content repositories are logically connectd to one another. Although this operationalization of content integration as "system interoperability" construct would have
had a greater distance to the actual production process in publishing companies, it
would have cast a slightly different, but certainly insightful light on content allocation.
Moreover, although content centralization and decentralization were picked as opposing extremes of a continuum that spans different content allocation modes in order to provide a simplified model of observable phenomena, they might fall short of
covering all relevant decision options for content allocation arrangements among
which the lines are certainly more blurred and not as choppy as as suggested in this
research study. The juxtaposition of a taxonomy of different content allocation

modes[187] would probably have delivered more precise, albeit more complex answers to the research questions of this study.

Second, although a variety of independent variables were thoroughly sorted out before they were integrated into the causal model, a complete picture with all potential influencing factors could not be provided. While a causal model whose dependent variable is accounted for by 100% is impossible to achieve, a more realistic picture could have been drawn, if more elaborate or additional decision criteria of complementary theoretical research domains (e.g., the theory of planned behavior) had been included. In particular, the introduction of more non-technical variables that rather tap into behavioral domains could enhance the explanation of content allocation. The research study would also have been better off, for instance, if more items had been integrated reflecting Porter's constructs for business strategy.

Furthermore, it is recommended to spend more time on enhancing the content specificity scales, which turned out to be weak predictors for relative production and transaction cost advantages[188]. This may also be due to the fact that respondents were asked to assess the specificity of those content modules that typically enter their media products and therefore may be considered as being representative for their own content portfolio. As publishing companies most often possess a great variety of content resources, both specific and unspecific, a sole judgement based on average content modules is too oversimplifying and distort real phenomena to a great extent. Upcoming research in this domain thus has to further delve into the intricacies of improving the construct and nomological validity of these variables. One possible antidote against this methodological shortcoming could, for instance, be to choose a lower level of analysis (see Figure 2.2-1) that would allow for integrating the perspective of editorial units or even of editors themselves.

Third, the study at hand relied exclusively on self-reported measures, which usually introduce a common response bias across constructs. Although the results of the validity and reliability tests carried out and reported in this study argue for sufficient confidence in those measures, future investigations using objective data would undoubtedly yield more powerful results. Although entailing much bigger efforts on the side of the researcher, the investigation of content databases of publishing companies and the interrogation of editors about their content access and usage behavior

---

[187] FIEDLER AND GROVER, for example, have developed a taxonomy of information technology structures for the investigation of its relationship to organizational structure (Fiedler/ Grover, 1996).

[188] In particular, not only constructs such as content specificity, but also content relatedness and transaction frequency and their interrelationships between one another have to be specified more thoroughly. These factors may be examined for their theoretical and empirical interconnectedness in the sense that all constructs tap into the conceptual realm of content reutilization. For instance, if requirements for sharing and exchanging content across editorial units are high due to a high level of content relatedness, content transaction frequency increases making content centralization a more and more vital content allocation option. This in turn would favor content reutilization, as a more centrally stored content portfolio could be better exploited.

would certainly produce more valid and reliable measures for content distribution and content integration. In addition, the study lacks the link to an objective performance criterion (e.g. return on assets (ROA) or return on investment (ROI)) that reflects the real market success of publishing firms in dependence of their content allocation behavior. Certainly, this study provided proxies for performance measures in the form of perceptual comparative advantage criteria. However, attitudinal data tends to be distorted not only by personal beliefs and desires, but also by effects of subjective norm.

For that reason, further insight into the content allocation behavior of publishing companies could have been provided by comparing planned (i.e. intended) and actual content allocation. The theory of planned behavior, which aims to predict and explain the behavior of individuals (Ajzen, 1991) and has already been applied fruitfully in MIS research (e.g. Mathieson, 1991), could have been used, for instance, to explain a possible gap between the intention and the actual behavior to allocate content in a certain way. As the intention of IS executives is influenced by individual attitude, subjective norm, and perceived behavioral control, the theory of planned behavior could have further enlightened the understanding of content allocation processes.

A weak point that goes along with the former one is that, in validating the content allocation model, only the perspective of IS executives (and to a lesser extent the perspective of CEOs) has been considered. Neither was an attempt made to empirically identify the person or group of persons deciding upon the actual content allocation decision, nor was investigated how real decisions on content allocation come about in publishing companies. Managers of individual editorial units, for instance, could have also been considered part of the target group.

Fourth, although all hypotheses were stated in associational terms, the logic behind them implies that comparative advantage and contingency variables are not just associated with, but cause higher or lower levels of content allocation. Because the data in this study is cross-sectional and snapshot-like, the ability to draw causal inferences is limited. Nonetheless, on an a priori basis, the results of this study are a promising foundation for future longitudinal studies that should be undertaken to examine the identified linkages. Such longitudinal research designs would also help researchers to examine the possibility that the effect of an improper fit between, for instance, IT governance practices, probably a recently developed mismatch, might not be fully reflected in a current content allocation configuration, but might affect content allocation after a couple of periods.

Fifth, the group samples for book, magazine, and newspaper publishing groups were not only not high enough in size to generate valid and reliable SEM-based parameter estimates in their own right, but also couldn't reflect real sample compositions in the population of publishing companies. Given this fait accompli, two consequences had to be drawn. On the one hand, the differences between book, magazine, and newspaper publishers could only be compared on the basis of descriptive findings, and not based on structural equation modeling. This also barred the way to more valuable insights into inter-group differences in content allocation practices. On the other hand, empirical findings from small samples with low response rates and distorted sample compositions may not be representative for a larger population. Thus, the generalizability (i.e. external validity) of the results presented in this research study has to be treated with care.

5.4 Future research

While these limitations must be kept in mind, when considering the findings, the pioneering character of this study should not be overseen. It is one of the first attempts to integrate multiple theoretical concepts that contribute to explain the content allocation phenomenon. Moreover, it is the only comparative empirical study, to date, that recognizes allocation dimension, content type and industry differences in the content allocation behavior of publishing organizations. Both the study limitations and the potential enhancements on the theoretical and methodological side open up avenues for future research.

First, the findings of this study need to be replicated across other settings (e.g., in the broadcast industry and other countries) in order to extend the external validity of the findings. The validity tests of the construct measures were very promising. However, researchers that want to replicate this model on the level of each publishing type are well advised to take care of the response rate and sample compositions. A meticulous analysis of the variances in content allocation in each publishing type (i.e. book, magazine, and newspaper) or even in each editorial unit might bring to light further interesting findings that were concealed and superposed by an analysis of variance emphasizing content allocation behavior in publishing companies. Moreover, if researchers intend to gather data from IS executives, the length of the questionnaire appears to be critical. A few constructs whose impact found little support in this study may be deleted. Moreover, researchers do not necessarily have to conduct questionnaire surveys. They can also use other empirical research methods, like case studies, to examine the theoretical framework. In this vein, researchers may even consider to examine the model on content allocation from other perspectives than that of the IS executive. It would be interesting to see how business unit managers or even editors would evaluate the constructs of this model.

Second, the static nature of this research study could be complemented by longitudinal investigations also replicating the findings across time. Of course, demanding longitudinal research is easier said than done. It requires a long breath by the researcher and a very profound understanding of content infrastructure management prior to entering into such an endeavor. It appears promising to pick out a few variables ex ante and to observe how and why they change over time. For example, it could be examined over multiple periods of time how changes in the content allocation configuration of an organization correspond with variations in other variables, like production costs, different types of IT-related and organizational variables. For such a

longitudinal research plan, case studies with a selection of companies may be considered. They allow taking into account emergent influences that the researcher is
not aware of when starting the research project. Moreover, it may be much easier to
convince a few senior IS executives of the benefits from their participation, than an
anonymous group of respondents, as it usually is the case in large scale surveys.

Third, further methodological work is needed to modify and enhance constructs,
which were provided in the study on hand. In particular, constructs which exhibited
critical values in construct validity (e.g., content specificity variables) should be reviewed carefully. As indicated in the chapter on the study's limitation, the inclusion of
further dimensions of content allocation as well as of additional features of distribution and integration would contribute not only to the advancement of content allocation research, but to the allocation of IT-related artifacts as a whole. Future work can
also extend this study and explain more variance in content allocation by incorporating non-rational factors that influence content allocation decisions. To this end, a
good starting point would be the development of analytical models that, for instance,
investigate the optimal degree of content allocation by means of counterbalancing
benefits from content bundling opportunities and costs from information overload and
content corruption. Cognitive or motivational characteristics could for example enter
the model as side conditions. The empirical results of this study also backed up the
notion that the benefits of content integration do not always provide sufficient benefits
to outweigh the costs in certain organizational contexts. Within the scope of such
models, the interesting research question of why a maximum of content integration is
most often not equivalent to the optimum could therefore also be addressed. Furthermore, it could be found that a maximum in content integration does not optimally
support organizational processes in every publishing organization. Therefore, another avenue for further research is to help practitioners get a grasp on better conceptualizations and methods for implementing "partial content integration arrangements" in publishing organizations.

Fourth, this study adopted a selective approach to the concept of fit. Although this
way of operationalization was appropriate for this rather production-oriented topic,
future studies may incorporate the interaction or systems view of fit as well. They
would offer the advantage that different modes of content allocation would not only
be benchmarked against each other by comparing relative efficiency criteria, but also
by objective market performance data. In addition to the relatedness factors included
in this study (i.e. content, production process, and market relatedness), other synergy
factors across editorial units may play a vital role in the determination of strategic and
operational advantages of particular content allocation modes. TANRIVERDI AND
VENKATRAMAN, for instance, suggest to assess whether the exploitation of a common corporate brand and common reputation across multiple businesses creates
synergies (Tanriverdi/ Venkatraman, 2005, p. 116). This potential avenue of extension particularly applies to brand-intensive industries such as the media industry. The
integration of brand-relatedness could therefore explain variance in content allocation

behavior over and beyond the variance explained by the three dimensions of knowledge relatedness examined in this study.

Fifth, future research on how content allocation can be embedded into content management processes provides an interesting research opportunity that would actively bridge the gap between academia and practice. Researchers may enter into companies acting as action researchers who not only seek to understand what practice is doing, but to actively shape and support their behavior. More critical social research may be one way towards that end. However, it should also be complemented by constructivist research approaches. This implies to actually develop tools that support and, thereby, improve the allocation practices of organizations. As mentioned before, the results of this research may serve as a basis to develop a content logistics system (e.g., as add-on to a content management application) that enables IT managers to optimally match content demand and supply during the production and bundling of content. Such a future research stream would also have to consider the possibilities arising from technologies fostering new ways of organizing content by means of metadata. Some few papers have already tackled the problem of how to take advantage and harness the capabilities of ontologies in the media industry in order to enhance content integration and distribution (Benlian/ Wiedemann/ Hess, 2004; Köhler/ Anding/ Hess, 2003).

Finally, another direction for future research on content allocation would be to more actively include neighboring disciplines, such as behavioral sciences, which, for instance, can add valuable insights into non-rational predictors of content allocation. Given the cross-functional nature of information systems and information systems research, there are manifold opportunities for collaborative research projects. Hopefully, this research project can serve as a solid starting point for upcoming research projects taking up similar research opportunities. It would also be desirable that some pieces of advice presented in the course of this research study are going to be of help in the future.

6 Conclusion

"Understanding in Information Systems research can be increased by inclusion of multiple explanation types [...]" (Hovorka, 2004, p. 4180)

The objectives of this research study were to shed light on the phenomenon 'content allocation' in publishing companies, to increase the understanding of the relationships between influencing factors and content allocation[189], and to deliver prescriptive and normative insights as to how to influence the determinant factors in order to manipulate content allocation. In particular, the analysis of content allocation was broken down to the distribution and integration of productive and archived content in book, magazine, and newspaper companies resulting in a more differentiated and informative picture

Based on the analysis of the state-of-the-art in MIS literature on the allocation of IT-related resources, a research gap with regard to the description and explanation of media content allocation in publishing companies was identified. In the course of sifting through related work it became evident that although the logic and reasoning for allocating IT-related resources in general was comprehensibly examined, neither media content nor publishing organizations had been focused yet. In order to understand the reasons and wider implications of the content allocation behavior of publishing companies, a multi-theoretical framework, which is based on the epistemological view of theoretical pluralism, was developed. Thus, in order to ensure that the content allocation practices of organizations are understood as completely as possible, multiple theoretical lenses have been integrated into a coherent framework shedding light on content allocation behavior from different selected angles.

This research study incorporated economic, strategic, and organizational dimensions of the content allocation decision by tying together concepts and constructs from transaction cost theory, resource-based view, and contingency theory into a cohesive whole refered to as framework of institutional performance. This framework was specified in a research model and empirically tested based on the content allocation behavior of 115 publishing organizations in Germany. To this end, the perspectives of IS executives were analyzed. This group was meant to be most inclined in the content allocation decision and to be best informed about the contingencies the IT infrastructure of the publishing company is exposed to. Moreover, it was assumed that the content allocation decision is influenced by multiple dimensions that should explain the degree of productive and archived content allocation. The empirical findings have widely supported this view.

---

[189] The relationship between explaining and understanding in MIS research is comprehensibly presented in Hovorka, 2004.

There is a consistent pattern of relationships that determine content distribution and integration, independent of the type of content as well as the type of publishing company. In particular, strategic arguments were found to have a profound impact on content integration, while content distribution was more influenced by a reasoning based on relative production costs and comparative operational benefits. Suppressing the variances between the different types of publishers, neither transaction costs nor organizational factors could unfold a high explanatory power. By contrast, the variances in the content allocation behavior of all publishing companies could be accounted for by IT-related factors to a substantial extent. In particular, infrastructural and administrative IT imperatives, as well as IT governance practices, which are moderated by IT usage-based path dependencies, were salient predictors of content allocation. These findings not only corroborate the outcomes of previous related work on the importance of technical requirements and the mode of IT governance, but also point to the relevance of behavioral factors in the process of content allocation decisions. Moreover, synergy effects between different sources of economies of scale based on content, production process, and market-based relatedness across editorial units were found to consistently explain comparative strategic and operational advantages in the allocation of content. This indicates not only the importance of reasonable cross-references between organizational units for an efficient design of content infrastructures, but also the necessity of complementary sources of relatedness.

On the level of the particular publisher sub-types, different forms of content allocation behavior could be identified. While book publishers show the most decentralized and isolated content allocation behavior compared to the others, newspaper publishers' content stock is located most centrally with editors having he most integrated access. Structural factors such as content transaction frequency, content reutilization practices and content devaluation speed proved to be relevant discriminating factors confirming the commonly recited structural differences in state-of-the-art literature.

In summarizing the results of this study, it may be concluded that the content allocation decision requires the consideration of multiple criteria. Both the characteristics of the content base (including the production process in which it is created and the markets it is offered to) and the overlapping layers of IT management and systems infrastructures a publishing firm has developed over time need to be carefully examined in order to rigorously evaluate and compare alternative content allocation options. In practice, it is frequently observed that the allocation behavior of IT-related resources is comparable to a pendulum's recurrent oscillations between centralization and decentralization – in particular due to upcoming technological trends pushing the one or the other extreme. A multi-theoretical model along with the overarching framework of institutional performance as put forth in this study offer the promise of a more profound conceptual and practical understanding of the complex dynamics underlying the evolutionary nature of IT-related resource allocation.

Hopefully, this research study has lived up to this promise by enriching existing conceptualizations and yielding practical knowledge about the allocation of media content in publishing companies.

Literature

Abell, P. (1975): Organizations as bargaining and influence systems, London.

Agarwal, R./ Prasad, J. (1997): The role of innovation characteristics and perceived voluntariness in the acceptance of information technology, in: *Decision Sciences*, 28, 3, p. 557-582.

Agarwal, R./ Prasad, J. (1998): The antecedents and consequences of user perceptions in information technology adoption, in: *Decision Support Systems*, 22, 1, p. 15-29.

Agarwal, R./ Sambamurthy, V. (2002): Principles and models for organizing the IT function, in: *MIS Quarterly Executive*, 1, 1, p. 1-16.

Ahituv, N./ Neumann, S./ Zviran, M. (1989): Factors affecting the policy for distributing computing resources, in: *MIS Quarterly*, 13, 4, p. 388-401.

Aiken, L. S./ Hage, J. (1968): Organizational interdependence and intra-organizational structure, in: *American Sociological Review*, 33, 6, p. 912-930.

Ailawadi, K. L./ Dant, R./ Grewal, D. (2004): The difference between perceptual and objective performance measures: An empirical analysis, in: *MSI Working Paper Series*, 1, p. 77-101.

Ajzen, I. (1991): The theory of planned behavior, in: *Organizational Behavior & Human Decision Processes*, 50, 3, p. 179-211.

AKEP (2004): Branchenbarometer Elektronisches Publizieren, Arbeitskreis Elektronisches Publizieren des Börsenvereins des Deutschen Buchhandels, Frankfurt am Main.

Albach, H. (1981): The nature of the firm – A production-theoretical viewpoint, in: *Journal of Institutional and Theoretical Economics*, 137, p. 717-722.

Alchian, A. A./ Demsetz, H. (1972): Production, information costs, and the economic organization, in: *American Economic Review*, 62, 5, p. 777-795.

Altmeppen, K.-D. (2000): Medienmanagement als Redaktions- und Produktionsmanagement, in: Karmasin, M., Winter, C.: *Grundlagen des Medienmanagements*, UTB - Wilhelm Fink Verlag, München, p. 41-58.

Amit, R./ Schoemaker, P. J. H. (1993): Strategic assets and organizational rent, in: *Strategic Management Journal*, 14, 1, p. 33-46.

Anding, M. (2004): Online Content Syndication - Theoretische Fundierung und praktische Ausgestaltung eines Geschäftsmodells der Medienindustrie, DUV, Wiesbaden.

Anding, M./ Hess, T. (2003): Was ist Content? Zur Definition und Systematisierung von Medieninhalten, Institut für Wirtschaftsinformatik und Neue Medien der Ludwig-Maximilians-Universität, München, Arbeitsbericht: 5/2003.

Anding, M./ Hess, T. (2004): Modularization, individualization and the first-copy-cost-effect: Shedding new light on the production and distribution of media content, Institut für

Wirtschaftsinformatik und Neue Medien der Ludwig-Maximilians-Universität, München, Arbeitsbericht: 1/2004.

Ang, S./ Cummings, L. L. (1997): Strategic response to institutional influences on information systems outsourcing, in: *Organization Science*, 8, 3, p. 235-256.

Ang, S./ Straub, D. (1998): Production and transaction economies and IS outsourcing: A study of the U.S. banking industry, in: *MIS Quartely*, 22, 4, p. 535-552.

Armstrong, J. S./ Overton, T. S. (1977): Estimating nonresponse bias in mail surveys, in: *Journal of Marketing Research*, 14, 3, p. 396-402.

Arrow, K. J. (1969): The organization of economic activity : Issues pertinent to the choice of market versus non-market allocation, in: *The Analysis and Evaluation of Public Expenditure: The PPB System*, U.S. Government Printing Office, Washington, DC, p. 39-73.

Arthur, B. (1989): Competing technologies, increasing returns, and lock-in by historical events, in: *Economic Journal*, 99, 394, p. 116-131.

Avison, D./ Jones, J./ Powell, P./ Wilson, D. (2004): Using and validating the strategic alignment model, in: *Journal of Strategic Information Systems*, 13, 3, p. 223-246.

Bacon, C. J. (1990): Organizational principles of systems decentralization, in: *Journal of Information Technology*, 5, 2, p. 84-93.

Bagozzi, R. P. (1981): Evaluating structural equation models with unobservable variables and measurement error: A comment, in: *Journal of Marketing Research*, XVIII, August, p. 375-381.

Bagozzi, R. P./ Fornell, C. (1982): Theoretical concepts, measurement, and meaning, in: Fornell, C.: *A Second Generation of Multivariate Analysis*, Praeger, New York, p. 5-23.

Bagozzi, R. P./ Phillips, L. (1982): Representing and testing organizational theories: A holistic construal, in: *Administrative Science Quarterly*, 27, 3, p. 459-489.

Bagozzi, R. P./ Yi, Y. (1988): On the evaluation of structural equation models, in: *Journal of the Academy of Marketing Science*, 16, 1, p. 74-94.

Bailey, K. D. (1994): Typologies and taxonomies: An introduction to classification techniques, Sage, Thousand Oaks, CA.

Bain, J. S. (1968): Industrial organization, John Wiley and Sons, New York.

Baker, D./ Cullen, J. B. (1993): The contingent effects of age, size, and change in size, in: *Academy of Management Journal*, 36, 6, p. 1251-1277.

Bamberger, I./ Wrona, T. (1995): Der Ressourcenansatz im Rahmen des Strategischen Management, Arbeitspapier Nr. 8 des Fachgebiets O&P der Universität Duisburg-Essen, Essen.

Bamberger, I./ Wrona, T. (1996): Der Ressourcenansatz und seine Bedeutung für die Strategische Unternehmensführung, in: *Zeitschrift für betriebswirtschaftliche Forschung*, 48, 8, p. 130-153.

Barclay, D. W./ Thompson, R. H./ Christopher, A. (1995): The partial least squares approach to causal modeling: Personal computer adoption and use as an illustration, in: *Technology Studies*, 2, 2 (Special Issue on Research Methodology), p. 285-309.

Barnes, W./ Gartland, M./ Stack, M. (2004): Old habits die hard: path dependency and behavioral lock-in, in: *Journal of Economic Issues*, 38, 2, p. 371-377.

Barney, J. (1991): Firm resources and sustained competitive advantage, in: *Journal of Management*, 17, 1, p. 99-120.

Barney, J. B. (2001): Resource-based theories of competitive advantage: A ten year retrospective on the resource-based view, in: *Journal of Management*, 27, 6, p. 643-650.

Baron, R. M./ Kenny, D. A. (1986): The moderator-mediator variable distinction in social psychological research: Conceptual, strategic and statistical considerations, in: *Journal of Personality and Social Psychology*, 51, 6, p. 1173-1182.

Barthélemy, J. (2001): The hidden costs of IT outsourcing, in: *Sloan Management Review*, 42, 3, p. 60-69.

Baruch, Y. (1999): Response rate in academic studies – A comparative analysis, in: *Human Relations*, 52, 4, p. 421-438.

Barzel, Y. (1997): Economic analysis of property rights, 2nd Edition, Cambridge University Press, Cambridge et al.

BDZV (2004): Zeitungen 2004, ZV Zeitungs-Verlag Service GmbH, Berlin.

Bechtold, S. (2002): Vom Urheber- zum Informationsrecht, Verlag C.H. Beck, München.

Benbasat, I./ Zmud, R. W. (1999): Empirical research in information systems: The practice of relevance, in: *MIS Quartely*, 23, 1, p. 3-16.

Benham, A./ Benham, L. (2004): The costs of exchange: An approach to measuring transactions costs, Ronald Coase Institute Working Papers, St. Louis, MI, Number 1.

Benjamin, R. I./ Blunt, J. (1992): Critical IT issues: The next ten years, in: *Sloan Management Review*, 33, 4, p. 13-19.

Benlian, A./ Hess, T. (2004): Identifikation und technische Bewertung von integrierten Datenverteilungsvarianten für eine effiziente Mehrfachnutzung multimedialer Medieninhalte, Institut für Wirtschaftsinformatik und Neue Medien der Ludwig-Maximilians-Universität, München, Arbeitsbericht: 3/2004.

Benlian, A./ Reitz, M./ Wilde, T./ Hess, T. (2005): Verbreitung, Anwendungsfelder und Wirtschaftlichkeit von XML in Print-Verlagen - Eine empirische Untersuchung, in: *Proceedings der 7. Internationalen Tagung Wirtschaftsinformatik 2005*, Bamberg, p. 211-230.

Benlian, A./ Wiedemann, F./ Hess, T. (2004): KeyTEx - An integrated prototype for semi-automatic metadata assignment and network-based content retrieval, in: *Proceedings of the 10th Americas Conference on Information Systems (AMCIS 2004)*, New York, NY, 3228-3238.

Betzin, J./ Henseler, J. (2005): Einführung in die Funktionsweise des PLS-Algorithmus, in: Bliemel, F., et al.: *Handbuch PLS-Pfadmodellierung. Methode, Anwendung, Praxisbeispiele*, Schäffer-Poeschel, Stuttgart, p. 49-70.

Beyer, J. M./ Trice, H. M. (1979): A reexamination of the relations between size and various components of organizational complexity, in: *Administrative Science Quarterly*, 24, 1, p. 48-64.

Bharadwaj, A. S. (2000): A resource-based perspective on information technology capability and firm performance: an empirical investigation, in: *MIS Quarterly*, 24, 1, p. 169-196.

Bharadwaj, A. S./ Bharadwaj, S. G./ Konsynski, B. R. (1995): The moderator role of information technology in firm performance: A conceptual model and research propositions, in: *International Conference on Information Systems (ICIS)*, Amsterdam, The Netherlands, p. 183-188.

Blau, P. (1970): A formal theory of differentiation in organizations, in: *American Sociological Review*, 35, 2, p. 201-218.

Bloomfield, B. P./ Coombs, R. (1992): Information technology, control and power: The centralization and decentralization debate revisited, in: *Journal of Management Studies*, 29, 4, p. 459-484.

Boerner, C./ Macher, J. (2001): Transaction cost economics: an assessment of empirical research in the social sciences, Walter A. Haas School of Business (UC Berkely) & Robert E. McDonough School of Business (Georgetown University), unpublished manuscript.

Bollen, K. A. (1984): Multiple indicators: Internal consistency or no necessary relationship, in: *Quality and Quantity*, 18, p. 377-385.

Bollen, K. A./ Stine, R. A. (1993): Bootstrapping goodness-of-fit measures in structural equation models, in: Bollen, K. A., Long, J. S.: *Testing Structural Equation Model*, Sage, Newbury Park, CA, p. 111-135.

Bortz, J./ Bongers, D. (1984): Lehrbuch der empirischen Forschung: Für Sozialwissenschaftler, Springer, Heidelberg.

Bortz, J./ Döring, N. (2002): Forschungsmethoden und Evaluation für Human- und Sozialwissenschaftler, 3rd Edition, Springer, Berlin et al.

Boynton, A. C./ Jacobs, G. C./ Zmud, R. W. (1992): Whose responsibility Is IT management?, in: *Sloan Management Review*, 33, 4, p. 32-38.

Boynton, A. C./ Zmud, R. W. (1987): Information technology planning in the 1990's: Directions for practice and research, in: *MIS Quarterly*, 11, 2, p. 59-71.

Breyer-Mayländer, T./ Seeger, C. (2004): Verlage vor neuen Herausforderungen. Krisenmanagement in der Pressebranche, ZV, Berlin.

Brosius, H.-B./ Koschel, F. (2005): Methoden der empirischen Kommunikationsforschung. Eine Einführung, 3rd Edition, VS Verlag für Sozialwissenschaftler, Wiesbaden.

Brown, C. V. (1997): Examining the emergence of hybrid IS governance solutions: Evidence from a single case site, in: *Information Systems Research*, 8, 1, p. 69-94.

Brown, C. V./ Magill, S. L. (1994): Alignment of the IS functions with the enterprise: Toward a model of antecedents, in: *MIS Quarterly*, 18, 4, p. 371-403.

Brown, C. V./ Magill, S. L. (1998): Reconceptualizing the context-design issue for the information systems function, in: *Organization Science*, 9, 2, p. 176-194.

Brynjolfsson, E. (1993): The productivity paradox of information technology, in: *Communications of ACM*, 36, 12, p. 67-77.

Buchanan, J. R./ Linowes, R. G. (1980): Understanding distributed data processing, in: *Harvard Business Review*, 58, 4, p. 143-153.

Bullock, H. E./ Harlow, L. L./ Mulaik, S. A. (1994): Causation issues in structural equation modeling research, in: *Structured Equation Modeling*, 1, 3, p. 253-267.

Burns, T./ Stalker, G. M. (1961): The management of innovation, Tavistock, London.

Burrell, G./ Morgan, G. (1979): Sociological paradigms and organizational analysis, Heinemann, London.

Burton, R./ Obel, B. (2004): Strategic organizational diagnosis and design: The dynamics of fit, 3rd Edition, Kluwer, Boston.

BVDB (2004): Buch und Buchhandel in Zahlen, Börsenverein des Deutschen Buchhandels, Frankfurt am Main.

Byrd, T. A. (2001): Information technology, core competencies, and sustained competitive advantage, in: *Information Resources Management Journal*, 14, 2, p. 41-52.

Campbell, D. T./ Fiske, D. W. (1959): Convergent and discriminant validation by the multitrait-multimethods matrix, in: *Psychological Bulletin*, 74, 2, p. 81-105.

Capgemini (2005): Paradigmenwechsel in Sicht. Studie IT-Trends 2005, München.

Capron, L./ Hulland, J. (1999): Redeployment of brands, sales forces, and general marketing management expertise following horizontal acquisitions: A resource-based view, in: *Journal of Marketing*, 63, 2, p. 41-54.

Carte, T. A./ Russell, C. J. (2003): In pursuit of moderation: Nine common errors and their solutions, in: *MIS Quarterly*, 27, 3, p. 479-501.

Carter, N. M. (1984): Computerization as a predominant technology: Its influences on the structure of newspaper organizations, in: *Academy of Management Journal*, 27, 2, p. 247-270.

Cash, J. I./ McFarlan, F. W./ McKenney, J. L. (1992): Corporate information systems management: The issues facing senior executives, 3rd Edition, Irwin, Homewood, IL.

Chalmers, A. F. (2001): Wege der Wissenschaft. Einführung in die Wissenschaftstheorie, 5th Edition, Springer, Berlin et al.

Chatterjee, S./ Wernerfelt, B. (1991): The link between resources and type of diversification: Theory and evidence, in: *Strategic Management Journal*, 12, 1, p. 33-48.

Cheon, M. J./ Grover, V./ Teng, J. T. C. (1995): Theoretical perspectives on the outsourcing of information Systems, in: *Journal of Information Technology*, 10, p. 209-210.

Child, J. (1973): Predicting and understanding organizational structure, in: *Administrative Science Quarterly*, 18, 2, p. 168-185.

Childers, T. L./ Ferrell, O. C. (1979): Response rates and perceived questionnaire length in mail surveys, in: *Journal of Marketing Research*, 16, 3, p. 429-431.

Chin, W. W. (1998a): Issues and opinion on structural equation modeling, in: *MIS Quarterly*, 22, 1, p. VII-XVI.

Chin, W. W. (1998b): The partial least squares approach for structural equation modeling, in: Marcoulides, G. A.: *Modern Methods for Business Research*, Lawrence Erlbaum Associates, Hillsdale, NJ, p. 295-336.

Chin, W. W./ Gopal, A. (1995): Adoption intention in GSS: Relative importance of beliefs, in: *The DATA BASE for Advances in Information Systems*, 26, 2, p. 42-63.

Chin, W. W./ Marcolin, B. L./ Newsted, P. R. (1996): A partial least squares latent variable modeling approach for measuring interaction effects: Results from a Monte Carlo simulation study and voice mail emotion/adoption study, in: *Proceedings of the seventeenth international conference on information systems*, Cleveland, Ohio, p. 21-40.

Chin, W. W./ Marcolin, B. L./ Newsted, P. R. (2003): A partial least squares latent variable modeling approach for measuring interaction effects: Results from a Monte Carlo simulation study and an electronic-mail emotion/adoption study, in: *Information Systems Research*, 14, 2, p. 189-217.

Chin, W. W./ Newsted, P. R. (1999): Structural equation modeling analysis with small samples using partial least squares, in: Hoyle, R. H.: *Statistical strategies for small sample research*, SAGE Publications, Thousand Oaks, London, p. 307-341.

Churchill, G. A. (1979): A paradigm for developing better measures of marketing constructs, in: *Journal of Marketing Research*, 16, 1, p. 64-73.

Chwelos, P./ Benbasat, I./ Dexter, A. S. (2001): Research report: Empirical test of an EDI adoption model, in: *Information Systems Journal*, 12, 3, p. 304-321.

Clemons, E. K./ Row, M. C. (1991): Sustaining IT advantage: The role of structural differences, in: *MIS Quarterly*, 15, 3, p. 275-292.

Clemons, E. K./ Row, M. C. (1993): Limits to interfirm coordination through information technology: Results of a field study in consumer packaged goods distribution, in: *Journal of Management Information Systems*, 10, 1, p. 73-95.

Coase, R. H. (1937): The nature of the firm, in: *Economica*, 16, 4, p. 386-405.

Cohen, J. (1988): Statistical power analysis for the behavioral sciences, 2nd Edition, Lawrence Erlbaum Associates, Hillsdale.

Commons, J. R. (1931): Institutional economics, in: *The American Economic Review*, 12, p. 648-657.

Conner, K. R. (1991): A historical comparison of resource-based theory and five schools of thought within industrial organization economics: Do we have a new theory of the firm?, in: Journal of Management, 17, 1, p. 121-154.

Cournot, A. (1924): Untersuchungen über die mathematischen Grundlagen der Theorie des Reichtums, Fischer, Jena.

Cyert, R. M./ March, J. G. (1963): A behavioral theory of the firm, Prentice-Hall, Englewood Cliffs, N.J.

Dadam, P. (1996): Verteilte Datenbanken und Client/Server-Systeme. Grundlagen, Konzepte, Realisierungsformen, Springer, Berlin et al.

Daft, R. L. (1989): Organization theory and design, 3rd Edition, West Publishing Co, St. Paul, MN.

Dagum, C. (1989): Scientific model building: Principles, methods, and history, in: Wold, H.: Theoretical empiricism: A general rationale for scientific model-building, Paragon House, New York, p. 113-152.

David, P. A. (1985): Clio and the economics of QWERTY, in: American Economic Review, 75, 2, p. 332-337.

David, P. A. (2000): Path dependence, its critics, and the quest for 'historical economics', Stanford University, Department of Economics, Working Paper: Nr. 00011.

Davis, F. D. (1989): Perceived usefulness, perceived ease of use, and user acceptance of information technology, in: MIS Quarterly, 13, 3, p. 319-339.

Dewar, R. D. (1978): Size, technology, complexity, and structural differentiation: Toward a theoretical synthesis, in: Administrative Science Quarterly, 23, 1, p. 111-136.

Dewar, R. D./ Whetten, D. A./ Boje, D. (1980): An examination of the reliability and validity of the Aiken and Hage scales of centralization, formalization, and task routineness, in: Administrative Science Quarterly, 25, 1, p. 120-128.

Diamantopoulos, A. (1999): Export performance measurement: Reflective versus formative indicators, in: International Marketing Review, 16, 6, p. 444-457.

Dibbern, J. (2004): Sourcing of application software services. Empirical evidence of cultural, industry and functional differences, Physica-Verlag, Heidelberg, New York.

Dibbern, J./ Heinzl, A./ Leibbrandt, S. (2003): Interpretation des Sourcings der Informationsverarbeitung. Hintergründe und Grenzen ökonomischer Einflussgrößen, in: Wirtschaftsinformatik, 45, 5, p. 533-540.

Dierickx, I./ Cool, K./ Barney, J. (1989): Asset Stock accumulation and sustainability of competitive advantage, in: Management Science, 35, 12, p. 1504-1514.

Dillman, D. A./ Sinclair, M. D./ Clark, J. R. (1993): Effects of questionnaire length, respondent-friendly design, and a difficult question on response rates for occupant-addressed census mail surveys, in: Public Opinion Quarterly, 57, 3, p. 289-304.

DiMaggio, P. J./ Powell, W. W. (1983): The iron cage revisited: Institutional isomorphism and collective rationality in organizational fields, in: *American Sociological Review*, 48, 2, p. 147-160.

Donald, M. N. (1967): Implications of non-response for the interpretation of mail questionnaire data, in: *Public Opinion Quarterly*, 24, 1, p. 99-114.

Doty, D. H./ Glick, W. H. (1993): Fit, equifinality, and organizational effectiveness: A test of two configurational theories, in: *Academy of Management Journal*, 36, 6, p. 1196-1250.

Drazin, R./ Van de Ven, A. H. (1985): Alternative forms of fit in contingency theory, in: *Administrative Science Quarterly*, 30, 4, p. 514-539.

Dreyer, B./ Grønhaug, K. (2004): Uncertainty, flexibility, and sustained competitive advantage, in: *Journal of Business Research*, 57, 5, p. 484-494.

Duncan, N. B. (1995): Capturing flexibility of information technology infrastructure: A study of resource characteristics and their measure, in: *Information Systems Research*, 12, 2, p. 37-57.

Duncan, W. J. (1979): Mail questionnaires in survey research: A review of response inducement techniques, in: *Journal of Management*, 5, 1, p. 39-55.

Eberhard, K. (1999): Einführung in die Erkenntnis- und Wissenschaftstheorie. Geschichte und Praxis der konkurrierenden Erkenntniswege, 2nd Edition, Verlag W. Kohlhammer, Stuttgart, Berlin, Köln.

Eggert, A./ Fassott, G. (2005): Zur Verwendung formativer und reflektiver Indikatoren in Strukturgleichungsmodellen: Bestandsaufnahme und Anwendungsempfehlungen, in: Bliemel, F., et al.: *Handbuch PLS-Pfadmodellierung. Methode, Anwendung, Praxisbeispiele*, Schäffer-Poeschel, Stuttgart, p. 31-38.

Eggert, A./ Fassott, G./ Helm, S. (2005): Identifizierung und Quantifizierung mediierender und moderierender Effekte in komplexen Kausalstrukturen, in: Bliemel, F., et al.: *Handbuch PLS-Pfadmodellierung. Methode, Anwendung, Praxisbeispiele*, Schäffer-Poeschel, Stuttgart, p. 101-116.

Ein-Dor, P./ Segev, E. (1982): Organizational context and MIS structure: Some empirical evidence, in: *MIS Quarterly*, 6, 3, p. 55-68.

Eisenhardt, K. M./ Martin, J. A. (2000): Dynamic capabilities: What are they?, in: *Strategic Management Journal*, 21, 10-11, p. 1105-1121.

Ensign, P. C. (2001): The concept of fit in organizational research, in: *International Journal of Organizational Theory & Behavior*, 4, 3&4, p. 287-306.

Farjoun, M. (1994): Beyond industry boundaries: Human expertise, diversification and resource-related industry groups, in: *Organization Science*, 5, 2, p. 185-199.

Farjoun, M. (1998): The independent and joint effects of the skill and physical bases of relatedness in diversification, in: *Strategic Management Journal*, 19, 7, p. 611-630.

Fassott, G. (2005): Die PLS-Pfadmodellierung: Entwicklungsrichtungen, Möglichkeiten, Grenzen., in: Bliemel, F., et al.: *Handbuch PLS-Pfadmodellierung - Methode, Anwendung, Praxisbeispiele,* Schäffer-Poeschel, Stuttgart.

Fennell, M. L. (1980): The effects of environmental characteristics on the structure of hospital clusters, in: *Administrative Science Quarterly,* 25, 3, p. 485-510.

Fiedler, K. D./ Grover, V. (1996): An empirically derived taxonomy of information technology structure and its relationship to organizational structure, in: *Journal of Management Information Systems,* 13, 1, p. 9-34.

Fischer, J. (1999): Informationswirtschaft: Anwendungsmanagement, Oldenbourg, München, Wien.

Fisseni, H.-J. (2004): Lehrbuch der psychologischen Diagnostik, 3rd Edition, Hogrefe, Göttingen.

Floyd, S. W./ Wooldridge, B. (1990): Path analysis of the relationship between competitive strategy, information technology, and financial performance, in: *Journal of Management Information Systems,* 7, 1, p. 47-64.

Fornell, C. (1982): Two structural equation models: LISREL and PLS applied to consumer exit-voice theory, in: *Journal of Marketing Research,* 19, 4, p. 440-452.

Fornell, C. (1989): The blending of theoretical and empirical knowledge in structural equations with unobservables, in: Wold, H.: *Theoretical empiricism: A general rationale for scientific model-building,* Paragon House, New York, p. 153-173.

Fornell, C./ Larcker, D. F. (1981): Evaluating structural equation models with unobservable variables and measurement error, in: *Journal of Marketing Research,* 18, 1, p. 39-50.

Foss, N. J./ Knudsen, C./ Montgomery, C. A. (1995): An exploration of common ground: Integrating evolutionary and strategic theories of the firm, in: Montgomery, C. A.: *Resource-based and evolutionary theories of the firm: towards a synthesis,* Kluwer Academic Publishers, Norwell, MA, p. 1-17.

Friedrichs, J. (1990): Methoden der empirischen Sozialforschung, 14th Edition, Westdeutscher Verlag, Opladen.

Fry, L. W./ Smith, D. A. (1987): Congruence, contingency, and theory building, in: *Academy of Management Review,* 12, 1, p. 117-132.

Furubotn, E. G./ Pejovich, S. (1972): Property rights and economic theory: a survey of recent literature, in: *Journal of Economic Literature,* 10, 4, p. 1137-1162.

George, J. F./ King, J. L. (1991): Examining the computing and centralization debate, in: *Communications of the ACM,* 34, 7, p. 63-72.

Gershenson, J. K./ Prasad, G. J./ Zhang, Y. (2003): Product modularity: definitions and benefits, in: *Journal of Engineering Design,* 14, 3, p. 295-313.

Gillespie, D. F./ Mileti, D. S. (1977): Technology and the study of organizations: An overview and appraisal, in: *Academy of Management Review,* 2, 1, p. 7-16.

Goodhue, D. L./ Quillard, J. A./ Rockart, J. F. (1988): Managing the data resource: a contingency perspective, in: MIS Quarterly, 12, 3, p. 372-392.

Goodhue, D. L./ Wybo, M. D./ Kirsch, L. J. (1992): The impact of data integration on the costs and benefits of information systems, in: MIS Quarterly, 16, 3, p. 293-311.

Goold, M./ Luchs, K. S. (1993): Why diversify? Four decades of management thinking, in: Academy of Management Executive, 7, 3, p. 7-25.

Gordon, J. R./ Gordon, S. R. (2000): Structuring the interaction between IT and business units, in: Information Systems Management, 17, 1, p. 7-16.

Götz, O./ Liehr-Gobbers, K. (2004): Analyse von Strukturgleichungsmodellen mit Hilfe der Partial-Least-Squares (PLS)-Methode, in: Die Betriebswirtschaft (DBW), 64, 6, p. 714-738.

Govindarajan, V. (1988): A contingency approach to strategy implementation at the business-unit level: Integrating administrative mechanisms with strategy, in: Academy of Management Journal, 31, 4, p. 828-853.

Grandon, E. E./ Pearson, J. M. (2003): Perceived strategic value and adoption of electronic commerce: An empirical study of small and medium sized businesses, in: Proceedings of the 36th Annual Hawaii International Conference on System Sciences (HICSS-36), Hawaii.

Grant, R. M. (1988): On 'dominant logic', relatedness and the link between diversity and performance, in: Strategic Management Journal, 9, 6, p. 639-642.

Grant, R. M. (1991): The resource-based theory of competitive advantage: Implications for strategy formulation, in: California Management Review, 33, 3, p. 114-135.

Gremillion, L. L. (1984): Organization size and information system use: An empirical study, in: Journal of Management Information Systems, 1, 2, p. 4-27.

Gresov, C. (1989): Exploring fit and misfit with multiple contingencies, in: Administrative Science Quarterly, 34, 3, p. 431-453.

Groenewegen, J./ Vromen, J. J. (1996): A case for theoretical pluralism, in: Groenewegen, J.: Transaction cost economics and beyond, Kluwer Academic Publishers, Boston et al., p. 365-380.

Gümbel, R. (1985): Handel, Markt und Ökonomik, Gabler Verlag, Wiesbaden.

Gupta, N. (1980): Some alternative definitions of size, in: Academy of Management Journal, 23, 4, p. 759-766.

Gurbaxani, V./ Whang, S. (1991): The impact of information systems on organizations and markets, in: Communications of ACM, 34, 1, p. 59-73.

Hage, J./ Aiken, M. (1967): Relationship of centralization to other structural properties, in: Administrative Science Quarterly, 12, 1, p. 93-117.

Hall, R. H. (1962): Intraorganizational structural variation: Application of the bureaucratic model, in: Administrative Science Quarterly, 7, 3, p. 295-308.

Hannan, M. T./ Freeman, J. (1989): Organizational ecology, Harvard University Press, Cambridge.

Harrison, J. S./ Hitt, M. A./ Hoskisson, R. E./ Ireland, R. D. (2001): Resource complementarity in business combinations: extending the logic to organizational alliances, in: *Journal of Management*, 27, 6, p. 679-690.

Heinrich, J. (2001): Medienökonomie. Band 1: Mediensystem, Zeitung, Zeitschrift, Anzeigenblatt, 2nd Edition, VS Verlag für Sozialwissenschaften, Wiesbaden.

Heinrich, L. J./ Roithmayr, F. (1985): Die Bestimmung des optimalen Distribuierungsgrades von Informationssystemen, in: *HMD*, 22, 121, p. 29-45.

Heinzl, A. (1993): Die Ausgliederung der betrieblichen Datenverarbeitung - eine empirische Untersuchung der Motive, Formen und Wirkungen, Schäffer-Poeschel, Stuttgart.

Henderson, B. D. (1960): The application and misapplication of the experience curve, in: *Journal of Business Strategy*, 4, 3, p. 3-9.

Henderson, B. D./ Venkatraman, N. (1993): Strategic alignment: Leveraging information technology for transforming organizations, in: *IBM Systems Journal*, 32, 1, p. 4-16.

Henderson, J. C./ Venkatraman, N. (1992): Strategic alignment: A model for organizational transformation through information technology, in: Kochan, T. A., Useem, M.: *Transforming Organizations*, Oxford, p. 97-117.

Henderson, R./ Cockburn, I. (1994): Measuring competence? Exploring firm effects in pharmaceutical research, in: *Strategic Management Journal*, 15, Winter Special Issue, p. 63-84.

Hennart, J.-F. (1994): The comparative institutional theory of the firm: some implications for corporate strategy, in: *Journal of Management Studies*, 31, 2, p. 193-207.

Henseler, J. (2005): Einführung in die PLS-Pfadmodellierung, in: *Wirtschaftswissenschaftliches Studium (Wist)*, 34, 2, p. 70-75.

Herrmann-Pillath, C. (2002): Grundriß der Evolutionsökonomik, Fink, München.

Hess, T. (2005a): Media companies between multiple utilisation and individualisation: an analysis for static contents, in: Zerdick, A., et al.: *E-merging media - Communication and the media economy of the future*, Springer, Berlin, Heidelberg, p. 57-74.

Hess, T. (2005b): Product platforms for the media industry, in: Picard, R. G.: *Media product portfolios: Issues in management of multiple products and services*, Lawrence Erlbaum Associates, Mahwah, NJ, p. 119-138.

Hess, T./ Ünlü, V. (2004): Systeme für das Management digitaler Rechte, in: *Wirtschaftsinformatik*, 46, 4, p. 273-280.

Hickson, D. J./ Hinings, B./ Lee, C. A./ Schneck, R. E./ Pennings, J. M. (1971): A strategic contingencies' theory of intraorganizational power, in: *Administrative Science Quarterly*, 1971, June, p. 216-229.

Hickson, D. J./ Pugh, D. S./ Pheysey, D. C. (1969): Operations technology and organizational structure: An empirical reappraisal, in: *Administrative Science Quarterly*, 14, 3, p. 378-397.

Hildebrandt, L./ Homburg, C. (1998): Editorial Preface, in: Hildebrandt, L., Homburg, C.: *Die Kausalanalyse*, Schäffer-Poeschel, Stuttgart, p. 5-6.

Hiltz, T./ Johnson, K. (1990): User satisfaction with computer-mediated communication systems, in: *Management Science*, 36, 6, p. 739-764.

Hinkin, T. R. (1995): A review of scale development practices in the study of organizations, in: *Journal of Management*, 21, 5, p. 967-988.

Hodgkinson, S. T. (1996): The role of the corporate IT function in the federal IT organization, in: Earl, M. J.: *Information management: The organizational dimension*, Oxford University Press, Oxford, p. 247-269.

Hohberger, S. (2001): Operationalisierung der Transaktionskostentheorie im Controlling, DUV, Wiesbaden.

Homburg, C./ Baumgartner, H. (1985): Beurteilug von Kausalmodellen: Bestandsaufnahme und Anwendungsfelder, in: *Marketing ZFP*, 17, 3, p. 162-176.

Homburg, C./ Dobratz, A. (1991): Iterative Modellselektion in der Kausalanalyse, in: *Zeitschrift für betriebswirtschaftliche Forschung*, 43, 3, p. 213-237.

Homburg, C./ Dobratz, A. (1992): Covariance structure analysis via specification searches, in: *Statistical Papers*, 32, 2, p. 119-142.

Homburg, C./ Giering, A. (1996): Konzeptualisierung und Operationalisierung komplexer Konstrukte - Ein Leitfaden für die Marketingforschung, in: *Marketing ZFP*, 18, 1, p. 5-24.

Hoopes, D. G./ Madsen, T. L./ Walker, G. (2003): Why is there a resource-based view? Toward a theory of competitive heterogeneity. Guest editors' introduction to the special issue, in: *Strategic Management Journal*, 24, 10, p. 889-902.

Hoskisson, R. E./ Hitt, M. A. (1990): Antecedents and performance outcomes of diversification: A review and critique of theoretical perspectives, in: *Journal of Management*, 16, 2, p. 461-509.

Hovorka, D. S. (2004): Explanation and understanding in information systems, in: *Proceedings of the 10th Americas Conference on Information Systems (AMCIS 2004)*, New York, NY, p. 4180-4188.

Huber, G. P. (1990): A theory of the effects of advanced information technologies on organizational design, intelligence, and decision making, in: *Academy of Management Review*, 15, 1, p. 47-71.

Huber, G. P./ Power, D. J. (1985): Retrospective reports of strategic-level managers: guidelines for increasing their accuracy, in: *Strategic Management Journal*, 6, 2, p. 171-180.

Hulland, J. (1999): Use of partial least squares (PLS) in strategic management research: a review of four recent studies, in: *Strategic Management Journal*, 20, 2, p. 195-204.

Ives, B./ Learmonth, G. (1984): The information system as a competitive weapon, in: *Communications of ACM*, 27, 12, p. 1193-1201.

Jaccard, J./ Wan, C. K. (1996): LISREL approaches to interaction effects in multiple regression, Sage, Thousands Oaks, CA.

Jain, H./ Ramamurthy, K./ Ryu, H.-S./ Yasai-Ardekani, M. (1998): Success of data resource management in distributed environments: an empirical investigation, in: *MIS Quarterly*, 22, 1, p. 1-29.

Jarvis, C. B./ Mackenzie, S. B./ Podsakoff, P. M./ Mick, D. G./ Bearden, W. O. (2003): A critical review of construct indicators and measurement model misspecification in marketing and consumer research, in: *Journal of Consumer Research*, 30, 2, p. 199-218.

Jasperson, J. S./ Carte, T. A./ Saunders, C. S./ Butler, B. S./ Croes, H. J. P./ Zheng, W. (2002): Review: Power and information technology research: A metatriangulation review, in: *MIS Quartely*, 26, 4, p. 397-459.

Jensen, M. C./ Meckling, W. H. (1976): Theory of the firm: Managerial behavior, agency costs and ownership structure, in: *Journal of Financial Economics*, 3, p. 305-360.

Jost, P.-J. (2001): Der Transaktionskostenansatz in der Betriebswirtschaftslehre, Schäffer-Poeschel, Stuttgart.

Kahai, P. S./ Carr, H. H./ Snyder, C. A. (2003): Technology and the decentralization of information systems, in: *Information Systems Management*, 20, 3, p. 51-60.

Kahai, P. S./ Snyder, C. A./ Carr, H. H. (2002): Decentralizing the IS function: Resources and locus of decisions, in: *Journal of Computer Information Systems*, Winter 2001-2002, p. 44-50.

Karahanna, E./ Straub, D. W. (1999): Information technology adoption across time: A cross-sectional comparison of pre-adoption and post-adoption beliefs, in: *MIS Quartely*, 23, 2, p. 183-213.

Keen, P. G. W. (1991): Shaping the future: Business design through information technology, Harvard Business Press, 1991, Cambridge, MA.

Kerlinger, F. N./ Lee, H. B. (2000): Foundations of behavioral research, 4th Edition, Wadsworth Publishing, Belmont, CA.

Kieser, A. (2001): Organisationstheorien, 4th Edition, W. Kohlhammer, Stuttgart, Berlin, Köln.

Kim, S./ Young-Soo, C. (2003): Critical success factors for IS outsourcing implementation from an interorganizational relationship perspective, in: *Journal of Computer Information Systems*, 43, 4, p. 81-90.

Kimberly, J. R. (1976): Organizational size and the structuralist perspective: A review, critique, and proposal, in: *Administrative Science Quarterly*, 21, 4, p. 571-597.

King, J. L. (1983): Centralized versus decentralized computing: Organizational considerations and management options, in: *Computing Surveys*, 15, 4, p. 319 - 349.

Klaas, P. (2004): Towards a concept of dynamic fit in contingency theory, University of Southern Denmark, Faculty of Social Sciences, Dept. of Organization and Management, Odense, Denmark.

Klatzky, S. R. (1970): Automation, size, and the locus of decision making: The cascade effect, in: *Journal of Business*, 43, 2, p. 141-151.

Klein, K. J./ Dansereau, F./ Hall, R. J. (1994): Levels issues in theory development, data collection, and analysis, in: *Academy of Management Review*, 19, 2, p. 195-229.

Knudsen, C. (1995): Theories of the firm, strategic management, and leadership, in: Montgomery, C. A.: *Resource-based and evolutionary theories of the firm: towards a synthesis*, Boston, Dordrecht, London, p. 179-217.

Kochhar, R. (1996): Explaining firm capital structure: The role of agency theory vs. transaction cost economics, in: *Strategic Management Journal*, 17, 9, p. 713-728.

Köhler, L. (2005): Produktinnovation in der Medienindustrie: Organisationskonzepte auf Basis von Produktplattformen, DUV, Wiesbaden.

Köhler, L./ Anding, M./ Hess, T. (2003): Exploiting the power of product platforms for the media industry – a conceptual framework for digital goods and its customization for content syndicators, in: *Proceedings of the third IFIP Conference on e-commerce, e-business and e-government*, Sao Paulo, p. 303-313.

Koopmans, T. C. (1957): The construction of economic knowledge, in: Koopmans, T. C.: *Three essays on the state of economic science*, New York, p. 127-166.

Kosiol, E. (1962): Organisation der Unternehmung, Gabler, Wiesbaden.

Krcmar, H. (1990): Bedeutung und Ziele von Informationssystem-Architekturen, in: *Wirtschaftsinformatik*, 32, 5, p. 395-402.

Krcmar, H. (2003): Informationsmanagement, 3rd Edition, Springer Verlag, Berlin et al.

Langolis, R./ Savage, D. (2001): Standards, modularity, and innovation: The case of medical practice, in: Garud, R., Karnoe, P.: *Path dependence and creation*, Lawrence Erlbaum Associates, London.

Larsen, K. R. T. (2003): A taxonomy of antecedents of information systems success: Variable analysis studies, in: *Journal of Management Information Systems*, 20, 2, p. 169-246.

Laskey, R. (1982): Centralization and decentralization: Key issues revisited, in: *Strategic Planning for Information Management Proceedings of the 14th Annual Conference of SIM*, Chicago, IL, p. 103-113.

Laux, H./ Liermann, F. (2005): Grundlagen der Organisation. Die Steuerung von Entscheidungen als Grundproblem der Betriebswirtschaftslehre, 6th Edition, Springer, Berlin et al.

Lawrence, P. R. (1993): The contingency approach to organization design, in: Golembiewski, T.: *Handbook of organizational behaviour*, Marcel Dekker, New York, p. 9-18.

Lawrence, P. R./ Lorsch, J. W. (1967): Organization and environment: Managing differentiation and integration, Boston.

Leavitt, H. J. (1965): Applied organizational change in industry: structural, technological and humanistic approaches, in: March, J. G.: Handbook of organizations, Rand McNally, Chicago, p. 1144-1170.

Leblebici, H. (1985): Transactions and organizational forms: A re-analysis, in: Organization Studies, 6, 2, p. 97-115.

Lee, A. S. (1999): Rigor and relevance in MIS research: Beyond the approach of positivism alone, in: MIS Quarterly, 23, 1, p. 29-33.

Lee, A. S./ Baskerville, R. L. (2003): Generalizing generalizability in information systems research, in: Information Systems Research, 14, 3, p. 221-243.

Lee, B./ Barua, A./ Whinston, A. B. (1997): Discovery and representation of casual relationships in MIS research: A methodological framework, in: MIS Quarterly, 21, 1, p. 109-136.

Lee, S./ Leifer, R. (1992): A framework for linking the structure of information systems with organizational requirements for information sharing, in: Journal of Management Information Systems, 8, 4, p. 27-44.

Lehman, J. A. (1986): Organizational size and information system sophistication, in: Journal of Management Information Systems, 2, 3, p. 78-86.

Leiblein, M. J./ Miller, D. J. (2003): An empirical examination of transaction- and firm-level influences on the vertical boundaries of the firm, in: Strategic Management Journal, 24, 9, p. 839-859.

Leifer, R. (1988): Matching computer-based information systems with organizational structures, in: MIS Quarterly, 12, 1, p. 63-73.

Lewis, B. R./ Snyder, C. A./ Rainer, R. K. (1995): An empirical assessment of the information resource management construct, in: Journal of Management Information Systems, 12, 1, p. 199-223.

Loch, K. D./ Carr, H. H./ Warkentin, M. E. (1992): Threats to information systems: Today's reality, yesterday's understanding, in: MIS Quartely, 16, 2, p. 173-186.

Lohmöller, J.-B. (1989a): Basic principles of model building: Specification, estimation, evaluation, in: Wold, H.: Theoretical empiricism: A general rationale for scientific model-building, Paragon House, New York.

Lohmöller, J.-B. (1989b): Latent variable path modeling with partial least squares, Physica-Verlag, Heidelberg.

Lucas, H. C./ Baroudi, J. (1994): The role of information technology in organization design, in: Journal of Management Information Systems, 10, 4, p. 9-23.

Madhok, A. (1996): The organization of economic activity: Transaction costs, firm capabilities, and the nature of governance, in: Organization Science, 7, 5, p. 577-590.

Mahoney, J. T./ Pandian, J. R. (1992): The resource-based view within the conversation of strategic management, in: *Strategic Management Journal*, 13, 2, p. 363-380.

Mann, H./ Whitney, D. (1947): On a test of whether one of two variables is stochastically larger than the other, in: *Annals of mathematical statistics*, 18, p. 50-60.

Markides, C./ Williamson, P. (1994): Related diversification, core competences and corporate performance, in: *Strategic Management Journal*, 15, Special Issue, p. 149-165.

Markides, C./ Williamson, P. (1996): Corporate diversification and organizational structure: A resource-based view, in: *Academy of Management Journal*, 39, 2, p. 340-367.

Markus, M. L./ Pfeffer, J. (1983): Power and the design and implementation of accounting and control systems, in: *Accounting, Organizations and Society*, 8, 2/3, p. 205-218.

Markus, M. L./ Robey, D. (1988): Information technology and organizational change: Causal structure in theory and research, in: *Management Science*, 34, 5, p. 583-598.

Marshall, A. (1890): Principles of economics, Macmillan, London.

Masten, S. E./ Meehan, J. W./ Snyder, E. A. (1991): The costs of organization, in: *Journal of Law, Economics and Organization*, 7, 1, p. 1-27.

Mata, F. J./ Fuerst, W. L./ Barney, J. B. (1995): Information technology and sustained competitive advantage: A resource-based analysis, in: *MIS Quarterly*, 19, 4, p. 487-505.

Mathieson, K. (1991): Predicting user intentions: Comparing the technology acceptance model with the theory of planned behavior, in: *Information Systems Research*, 2, 3, p. 173-191.

Mathieson, K./ Peacock, E./ Chin, W. W. (2001): Extending the technology acceptance model: the influence of perceived user resources, in: *The DATA BASE for Advances in Information Systems*, 32, 3, p. 86-112.

McFarlan, F. W. (1984): Information technology changes the way you compete, in: *Harvard Business Review*, 62, 3, p. 98-103.

McFarlan, F. W./ McKenney, J. L. (1983): Corporate information systems management, Richard D. Irwin, Homewood, IL.

McKelvey, B./ Aldrich, H. E. (1983): Populations, natural selection, and applied organizational science, in: *Administrative Science Quarterly*, 28, p. 101-128.

McKenney, J. L./ McFarlan, F. W. (1982): The information archipelago-maps and bridges, in: *Harvard Business Review*, 60, 5, p. 109-119.

Melville, N./ Kraemer, K./ Gurbaxani, V. (2004): Information technology and organizational performance: An integrative model of IT business value, in: *MIS Quarterly*, 28, 2, p. 283-322.

Ménard, C. (1996): Inside the black box: The variety of hierarchical forms, in: Groenewegen, J.: *Transaction cost economics and beyond*, Kluwer Academic Press, Amsterdam, p. 149-170.

Ménard, C. (1997): Internal characteristics of formal organizations, in: Ménard, C.: Transaction cost economics: Recent developments, Edward Elgar, Aldershot, p. 30-58.

Mertens, P. (1985): Aufbauorganisation der Datenverarbeitung. Zentralisierung - Dezentralisierung - Informationszentrum, Gabler, Wiesbaden.

Mertens, P./ Bodendorf, F./ König, W./ Picot, A./ Schumann, M./ Hess, T. (2005): Grundzüge der Wirtschaftsinformatik, 9th Edition, Berlin et al.

Mertens, P./ Knolmayer, G. (1998): Organisation der Informationsverarbeitung: Grundlagen - Aufbau - Arbeitsteilung, 3rd Edition, Gabler, Wiesbaden.

Meyer, M./ Lehnerd, A. P. (1997): The power of product platforms: Building value and cost leadership, Free Press, New York.

Michaelis, E. (1985): Organisation unternehmerischer Aufgaben - Transaktionskosten als Beurteilungskriterium, Peter Lang, Frankfurt am Main, Bern, New York.

Michalk, S. (2004): Pressemitteilung zur VDZ Jahrespressekonferenz 2004: "Verlegerverband feiert 75-jähriges Bestehen - Gesetze und Verordnungen gefährden Pressefreiheit und Pressevielfalt", Verband Deutscher Zeitschriftenverleger (VDZ), Berlin.

Miles, R. E./ Snow, C. C. (1978): Organizational strategy, structure and process, McGraw-Hill Book Company, New York, NY.

Milgrom, P./ Roberts, J. (1992): Economics, organization & management, Prentice Hall,

Milgrom, P./ Roberts, J. (1995): Complementarities and fit: Strategy, structure, and organizational change in manufacturing, in: Journal of Accounting & Economics, 19, 2/3, p. 179-208.

Miller, D. (1981): Toward a new contingency approach: The search for organizational gestalts, in: Journal of Management Studies, 18, 1, p. 1-26.

Miller, D. (1988): Relating Porter's business strategies to environment and structure: Analysis and performance implications, in: Academy of Management Journal, 31, 2, p. 280-308.

Mintzberg, H. (1979): The structuring of organizations, Prentice-Hall, Englewood Cliffs.

Mirer, T. W. (1995): Economic statistics and econometrics, Prentice Hall, Upper Saddle River, NJ.

Montgomery, C. A./ Wernerfelt, B. (1988): Diversification, Richardian rents, and Tobin's q, in: RAND Journal of Economics, 19, 4, p. 623-632.

Moore, G. C./ Benbasat, I. (1991): Development of an instrument to measure the perceptions of adopting an information technology innovation, in: Information Systems Research, 2, 3, p. 192-222.

Morgan, G. (1980): Paradigms, metaphors, and puzzle solving in organization theory, in: Administrative Science Quarterly, 25, 4, p. 605-622.

Morgan, G. (1986): Images of organization, Sage Publications, Thousand Oaks, London, New Delhi.

Nault, B. R. (1998): Information technology and organization design: Locating decisions and information, in: *Management Science*, 44, 10, p. 1321-1335.

Nayyar, P. R. (1992): On the measurement of corporate diversification strategy: evidence from large U.S. service firms, in: *Strategic Management Journal*, 13, 3, p. 219-235.

Nayyar, P. R./ Kazanjian, R. K. (1993): Organizing to attain potential benefits from information asymmetries and economies of scope in related diversified firms, in: *Academy of Management Review*, 18, 4, p. 735-759.

Nelson, R. R./ Winter, S. G. (1982): An evolutionary theory of economic change, Belknap Press of Harvard University Press, Cambridge, MA.

Netemeyer, R. G./ Bearden, W. O./ Sharma, S. (2003): Scaling procedures: Issues and applications, Sage Publications, Thousand Oaks et al.

Nevitt, J./ Hancock, G. R. (2001): Performance of bootstrapping approaches to model test statistics and parameter standard error estimation in structural equation modeling, in: *Structured Equation Modeling*, 8, 3, p. 353–377.

Newkirk, H. E./ Lederer, A. L. (2004): The impact of incremental strategic information systems planning in an uncertain environment, in: *Proceedings of the Tenth Americas Conference on Information Systems*, New York, p. 3668-3678.

Nicolai, A. T. v. (2004): Der "trade-off" zwischen "rigour" und "relevance" und seine Konsequenzen für die Managementwissenschaften, in: *Zeitschrift für Betriebswirtschaft*, 74, 2, p. 99-118.

Olson, M. H./ Chervany, N. L. (1980): The relationship between organizational characteristics and the structure of the information services function, in: *MIS Quarterly*, 4, 2, p. 57-68.

Osgood, C. E./ Suci, G. J. T./ Tannenmann, P. H. (1957): The measurement of meaning, University of Ilinois Press, Urbana, IL.

Österle, H./ Brenner, W./ Hilbers, K. (1992): Unternehmensführung und Informationssystem - Der Ansatz des St. Galler Informationssystem-Managements, 2nd Edition, Teubner, Stuttgart.

Österle, H./ Riehm, R./ Vogler, P. (1996): Middleware. Grundlagen, Produkte und Anwendungsbeispiele für die Integration heterogener Welten, Vieweg, Wiesbaden.

Ouchi, W. G. (1980): Markets, bureaucracies, and clans, in: *Administrative Science Quarterly*, 25, 1, p. 129-141.

Peak, D. A./ Azadmanesh, M. H. (1997): Centralization/decentralization cycles in computing: Market evidence, in: *Information & Management*, 31, 6, p. 303-317.

Penrose, E. T. (1959): The theory of the growth of the firm, Blackwell, New York.

Perrow, C. (1967): A framework for comparative organizational analysis, in: *American Sociological Review*, 32, 2, p. 194-208.

Perrow, C. (1970): Organizational analysis: A sociological review, Brooks/Cole, Belmont, CA.

Peter, J./ Churchill, G. (1986): Relationships among research design choices and psychometric properties of rating scales: A meta-analysis, in: *Journal of Marketing Research*, 23, 2, p. 1-10.

Peteraf, M. (1993): The cornerstones of competitive advantage: a resource-based view, in: *Strategic Management Journal*, 14, 3, p. 179-191.

Peterson, R. R./ O'Callaghan, R./ Ribbers, P. M. A. (2000): Information technology governance by design: investigating hybrid configurations and integration mechanisms, in: *Proceedings of the twenty first International Conference on Information Systems*, Brisbane, Queensland, Australia, p. 435-452.

Pettigrew, A. M. (1973): The politics of organizational decision-making, Tavistock Publications, London.

Pfeffer, J. (1981): Power in organizations, Pitman Publ. Co., Marshfield, MA.

Philips, A. (1976): A critique of empirical studies of relations between market structure and profitability, in: *Journal of Industrial Economics*, 24, 4, p. 241-249.

Picot, A. (1991): Ein neuer Ansatz zur Gestaltung der Leistungstiefe, in: *Zeitschrift für Betriebswirtschaft*, 43, 4, p. 336-357.

Picot, A. (1992): Transaktionskostenansatz in der Organisationstheorie: Stand der Diskussion und Aussagewert, in: *Die Betriebswirtschaft (DBW)*, 42, p. 267-284.

Picot, A./ Dietl, H./ Franck, E. (2002): Organisation. Eine ökonomische Perspektive, 4th Edition, Schäffer-Poeschel, Stuttgart.

Picot, A./ Reichwald, R./ Wigand, R. (2003): Die grenzenlose Unternehmung. Information, Organisation und Management, 5th Edition, Gabler Verlag, Wiesbaden.

Picot, A./ Wenger, E. (1988): The employment relation from the transaction cost perspective, in: Dlugos, G., et al.: *Management under different labour market and employment systems*, Berlin, p. 29-43.

Popper, K. (1994): Die Logik der Forschung, 10th Edition, J.V.B. Mohr, Tübingen.

Poppo, L./ Zenger, T. R. (1998): Testing alternative theories of the firm: transaction cost, knowledge-based, and measurement explanations for make-or-buy decisions in information services, in: *Strategic Management Journal*, 19, 9, p. 853-877.

Porter, M. E. (1979): How competitive forces shape strategy, in: *Harvard Business Review*, 57, 2, p. 137-145.

Porter, M. E. (1980): Competitive strategy: Techniques for analyzing industries and competitors, Free Press, New York.

Porter, M. E. (1981): The contributions of industrial organization to strategic management, in: *Academy of Management Review*, 6, 4, p. 609-620.

Porter, M. E. (1985): Competitive advantage: Creating and sustaining superior performance, Free Press, New York, London.

Porter, M. E. (1996): What is strategy?, in: *Harvard Business Review*, 74, 6, p. 61-78.

Porter, M. E./ Millar, V. E. (1985): How information gives you competitive advantage, in: *Harvard Business Review*, 63, 4, p. 149-160.

Powell, T. C. (1992): Organizational alignment as competitive advantage, in: *Strategic Management Journal*, 13, 2, p. 119-134.

Powell, T. C./ Dent-Micallef, A. (1997): Information technology as competitive advantage: the role of human, business, and technology resources, in: *Strategic Management Journal*, 18, 5, p. 375-405.

Prahalad, C. K./ Bettis, R. A. (1986): The dominant logic: a new linkage between diversity and performance, in: *Strategic Management Journal*, 7, 6, p. 485-501.

Premkumar, G./ Ramamurthy, K. (1994): Implementation of electronic data interchange: An innovation diffusion perspective, in: *Journal of Management Information Systems*, 11, 2, p. 157-186.

Pugh, D. S./ Hickson, D. J. (1969): The context of organization structure, in: *Administrative Science Quarterly*, 14, 1, p. 91-114.

Pugh, D. S./ Hickson, D. J./ Hinings, C. R. (1969): An empirical taxonomy of structures of work organizations, in: *Administrative Science Quarterly*, 14, 1, p. 115-126.

Pugh, D. S./ Hickson, D. J./ Hinings, C. R./ Turner, C. (1968): Dimensions of Organizational Structure, in: *Administrative Science Quarterly*, 13, 1, p. 65-105.

Ragu-Nathan, B. S./ Apigian, C. H./ Ragu-Nathan, T. S./ Tu, Q. (2004): A path analytic study of the effect of top management support for information systems performance, in: *OMEGA: International Journal of Management Science*, 32, 6, p. 459-471.

Ragu-Nathan, B. S./ Ragu-Nathan, T. S./ Tu, Q. (1999): Dimensionality of the strategic grid framework: The construct and its measurement, in: *Information Systems Research*, 10, 4, p. 343-355.

Ramanujam, V./ Varadarajan, P. (1989): Research on corporate diversification: a synthesis, in: *Strategic Management Journal*, 10, 6, p. 523-552.

Ravichandran, T./ Lertwongsatien, C. (2005): Effect of information systems resources and capabilities on firm performance: A resource-based perspective, in: *Journal of Management Information Systems*, 21, 4, p. 237-276.

Ravichandran, T./ Rai, A. (2000): Quality management in systems development: an organizational system perspective, in: *MIS Quartely*, 24, 3, p. 381-415.

Rawolle, J. (2002): Content Management integrierter Medienprodukte. Ein XML-basierter Ansatz, Deutscher Universitätsverlag, Wiesbaden.

Rawolle, J./ Hess, T. (2001): XML in der Medienindustrie - Ökonomische Aspekte, in: Turowski, K., Fellner, J.: *XML in der betrieblichen Praxis - Standards, Möglichkeiten, Praxisbeispiele*, Dpunkt Verlag, Heidelberg, p. 229-244.

Raymond, L. (1985): Organizational characteristics and MIS success in the context of small business, in: *MIS Quartely*, 9, 1, p. 37-52.

Raymond, L. (1990): Organizational context and information systems success: A contingency approach, in: *Journal of Management Information Systems*, 6, 4, p. 5-20.

Reed, R. (1990): Causal ambiguity, barriers to imitation, and sustainable competitive advantage, in: *Academy of Management Review*, 15, 1, p. 88-102.

Reitze, H. (2004): Media Perspektiven. Basisdaten - Daten zur Mediensituation in Deutschland 2004, Arbeitsgemeinschaft der ARD-Werbegesellschaften, Frankfurt am Main.

Richter, R./ Furubotn, E. G. (2003): Neue Institutionenökonomik: Eine Einführung und kritische Würdigung, 3rd Edition, Mohr Siebeck, Tübingen.

Rindfleisch, A./ Heide, J. B. (1997): Transaction cost analysis: Past, present, and future applications, in: *Journal of Marketing*, 61, 4, p. 30-54.

Ringle, C. M. (2004): Gütemaße für den Partial Least Squares-Ansatz zur Bestimmung von Kausalmodellen, Institut für Industriebetriebslehre und Organisation, Universität Hamburg Nr. 16/2004.

Ringle, C. M./ Wende, S./ Will, A. (2005): SmartPLS, University of Hamburg, Hamburg, http://www.smartpls.de (Last Access: 01.11.05).

Robertson, D./ Ulrich, K. T. (1998): Planning for product platforms, in: *Sloan Management Review*, 39, 4, p. 19-31.

Robins, J./ Wiersema, M. F. (1995): A resource-based approach to the multibusiness firm: Empirical analysis of portfolio interrelationships and corporate financial performance, in: *Strategic Management Journal*, 16, 4, p. 277-299.

Rockart, J. F./ Bullen, C. V./ Leventer, J. S. (1977): Centralization vs. decentralization of information systems, Center for Information Systems Research, MIT Sloan School (Unpublished Manuscript), Cambridge, MA.

Rodgers, W./ Pavlou, P. (2003): Developing a predictive model: A comparative study of the partial least squares vs. maximum likelihood techniques, Working Paper at the Graduate School of Management, University of California, Riverside.

Rofrano, J. J. (1992): Design considerations for distributed applications, in: *IBM Systems Journal*, 31, 3, p. 564-589.

Rogers, E. M. (1983): Diffusion of innovations, 3rd Edition, The Free Press, New York.

Ross, J. W. (2003): Creating a strategic IT architecture competency: Learning in stages, in: *MIS Quarterly Executive*, 2, 1, p. 31-43.

Rumelt, R. P. (1974): Strategy, structure, and economic performance, Harvard University Press, Cambridge, MA.

Sambamurthy, V./ Bharadwaj, A. S./ Grover, V. (2003): Shaping agility through digital options: Reconceptualizing the role of information technology in contemporary firms, in: *MIS Quarterly*, 27, 2, p. 237-263.

Sambamurthy, V./ Chin, W. W. (1994): The effects of group attitudes towards alternative GDSS designs on the decision-making performance of computer-supported groups, in: *Decision Sciences*, 25, 2, p. 215-242.

Sambamurthy, V./ Zmud, R. W. (1999): Arrangements for IT governance: a theory of multiple contingencies, in: *MIS Quarterly*, 23, 2, p. 261-290.

Santhanam, R./ Hartono, E. (2003): Issues in linking information technology capability to firm performance, in: *MIS Quarterly*, 27, 1, p. 125-153.

Schek, M. (2005): Automatische Klassifizierung und Visualisierung im Archiv der Süddeutschen Zeitung, in: *Medienwirtschaft*, 2, 1, p. 20-24.

Schilling, M. A. (2000): Toward a general modular systems theory and its application to interfirm product modularity, in: *Academy of Management Review*, 25, 2, p. 312-334.

Schnell, R./ Hill, P. B./ Esser, E. (2005): Methoden der empirischen Sozialforschung, 7th Edition, Oldenbourg, München, Berlin.

Schoonhoven, C. B. (1981): Problems with contingency theory: Testing assumptions hidden within the language of contingency theory, in: *Administrative Science Quarterly*, 26, 3, p. 349-377.

Schriesheim, C. A./ Powers, K. J./ Scandura, T. A./ Gardiner, C. C./ Lankau, M. J. (1993): Improving construct measurement in management research: Comments and a quantitative approach for assessing the theoretical content adequacy of paper-and-pencil survey-type instruments, in: *Journal of Management*, 19, 2, p. 385-417.

Schulze, B. (2005): Mehrfachnutzung von Medieninhalten: Entwicklung, Anwendung und Bewertung eines Managementkonzepts für die Medienindustrie, Josef Eul Verlag, Lohmar.

Schulze, B./ Hess, T./ Eggers, B. (2004): The Internet's impact on content utilization chains: An exploratory case study on leading publishers in Germany, in: *The International Journal on Media Management*, 6, 3, p. 12-22.

Schumann, M./ Hess, T. (2005): Grundfragen der Medienwirtschaft, 3rd Edition, Springer-Verlag, Berlin, Heidelberg, New York.

Schütz, W. J. (2001): Redaktionelle und verlegerische Struktur der deutschen Tagespresse, in: *Media Perspektiven*, 12, p. 633-642.

Schütz, W. J. (2005): Redaktionelle und verlegerische Struktur der deutschen Tagespresse, in: *Media Perspektiven*, 5, p. 233-242.

Scott, W. (2003): Organizations: Rational, natural and open systems, 5th (International) Edition, Prentice Hall, Englewood Cliffs, NJ.

Seidler, J. (1974): On using informants: A technique for collecting quantitative data and controlling for measurement error in organizational analysis, in: *American Sociological Review*, 39, 6, p. 816-831.

Seth, A./ Thomas, H. (1994): Theories of the firm: Implications for strategy research, in: *Journal of Management*, 31, 2, p. 165-190.

Shapiro, C./ Varian, H. R. (1998): Information rules – a strategic guide to the network economy, Harvard Business Press, Boston, MA.

Silverman, B. S. (1999): Technological resources and the direction of corporate diversification: Toward an integration of the resource-based view and transaction cost economics, in: *Management Science*, 45, 8, p. 1109-1124.

Simon, H. A. (1957): Models of man - Social and rational, John Wiley & Sons, New York.

Simon, H. A. (1959): Theories of decision-making in economics and behavioral science, in: *American Economic Review*, 49, p. 253-283.

Simon, H. A. (1965): Administrative behavior, 2nd Edition, Free Press, New York.

Simon, H. A. (1969): The sciences of the artificial, MIT Press, Cambridge, MA.

Simon, J. (1978): Basic research methods in social sciences: Art of empirical investigation, 2nd Edition, Random House, New York.

Skinner, B. F. (1938): The behavior of organisms, New York.

Smith, J. B./ Barclay, D. W. (1997): The effects of organizational differences and trust on the affectiveness of selling partner relationships, in: *Journal of Marketing*, 61, 1, p. 3-21.

Snell, S. A./ Dean Jr., J. W. (1992): Integrated manufacturing and human resource management: A human capital perspective, in: *Academy of Management Journal*, 35, 3, p. 467-504.

Spinner, H. F. (1974): Pluralismus als Erkenntnismodell, Suhrkamp Verlag, Frankfurt.

Stamer, S. (2002): Technologie als Enabler für effizientes Cross-Media Publishing, in: Müller-Kalthoff, B.: *Cross-Media Management. Content-Strategien erfolgreich umsetzen*, Springer-Verlag, p. 89-124.

Staples, D. S./ Seddon, P. (2004): Testing the technology-to-performance chain model, in: *Journal of Organizational and End User Computing*, 16, 4, p. 17-36.

Straub, D. (1989): Validating instruments in MIS research, in: *MIS Quartely*, 13, 2, p. 147-169.

Straub, D./ Boudreau, M.-C./ Gefen, D. (2004): Validation guidelines for IS positivist research, in: *Communications of AIS*, 13, 24, p. 380-427.

Straub, D. W. (1998): Coping with systems risk: Security planning models for management decision making, in: *MIS Quartely*, 22, 4, p. 441-469.

Subramanian, G. H./ Nosek, J. T. (2001): An empirical study of the measurement and instrument validation of perceived strategy value of information systems, in: *Journal of Computer Information Systems*, 41, 3, p. 64-69.

Sudman, S./ Bradburn, N. M. (1982): Asking questions: A practical guide to questionnaire design, Jossey-Bass Publishers, San Francisco.

Sutton, R. I./ Staw, B. M. (1995): What theory is not, in: *Administrative Science Quarterly*, 40, 3, p. 371-384.

Szilagyi, A. D./ Wallace, M. W. (1980): Organizational behavior and performance, 2nd Edition, Goodyear, Santa Monica, CA.

Tanenbaum, A. S./ van Steen, M. (2002): Distributed systems - principles and paradigms, Prentice Hall, Upper Saddle River.

Tanriverdi, H. (2005): Information technology relatedness, knowledge management capability, and performance of multibusiness firms, in: *MIS Quartely*, 29, 2, p. 311-334.

Tanriverdi, H./ Venkatraman, N. (2005): Knowledge relatedness and the performance of multibusiness firms, in: *Strategic Management Journal*, 26, 2, p. 97-119.

Tavakolian, H. (1989): Linking the information technology structure with organizational competitive strategy: A survey, in: *MIS Quarterly*, 13, 3, p. 308-317.

Taylor, J. R./ Tucker, C. C. (1989): Reducing data processing costs through centralized procurement, in: *MIS Quarterly*, 1989, December, p. 486-499.

Taylor, W. A. (2004): Computer-mediated knowledge sharing and individual user differences: an exploratory study, in: *European Journal of Information Systems*, 13, 1, p. 52-64.

Teece, D. J. (1980): Economies of scope and the scope of the enterprise, in: *Journal of Economic Behavior & Organization*, 1, 3, p. 223-247.

Tenenhaus, M./ Vinzi, V. E./ Chatelin, Y.-M./ Lauro, C. (2005): PLS path modeling, in: *Computational Statistics & Data Analysis*, 48, 1, p. 159-205.

Thompson, J. D. (1967): Organizations in action. Social science bases of administrative theory, McGraw-Hill, New York.

Tosi Jr., H. L. (1984): Contingency theory: Some suggested directions, in: *Journal of Management*, 10, 1, p. 9-26.

Tractinsky, N./ Jarvenpaa, S. L. (1995): Information systems design decisions in a global versus domestic context, in: *MIS Quartely*, 19, 4, p. 507-534.

Tsai, W. (2004): Social capital, strategic relatedness and the formation of intraorganizational linkages, in: *Strategic Management Journal*, 21, 9, p. 925-939.

Tushman, M. L. (1977): A political approach to organizations: A review and rationale, in: *Academy of Management Review*, 2, 2, p. 206-216.

Van de Ven, A. H./ Ferry, D. L. (1980): Measuring and assessing organizations, Wiley, New York.

van Eimeren, B./ Ridder, C.-M. (2002): Mediennutzung im neuen Jahrtausend - Langzeittrends und Entwicklung in Deutschland, in: Müller-Kalthoff, B.: *Cross-Media Management. Content-Strategien erfolgreich umsetzen*, Springer Verlag, Berlin et. al., p. 61-88.

van Kranenburg, H. L. (2005): Product portfolios, diversification, and sustainability of media firms, in: Picard, R. G.: *Media product portfolios. Issues in management of multiple products and services*, Lawrence Erlbaum Assiciates, Mahwah, NJ, p. 23-40.

Varian, H. R. (2002): Intermediate microeconomics: A modern approach, 6th Edition, W. W. Norton & Company, Berkeley, CA.

Vázquez, X. H. (2004): Allocating decision rights on the shop floor: A perspective from transaction cost economics and organization theory, in: *Organization Science*, 15, 4, p. 463-480.

Venaik, S./ Midgley, D. F./ Devinney, T. M. (2001): Autonomy, networking and interunit learning in a model of mnc subsidiary innovation and performance, Working Paper of the Australian Graduate School of Management, Sydney.

Venkatraman, N. (1989): The concept of fit in strategy research: toward verbal and statistical correspondence, in: *Academy of Management Review*, 4, 3, p. 423-444.

Vitale, M./ Ives, B./ Beath, C. M. (1986): Linking information technology and corporate strategy: An organizational view, in: *Proceedings of the Seventh International Conference on Information Systems (ICIS 1986)*, San Diego, CA, p. 265-276.

Vizjak, A./ Ringlstetter, M. (2001): Medienmanagement: Content gewinnbringend nutzen. Trends, Business-Modelle, Erfolgsfaktoren, Gabler Verlag, Wiesbaden.

Völker, R./ Voit, E. (2000): Planung und Bewertung von Produktplattformen, in: *Kostenrechnungspraxis*, 44, 3, p. 137-143.

von der Lippe, P./ Kladropa, A. (2002): Repräsentativität von Stichproben, in: *Marketing ZFP*, 24, 2, p. 139-145.

von Simson, E. M. (1990): The 'centrally decentralized' IS organization, in: *Harvard Business Review*, 68, 4, p. 158-162.

von Walter, B./ Hess, T. (2004): A property rights view on the impact of file sharing on music business models – why iTunes is a remedy and MusicNet is not, in: *Proceedings of the 10th Americas Conference on Information Systems (AMCIS 2004)*, New York, NY, p. 2496-2506.

Wade, M./ Hulland, J. (2004): Review: The resource-based view and information systems research: review, extension, and suggestions for future research, in: *MIS Quarterly*, 28, 1, p. 107-142.

Wang, N. (2003): Measuring transaction costs: An incomplete survey, Ronald Coase Institute Working Papers, St. Louis, MI, Number 2.

Watson, J. B. (1913): Psychology as the behaviorist views it, in: *Psychological Review*, 20, p. 158-177.

Weber, M. (1998): Verteilte Systeme, Spektrum Akademischer Verlag, Heidelberg, Berlin.

Weill, P./ Olson, M. H. (1989): An assessment of the contingency theory of management information systems, in: *Journal of Management Information Systems*, 6, 1, p. 59-85.

Weill, P./ Ross, J. W. (2004): IT governance. How top performers manage IT decision rights for superior results, Harvard Business School Press, Boston, MA.

Weill, P./ Woodham, R. (2002): Don't just lead, govern: Implementing effective IT governance, MIT Center for Information Systems Research, Cambridge, MA, CISR Working Paper: 326.

Wernerfelt, B. (1984): A resource-based view of the firm, in: *Strategic Management Journal*, 5, p. 171-180.

Whetten, D. A. (1989): What constitutes a theoretical contribution?, in: *Academy of Management Review*, 14, 4, p. 490-495.

Willcocks, L. P./ Lester, S. (2000): Information technology and organizational performance: Beyond the IT productivity paradox, in: Galliers, R. D., et al.: *Strategic information systems: Challenges and strategies in managing information systems*, Butterworth-Heinemann, Oxford et al., p. 551-572.

Williamson, O. E. (1973): Markets and hierarchies: Some elementary considerations, in: *American Economic Review*, 63, 2, p. 316-325.

Williamson, O. E. (1975): Market and hierarchies: Analysis and antitrust implications, The Free Press, New York.

Williamson, O. E. (1981): The economics of organization: The transaction cost approach, in: *American Journal of Sociology*, 87, 3, p. 548-577.

Williamson, O. E. (1984): The economics of governance: Framework and implications, in: *Journal of Institutional and Theoretical Economics (JITE)*, 140, p. 195-223.

Williamson, O. E. (1985): The economic institutions of capitalism: firms, markets, relational contracting, The Free Press, New York.

Williamson, O. E. (1989): Transaction cost economics, in: Schmalensee, R., Willig, R. D.: *Handbook of Industrial Organization*, Elsevier, Amsterdam, p. 135-182.

Williamson, O. E. (1990a): Die ökonomischen Institutionen des Kapitalismus: Unternehmen, Märkte, Kooperationen, Mohr, Tübingen.

Williamson, O. E. (1990b): Transaction cost economics, in: Schmalensee, R., Willig, R. D.: *Handbook of Industrial Organization*, Amsterdam et al., p. 135-182.

Williamson, O. E. (1993): Calculativeness, trust, and economic organization, in: *Journal of Law and Economics*, 36, 1, p. 453-486.

Williamson, O. E. (1996): Transaction-cost economics: The governance of contractual relations, in: Buckley, P. J., Michie, J.: *Firms, organizations and contracts*, Oxford University Press, New York et al., p. 168-198.

Windsperger, J. (2001): Strategie und Organisationsstruktur, in: Jost, P.-J.: *Der Transaktionskostenansatz in der Betriebswirtschaftlehre*, Schäffer-Poeschel, Stuttgart, p. 155-181.

Wirtz, B. W. (2005): Medien- und Internetmanagement, 4th Edition, Gabler Verlag, Wiesbaden.

Wold, H. (1989a): Introduction to the second generation of multivariate analysis, in: Wold, H.: *Theoretical empiricism: A general rationale for scientific model-building*, Paragon House, New York, p. vii-xl.

Wold, H. (1989b): Theoretical empiricism: A general rationale for scientific model-building, Paragon House, New York.

Woodruff, R. B. (1997): Customer value: the next source for competitive advantage, in: *Journal of the Academy of Marketing Science*, 25, 2, p. 139-153.

Woodward, J. (1965): Industrial organization: Theory and practice, Oxford University Press, London.

Yasai-Ardekani, M. (1989): Effects of environmental scarcity and munificence on the relationship of context to organizational structure, in: *Academy of Management Journal*, 32, 1, p. 131-156.

Zachman, J. A. (1997): A framework for information systems architecture, in: *IBM Systems Journal*, 26, 3, p. 454-470.

Zerdick, A./ Picot, A./ Schrape, K./ Artope, A./ Goldhammer, K./ Heger, D. K./ Lange, U. T./ Vierkant, E./ Lopez-Escobar, E./ Silverstone, R. (2001): Die Internet-Ökonomie. Strategien für die digitale Wirtschaft (European Communication Council Report), Springer Verlag, Berlin, Heidelberg, New York.

Zhu, K./ Kraemer, K. L./ Gurbaxani, V./ Xu, S. (2005): Migration to open-standard interorganizational systems: Network effects, switching costs, and path dependency, Paper presented at a workshop at the MIS Research Center of the University of Minnesota (forthcoming MIS Quartely paper in 2006).

Zinnbauer, M./ Eberl, M. (2004): Die Überprüfung von Spezifikation und Güte von Strukturgleichungsmodellen: Verfahren und Anwendung, in: *Schriften zur Empirischen Forschung und Quantitativen Unternehmensplanung (EFOplan)*, Heft 21, p. 1-33.

Zmud, R. W. (1984): Design alternatives for organizing information systems activities, in: *MIS Quarterly*, 8, 2, p. 79-93.

Appendix

Appendix A: State-of-the-art in content allocation research

Study			Methodology				Reference Theories			
			Empirical		Non-empirical					
Year	Author(s)	Publication Outlet	Exploratory	Inductive	Conceptual	Mathematical	Economic	Strategic	Contingency-based	Non
1977	Rockart et al.	Mono			✓					✓
1980	Olson et al.	MISQ	✓						✓	
	Buchanan et al.	HBR			✓				✓	
	Buchanan et al.	HBR			✓				✓	
1982	Ein-Dor et al.	MISQ	✓						✓	
	Laskey	SPIM			✓				✓	
1983	King	CS			✓					✓
1984	Zmud	MIS			✓				✓	
	Carter	AMJ	✓						✓	
1985	Heinrich et al.	HMD			✓					✓
1988	Leifer	MISQ	✓							✓
1988	Goodhue et al.	MISQ	✓		(✓)				✓	
1989	Tavakolian et al.	MISQ		✓				✓	✓	
	Ahituv et al.	MISQ		✓					✓	
	Taylor et al.	MISQ	✓							✓
1990	Huber	ACR			✓				✓	
	von Simson	HBR	(✓)		✓			✓		
	Bacon	JIT	✓						✓	
1991	George et al.	CACM			✓					✓
	Gurbaxani et al.	CACM			✓		✓			
1992	Rofrano	IBM SJ			✓				✓	
	Goodhue et al.	MISQ	(✓)		✓					✓
	Lee et al.	JMIS			✓				✓	
	Boynton et al.	SMR			✓					✓
	Brown et al.	WP			✓				✓	
	Bloomfield et al.	JMS	(✓)		✓					✓
1994	Brown et al.	MISQ	✓					✓	✓	✓
1995	Tractinsky et al.	MISQ	✓						✓	
1996	Fiedler et al.	JMIS	✓	✓					✓	
1997	Brown	ISR	✓					✓	✓	
	Peak et al.	IM	✓							✓
1998	Jain et al.	MISQ	✓	✓					✓	
	Brown et al.	OS			✓			✓	✓	
	Nault	MS				✓	✓			
1999	Sambamurthy et al.	MISQ	✓				✓	✓	✓	
2000	Gordon et al.	ISM	✓						✓	
	Peterson et al.	ICIS	✓						✓	
2002	Kahai et al.	JCIS		✓					✓	
	Agarwal et al.	MISQ Ex			✓					✓
2003	Kahai et al.	ISM	✓						✓	
	Total	40	17	8	20	1	4	6	26	11

Table Appendix-A1: Reference theories and methodologies in prior related research studies

The preceding table illustrates reference theories and methodologies used in prior related research studies. As it was impossible to assign always only one reference theory and methodology to a publication outlet, multiple assignments were sometimes necessary.

The following table provides an overview of the major publication outlets, in which articles have been published on the determinants of and reasons for the allocation of IT-related resources.

IS Journals		Management Journals	
CACM	Communications of the Association for Computing Machinery	ACR	Academy of Management Review
CS	Computer Surveys	AMJ	Academy of Management Journal
JIT	Journal of Information Technology	JMS	Journal of Management Studies
JMIS	Journal of Management Information Systems	MS	Management Science
JCIT	Journal of Computer Information Systems	OS	Organization Science
IM	Information and Management	**Other**	
IBM SJ	IBM Systems Journal	Mono	Monography
ISM	Information Systems Management	WP	Working Paper
ISR	Information Systems Research		
MISQ	Management Information Systems Quarterly		

Table Appendix-A2: Publication outlets on the allocation of IT-related resources (Part I)

IS Conferences		Applied Management Journals	
ICIS	International Conference of Information Systems (ICIS)	MISQ Ex	Management Information Systems Quarterly Executive
SPIM	Conference on Strategic Planning for Information Management	HBR	Harvard Business Review
		HMD	HMD – Praxis der Wirtschaftsinformatik (formerly known as "Handbuch der modernen Datenverarbeitung")
		SMR	Sloan Management Review

Table Appendix-A3: Publication outlets on the allocation of IT-related resources (Part II)

Appendix B1: Initial Print cover letter

Ludwig-Maximilians-Universität München	Prof. Dr. Thomas Hess
	Ludwigstraße 28
Institut für Wirtschaftsinformatik und Neue Medien	D-80539 München
Leitung: Prof. Dr. Thomas Hess	Tel. 089-2180-6391
	Fax 089-2180-13541
	Email: thess@bwl.uni-muenchen.de
	WWW: www.wi.bwl.uni-muenchen.de
«Name_Verlag»	
«zHd» «Anrede_HF_Kopf» «Nachname»	
«Straße__HausNr»	München, den 01.Februar 2005
«Postleitzahl» «Ort»	

Mehrfachnutzung von Medieninhalten – zentralisierte oder dezentralisierte Datenhaltung?

«Anrede_HF» «Anrede_Floskel» «Nachname»,

in der Verlagsbranche ist das Thema der **Mehrfachnutzung von Medieninhalten** zurzeit in aller Munde. Eine wichtige technische Voraussetzung dafür ist die zweckmäßige Organisation und Bereitstellung von Medieninhalten. Doch an welchen Stellschrauben muss in der Verlagspraxis gedreht werden, um eine optimale Verteilung und Integration von Medieninhalten zu erreichen?

Der **AKEP** (Arbeitskreis Elektronische Publizieren) des Börsenvereins des Deutschen Buchhandels und das Institut für Wirtschaftsinformatik und Neue Medien (**WIM**) der Ludwig-Maximilians-Universität München führen eine gemeinsame **Branchenstudie** zur Untersuchung dieser Fragestellung durch. In einer ersten Studienphase sollen technisch-infrastrukturelle Einflussfaktoren einer effizienten Umsetzung der Mehrfachnutzung von Medieninhalten untersucht werden.

Zu diesem Zweck bitten wir Sie, den beiliegenden Fragebogen auszufüllen und im beigefügten Freiumschlag bis spätestens 1. April 2005 an uns zurückzusenden.

Idealerweise sollte der Fragebogen von einer Person ausgefüllt werden, die sowohl die technische Situation, als auch die kaufmännische Komponente dieser Fragestellung in Ihrem Verlag einschätzen kann und auch verantwortet (z.B. IT- bzw. Herstellungsleiter). Dabei beziehen wir uns auf den (rechtlich selbständigen) Tochterverlag, nicht die übergeordnete Verlagsgruppe.

Wenn Sie den Fragebogen beantworten, erhalten Sie von uns die Auswertung der **Studienergebnisse**. Auf diese Weise haben Sie die Möglichkeit, Ihre Inhalte-Organisation mit anderen Verlagen in ganz Deutschland zu vergleichen. Zudem erhalten Sie eine **fundierte Analyse und Handlungsempfehlungen** für Verlage Ihrer Unternehmensgröße aus unabhängiger Hand.

Mitmachen lohnt sich: Nehmen Sie an unserer Verlosung teil und gewinnen Sie einen von **fünf Apple iPod Shuffle** (mit 512 MB) oder sogar **einen Apple iPod** (mit 20 GB).

Alle von Ihnen gemachten Angaben werden natürlich **anonym und streng vertraulich** behandelt. Vielen Dank im Voraus für Ihre Mitarbeit.

Mit freundlichen Grüßen

Prof. Dr. Thomas Hess

Appendix B2: Follow-up E-Mail cover letter

Betreff: Wissenschaftliche Studie zur Mehrfachnutzung von Medieninhalten - Mitmachen und gewinnen

«Anrede_HF» «Anrede_Floskel» «Nachname»,

vor einigen Wochen haben wir Ihnen einen Fragebogen zugesandt, mit dessen Hilfe wir Ihre persönliche Einschätzung zur Frage der optimalen technisch-infrastrukturellen Unterstützung einer **Mehrfachnutzung von Medieninhalten** erheben wollen.

Erste Auswertungen der bisherigen Antworten deuten bereits auf sehr interessante Ergebnisse hin. Wir konnten z.b. bisher feststellen, dass Buch-, Zeitschriften- und Zeitungsverlage **unterschiedliche Praktiken bei der Verteilung und Integration von Medieninhalten** an den Tag legen. Als wichtige Entscheidungskriterien für die Wahl einer geeigneten Medieninhalte-Infrastruktur kristallisieren sich bisher insbesondere Produktionskosten sowie operative Nutzenfaktoren heraus. Insofern möchten wir mit diesem Schreiben erneut Ihr Interesse zur Teilnahme an unserer Studie wecken.

Weitere Details der Gemeinschaftsstudie des **AKEP** (Arbeitskreis Elektronische Publizieren) des Börsenvereins des Deutschen Buchhandels und des Instituts für Wirtschaftsinformatik und Neue Medien (**WIM**) der Ludwig-Maximilians-Universität München können Sie unter http://www.wi.bwl.uni-muenchen.de/query/mehrfachnutzung.asp (Login: user; Passwort: akep) nachlesen.

Wir bitten Sie daher, den beiliegenden Fragebogen auszufüllen und bis spätestens 1. April 2005 an uns zurückzusenden. Alternativ können Sie sich den Fragebogen in anderen Formaten unter http://www.wi.bwl.uni-muenchen.de/query/mehrfachnutzung.asp (Login: user; Passwort: akep) herunterladen.

Idealerweise sollte der Fragebogen von einer Person ausgefüllt werden, die sowohl die technische Situation, als auch die kaufmännische Komponente dieser Fragestellung in Ihrem Verlag einschätzen kann und auch verantwortet (z.B. IT- bzw. Herstellungsleiter). Dabei beziehen wir uns auf den (rechtlich selbständigen) Tochterverlag, nicht die übergeordnete Verlagsgruppe.

Wenn Sie den Fragebogen beantworten, erhalten Sie von uns die Auswertung der **Studienergebnisse**. Auf diese Weise haben Sie die Möglichkeit, Ihre Inhalte-Organisation mit anderen Verlagen in ganz Deutschland zu vergleichen. Zudem erhalten Sie eine **fundierte Analyse und Handlungsempfehlungen** für Verlage Ihrer Unternehmensgröße aus unabhängiger Hand.

> Mitmachen lohnt sich: Nehmen Sie an unserer Verlosung teil und gewinnen Sie einen von **fünf Apple iPod Shuffle** (mit 512 MB) oder sogar **einen Apple iPod** (mit 20 GB).

Alle von Ihnen gemachten Angaben werden natürlich **anonym und streng vertraulich** behandelt. Vielen Dank im Voraus für Ihre Mitarbeit.

Mit freundlichen Grüßen

Prof. Dr. Thomas Hess

Appendix C1: Questionnaire in German

Fragebogen zur Mehrfachnutzungsstudie 2005

Technisch-infrastrukturelle Voraussetzungen für eine erfolgreiche Mehrfachnutzung von Medieninhalten in Verlagen

---

Vertraulicher Fragebogen für den Leiter der Informationsverarbeitung bzw. einer Führungskraft mit technisch-organisatorischer sowie betriebswirtschaftlicher Verantwortung

Allgemeine Hinweise zu den Fragen

(Bitte vor dem Ausfüllen des Fragebogens durchlesen!)

▷ In den nachfolgenden Fragen werden mit **Medieninhalten** (synonym auch **Content**) **digitalisierte redaktionelle Inhalte gemeint**, d.h. analoge bzw. Werbeinhalte sollen explizit **nicht** berücksichtigt werden. Einige der folgenden Fragen beziehen sich zudem auf zwei unterschiedliche Arten von redaktionellen Medieninhalten in Ihrem Unternehmen (Bitte versuchen Sie auch dann, wenn Sie in der Praxis Produktiv- und Archivinhalte nicht voneinander trennen, eine **Unterscheidung** vorzunehmen):

▷ A) Unter „**Produktivinhalte**" werden im Folgenden *aktuelle* redaktionelle Inhalte verstanden, welche im täglichen Produktions- bzw. Überarbeitungsprozess (z.B. für die aktuelle Ausgabe einer Zeitschrift, Zeitung oder eines Buches) erstellt bzw. extern abgerufen und genutzt werden.

   B) Unter „**Archivinhalte**" werden dagegen im Folgenden *alte* Inhalte (d.h., die bereits in einer alten Ausgabe erschienen sind) verstanden, auf die während des aktuellen täglichen Herstellungs- bzw. Überarbeitungsprozess über eine Archiv-Datenbank zugegriffen werden kann.

▷ In den nachfolgenden Fragen werden **Redaktionsmitarbeiter** als diejenigen Mitarbeiter angesprochen, die Medieninhalte erstellen, bündeln und bearbeiten. Sollten Sie in Ihrem Unternehmen keine Redaktionen, sondern im weitesten Sinne **vergleichbare Organisationseinheiten** (z.B. Ressorts, Objekte, Lektorate, etc.) haben, beziehen Sie sich in Ihren Antworten auf diese.

▷ Der Begriff „**Verlag**" bezieht sich auf den **rechtlich selbständigen Verlag bzw. Tochterverlag einer Verlagsgruppe**, dem Sie angehören, und für dessen Management und Koordination der Informationsverarbeitung Sie die Verantwortung tragen. Sollten Sie einem **rechtlich selbständigen Tochterverlag einer Verlagsgruppe** angehören, würden wir uns sehr freuen, wenn Sie den **Fragebogen auch an Kollegen (mit vergleichbarem fachlichen Hintergrund)** anderer Tochterverlage Ihrer Verlagsgruppe weiterleiten könnten.

▷ Es gibt keine richtigen oder falschen Antworten. Wir sind an Ihrer **persönlichen Meinung** interessiert. Es ist sehr wichtig für uns, dass Sie **alle** Fragen beantworten.

Ihre Antworten werden anonym und streng vertraulich behandelt!

Herzlichen Dank für Ihre Unterstützung!

Arbeitskreis
Elektronisches Publizieren
Börsenverein des
Deutschen Buchhandels

Prof. Dr. Thomas Hess
Dipl.-Kfm. Alexander Benlian, M.A.

Arnould de Kemp
Cornelia Waldenmaier

Nehmen Sie an unserer Verlosung teil
und gewinnen Sie einen von fünf
Apple iPod shuffle (512 MB) oder
einen iPod (20 GB)!

Der Fragebogen beginnt auf der nächsten Seite und umfasst 5 Seiten ...

1) Fragen zur Verteilung und Integration von Medieninhalten

(i) Unter der „Zentralisierung von Medieninhalten" wird die Speicherung von Medieninhalten in einer oder in wenigen Datenbanken gemeint, die verlagsweit (global) zugänglich sind, wohingegen die „Dezentralisierung von Medieninhalten" die Speicherung von Medieninhalten auf vielen getrennten, jeweils in den Redaktionen befindlichen Datenbanken bezeichnet.

Bitte pro Spalte nur ein Kästchen ankreuzen

Werden Produktiv- und Archivinhalte **innerhalb Ihres Verlages** oder **extern bei Dienstleistern** gespeichert?

Produktivinhalte werden *vorwiegend* gespeichert …	**Archivinhalte** werden *vorwiegend* gespeichert …
☐ … innerhalb unserer Organisation	☐ … innerhalb unserer Organisation
☐ … unternehmensextern bei einem Dienstleister	☐ … unternehmensextern bei einem Dienstleister

(i) Wenn Ihre Produktiv- bzw. Archivinhalte vorwiegend extern bei einem Dienstleister gespeichert werden, kreuzen Sie bitte im Folgenden so an, dass Ihre Haltung von Produktiv- bzw. Archivinhalten völlig zentralisiert ist.

Verteilung der Medieninhalte in Ihrem Verlag

Bitte pro Spalte nur ein Kästchen ankreuzen

Bitte geben Sie für Produktiv- und Archivinhalte jeweils getrennt an, wo deren vorwiegender Speicherort in Ihrer Organisation liegt (Ist) bzw. idealer Weise liegen sollte (Soll).	**Produktivinhalte**		**Archivinhalte**	
	Ist	**Soll**	**Ist**	**Soll**
Die Inhalte unseres Verlags werden auf einem zentralen Datenspeicher (z.B. in einer IT-Abteilung oder in einer Redaktion) gehalten.	☐	☐	☐	☐
Die Inhalte unseres Verlags werden auf einigen wenigen zentralen Datenspeichern (z.B. in einer IT-Abteilung oder in wenigen, aber nicht in allen Redaktionen) gehalten.	☐	☐	☐	☐
Die Inhalte unseres Verlags werden verlagsweit auf mehreren, pro Redaktion jedoch jeweils nur auf einem Datenspeicher (z.B. eine globale Dahlten Datenbank pro Redaktion) gehalten.	☐	☐	☐	☐
Die Inhalte unseres Verlags werden verlagsweit auf mehreren, pro Redaktion jeweils auf wenigen dezentralen Datenspeichern (z.B. einige wenige getrennte Datenbanken pro Redaktion) gehalten.	☐	☐	☐	☐
Die Inhalte unseres Verlags werden verlagsweit auf mehreren, pro Redaktion auf nahezu allen dezentralen Datenspeichern (z.B. viele getrennte Datenbanken pro Redaktion) gehalten.	☐	☐	☐	☐

Bitte in jedes Feld einen Wert eintragen

Bitte schätzen Sie für **Produktiv- und Archivinhalte** Ihres Verlags jeweils getrennt nach **Ist- und Sollsituation**, …	**Produktivinhalte**		**Archivinhalte**	
	Ist	**Soll**	**Ist**	**Soll**
… bezogen auf den Gesamtbestand an Inhalten den **prozentualen Anteil** (0 bis 100%) **von in zentralen Datenbanken gespeicherten** Inhalten.	%	%	%	%
… die **Anzahl an Mitarbeitern**, die zur Administration von zentralen Datenbanken bzw. Netzwerkordnern mit gespeicherten Inhalten eingesetzt werden.				

Integration der Medieninhalte in Ihrem Verlag

Bitte pro Spalte nur ein Kästchen ankreuzen

Bitte kreuzen Sie im Folgenden an, inwieweit Redaktionsmitarbeiter Zugriff auf **Produktiv- bzw. Archivinhalte** in Ihrem Verlag haben (**Ist**) und idealer Weise haben sollten (**Soll**):	**Produktivinhalte**		**Archivinhalte**	
Jeder redaktionelle Mitarbeiter kann zur Unterstützung der eigenen Arbeit …	**Ist**	**Soll**	**Ist**	**Soll**
… auf sämtliche, dem Verlag zugängliche Inhalte zugreifen.	☐	☐	☐	☐
… auf Inhalte der eigenen und weiteren ausgewählten Redaktionen zugreifen.	☐	☐	☐	☐
… ausschließlich auf alle Inhalte der eigenen Redaktion zugreifen.	☐	☐	☐	☐
… auf Inhalte einiger Kollegen in der eigenen Redaktion zugreifen.	☐	☐	☐	☐
… nur auf Inhalte zugreifen, die er selbst erstellt hat.	☐	☐	☐	☐

Bitte in jedes Feld einen Wert eintragen

Bitte schätzen Sie für **Produktiv- und Archivinhalte** Ihres Verlags jeweils getrennt nach **Ist- und Sollsituation**, …	**Produktivinhalte**		**Archivinhalte**	
	Ist	**Soll**	**Ist**	**Soll**
… auf wie viel **Prozent** (von 0 bis 100%) **des Gesamtbestandes** an Inhalten Redaktionsmitarbeiter Ihres Verlages durchschnittlich zugreifen können (sollten).	%	%	%	%
… die **Anzahl an Mitarbeitern**, die zur Konfiguration von Zugriffsrechten auf Inhalte eingesetzt werden (sollten).				
… wie viel **Prozent** (von 0 bis 100%) Ihrer Inhalte in weiteren Medienprodukten wieder bzw. mehrfach verwendet/verwertet werden (sollten).	%	%	%	%

2) Fragen zu Kosten-Nutzen-Argumenten bei der Verteilung u. Integration von Medieninhalten

Produktionskosten

1 = trifft gar nicht zu 2 = trifft weniger zu 3 = trifft teils zu - teils nicht zu 4 = trifft eher zu 5 = trifft voll zu									
Bitte geben Sie für folgende Aussagen an, inwieweit diese jeweils für **Produktiv- u. Archivinhalte** (Ist-Situation) zutreffen:	... Produktivinhalte ...					... Archivinhalte ...				
Bezogen auf die Erstellung und Bearbeitung von Inhalten ...	1	2	3	4	5	1	2	3	4	5
... arbeiten unsere Redaktionsmitarbeiter kosteneffizienter, wenn sie auf Inhalte zugreifen können, die an zentraler Stelle gespeichert werden.	☐	☐	☐	☐	☐	☐	☐	☐	☐	☐
... arbeiten unsere Mitarbeiter schneller, wenn sie auf Inhalte zugreifen können, die an einer zentralen Stelle gespeichert werden.	☐	☐	☐	☐	☐	☐	☐	☐	☐	☐
... können wir Medienprodukte kostengünstiger erzeugen, wenn unsere Redaktionsmitarbeiter auf zentral gespeicherte Inhalte zugreifen können.	☐	☐	☐	☐	☐	☐	☐	☐	☐	☐

Koordinationskosten

ⓘ Koordinationskosten sind alle Kosten außer den direkten Herstellungskosten und treten in Form von Reibungsverlusten (z.B. Wartezeiten bzw. Verzögerungen bei der Übertragung von Medieninhalten) bzw. Managementkosten (z.B. Versions- oder Metadaten-Management) auf.

1 = trifft gar nicht zu 2 = trifft weniger zu 3 = trifft teils zu - teils nicht zu 4 = trifft eher zu 5 = trifft voll zu									
Bitte geben Sie für folgende Aussagen an, inwieweit diese jeweils für **Produktiv- u. Archivinhalte** (Ist-Situation) zutreffen:	... Produktivinhalte ...					... Archivinhalte ...				
Bezogen auf die Erstellung und Bearbeitung von Inhalten ...	1	2	3	4	5	1	2	3	4	5
... fallen geringere Recherchekosten an, wenn unsere Redaktionsmitarbeiter auf Inhalte zugreifen können, die zentral gespeichert werden.	☐	☐	☐	☐	☐	☐	☐	☐	☐	☐
... kommt es zu geringeren Abstimmungsschwierigkeiten (evtl. Doppelarbeit), wenn unsere Redaktionsmitarbeiter auf Inhalte zugreifen können, die zentral gespeichert werden.	☐	☐	☐	☐	☐	☐	☐	☐	☐	☐
... fallen geringere Managementkosten (z.B. für die Versionskontrolle oder die Metadaten-Auszeichnung) an, wenn unsere Redaktionsmitarbeiter auf Inhalte zugreifen können, die zentral gespeichert werden.	☐	☐	☐	☐	☐	☐	☐	☐	☐	☐
... fallen geringere Reibungsverluste in Form von Wartezeiten bzw. Verzögerungen bei der Suche und beim Austausch an, wenn unsere Redaktionsmitarbeiter auf Inhalte zugreifen können, die zentral gespeichert werden.	☐	☐	☐	☐	☐	☐	☐	☐	☐	☐

Strategischer Nutzen

1 = trifft gar nicht zu 2 = trifft weniger zu 3 = trifft teils zu - teils nicht zu 4 = trifft eher zu 5 = trifft voll zu									
Bitte geben Sie für folgende Aussagen an, inwieweit diese jeweils für **Produktiv- u. Archivinhalte** (Ist-Situation) zutreffen:	... Produktivinhalte ...					... Archivinhalte ...				
	1	2	3	4	5	1	2	3	4	5
Das Erreichen unserer strategischen Ziele wird gestärkt, wenn unsere Redaktionsmitarbeiter auf Inhalte zugreifen können, die zentral gespeichert werden.	☐	☐	☐	☐	☐	☐	☐	☐	☐	☐
Die Fähigkeit unserer Organisation, einen Beitrag zum erfolgreichen Bestehen gegenüber unseren Wettbewerbern zu leisten, wird gestärkt, wenn unsere Redaktionsmitarbeiter auf Inhalte zugreifen können, die zentral gespeichert werden.	☐	☐	☐	☐	☐	☐	☐	☐	☐	☐
Das Erzielen von Synergieeffekten (wie z.B. durch eine Mehrfachverwertung von Medieninhalten) wird gestärkt, wenn unsere Redaktionsmitarbeiter auf Inhalte zugreifen können, die zentral gespeichert werden.	☐	☐	☐	☐	☐	☐	☐	☐	☐	☐

Operativer Nutzen

1 = trifft gar nicht zu 2 = trifft weniger zu 3 = trifft teils zu - teils nicht zu 4 = trifft eher zu 5 = trifft voll zu									
Bitte geben Sie für folgende Aussagen an, inwieweit diese jeweils für **Produktiv- u. Archivinhalte** (Ist-Situation) zutreffen:	... Produktivinhalte ...					... Archivinhalte ...				
	1	2	3	4	5	1	2	3	4	5
Die Effizienz des Content-Workflows im alltäglichen Betrieb wird gestärkt, wenn unsere Redaktionsmitarbeiter auf Inhalte zugreifen können, die zentral gespeichert werden.	☐	☐	☐	☐	☐	☐	☐	☐	☐	☐
Die redaktionelle Erstellung von Inhalten im alltäglichen Betrieb ist effizienter, wenn unsere Redaktionsmitarbeiter auf Inhalte zugreifen können, die zentral gespeichert werden.	☐	☐	☐	☐	☐	☐	☐	☐	☐	☐
Die redaktionelle Erstellung von Inhalten im alltäglichen Betrieb ist aufgrund der einfacheren Mehrfachverwendung schneller, wenn unsere Redaktionsmitarbeiter auf Inhalte zugreifen können, die zentral gespeichert werden.	☐	☐	☐	☐	☐	☐	☐	☐	☐	☐
Der reibungslose Ablauf unserer täglichen Produktionsprozesse wird gestärkt, wenn unsere Redaktionsmitarbeiter auf Inhalte zugreifen können, die zentral gespeichert werden.	☐	☐	☐	☐	☐	☐	☐	☐	☐	☐

3) Fragen zu den Charakteristika der Medieninhalte in Ihrem Unternehmen

Charakterisierung der eigenen Medieninhalte

Bitte geben Sie eine Einschätzung Ihrer Medieninhalte ab

Die Medieninhalte, die typischerweise in unsere umsatzstärksten Medienprodukte fließen, lassen sich folgendermaßen beschreiben...

	1	2	3	4	5	6	7	
1. Bezogen auf die Thematik der Medieninhalte								
... sprechen sehr enge Zielgruppe an	☐	☐	☐	☐	☐	☐	☐	... sprechen sehr breite Zielgruppe an
... thematisch speziell	☐	☐	☐	☐	☐	☐	☐	... thematisch generell
... schwer mehrfach verwertbar	☐	☐	☐	☐	☐	☐	☐	... einfach mehrfach verwertbar
... schnell entwertet (hochaktuell)	☐	☐	☐	☐	☐	☐	☐	... langsam entwertet (zeitlos)
2. Bezogen auf die Struktur bzw. den Aufbau der Medieninhalte								
... monolithisch bzw. starr	☐	☐	☐	☐	☐	☐	☐	... modular
... schlecht strukturierbar	☐	☐	☐	☐	☐	☐	☐	... gut strukturierbar
... komplexe Struktur	☐	☐	☐	☐	☐	☐	☐	... einfache Struktur
3. Bezogen auf das Layout der Medieninhalte								
... nicht flexibel konvertierbar	☐	☐	☐	☐	☐	☐	☐	... flexibel konvertierbar
... individualisiert	☐	☐	☐	☐	☐	☐	☐	... standardisiert
... layoutabhängig	☐	☐	☐	☐	☐	☐	☐	... layoutunabhängig

Ähnlichkeit von Medieninhalten, Märkten und Prozessen über Redaktionen hinweg

1 = einzigartig in allen Redaktionen 2 = einzigartig in fast allen Redaktionen 3 = einzigartig in ca. der Hälfte 4 = ähnlich in fast allen Redaktionen 5 = ähnlich in allen Redaktionen der Redaktionen					
Bitte geben Sie im Folgenden an, wie **ähnlich** sich die **Produkte, Produktionsprozesse und bedienten Kunden bzw. Märkte der einzelnen Redaktionen untereinander** sind.	1	2	3	4	5
1. Ähnlichkeit der Medienprodukte zwischen Redaktionen					
Unsere Texte, Bilder und sonstigen Medieninhalte sind thematisch ...	☐	☐	☐	☐	☐
Die Struktur bzw. der Aufbau unserer Medieninhalte ist ...	☐	☐	☐	☐	☐
Das Layout bzw. die Aufmachung unserer Medieninhalte ist ...	☐	☐	☐	☐	☐
2. Ähnlichkeit der Prozesse und Technologien zwischen Redaktionen					
Der Komplexitätsgrad der Prozessschritte zur Erstellung der Medienprodukte ist ...	☐	☐	☐	☐	☐
Die Dauer und Anzahl von Bearbeitungszyklen von Medieninhalten sind ...	☐	☐	☐	☐	☐
Die fachlich-technischen Qualifikationen zur Erstellung unserer Medieninhalte sind ...	☐	☐	☐	☐	☐
Die verwendeten Technologien bzw. Systeme zur Erstellung der Medieninhalte sind ...	☐	☐	☐	☐	☐
3. Ähnlichkeit von bedienten Märkten zwischen Redaktionen					
Die Präferenzen, Bedürfnisse und das Kaufverhalten unserer Kundengruppen sind ...	☐	☐	☐	☐	☐
Die Charakteristika unserer Kunden sind ...	☐	☐	☐	☐	☐
Das Marktumfeld in den einzelnen Produktbereichen ist ...	☐	☐	☐	☐	☐

Intensität der Wechselbeziehungen zwischen Redaktionen Ihres Verlags

1 = trifft gar nicht zu 2 = trifft weniger zu 3 = teils zu - teils nicht zu 4 = trifft eher zu 5 = trifft voll zu					
Bitte geben Sie an, inwieweit die folgenden Aussagen zutreffen, dass einzelne Redaktionen in Ihrem Verlag **bezogen auf Medieninhalte**...	1	2	3	4	5
... voneinander unabhängig arbeiten.	☐	☐	☐	☐	☐
... zueinander in einer einseitigen Input- oder Outputbeziehung stehen.	☐	☐	☐	☐	☐
... in wechselseitigen Austauschbeziehungen zusammenarbeiten.	☐	☐	☐	☐	☐
... in redaktionsübergreifenden Projekten zusammenarbeiten.	☐	☐	☐	☐	☐

Einschätzung der strategischen Bedeutung Ihrer Medieninhalten

1 = trifft gar nicht zu 2 = trifft weniger zu 3 = trifft teils zu - teils nicht zu 4 = trifft eher zu 5 = trifft voll zu					
Bitte geben Sie für folgende Aussagen an, inwieweit diese für Ihre Medieninhalte im Durchschnitt zutreffen:	1	2	3	4	5
Unsere Medieninhalte heben sich in ihrer *Einzigartigkeit* von den Medieninhalten anderer Wettbewerber ab.	☐	☐	☐	☐	☐
Gegenüber unseren Wettbewerbern haben wir den strategischen Vorteil, *schwer imitierbare bzw. substituierbare* Medieninhalte zu besitzen.	☐	☐	☐	☐	☐
Unsere Medieninhalte besitzen ein *höheres Verwertungspotenzial* als die Medieninhalte unserer Wettbewerber.	☐	☐	☐	☐	☐

4) Allgemeine Fragen zur IT-Organisation und -Infrastruktur in Ihrem Verlag

Organisation der Informationsverarbeitung

Bitte hier nur ein Kästchen ankreuzen

In welcher Form sind IT-Aufgaben bzw. die Informationsverarbeitung in Ihre Verlagsorganisation eingegliedert?

- ☐ Als Stabstelle (nur beratende Funktion)
- ☐ Als eigener Hauptbereich neben den Fachbereichen (wie z.B. Redaktionen, Marketing, Vertrieb, etc.)
- ☐ Als Querschnittsfunktion (zentrale IT-Abteilung und dezentrale IT-Instanzen eingebettet in einer oder in mehreren Redaktionen)
- ☐ Als Linieninstanz (z.B. IT-Mitarbeiter eingebettet in einen oder mehrere Fachbereiche/Redaktionen)
- ☐ Als IT-Dienstleister in der Verlagsgruppe   ☐ Ausgelagert an externen IT-Dienstleister

Zentralisierungsgrad der Informationsverarbeitung

1 = trifft gar nicht zu 2 = trifft weniger zu 3 = trifft teils zu - teils nicht zu 4 = trifft eher zu 5 = trifft voll zu					
Bitte geben Sie an, inwieweit die folgenden Aussagen für Ihren Verlag zutreffen.	1	2	3	4	5
Das Management aller Aufgaben der Informationsverarbeitung wird von einer zentralen EDV- bzw. IT-Abteilung verrichtet.	☐	☐	☐	☐	☐
Datenbanken, in denen Medieninhalte gespeichert werden, werden von einer zentralen IT-Abteilung administriert.	☐	☐	☐	☐	☐
Die einzelnen Bearbeitungsschritte bei der Erstellung von Medieninhalten werden von einer zentralen DV- bzw. IT-Abteilung unterstützt bzw. kontrolliert.	☐	☐	☐	☐	☐

Abhängigkeit von vergangenen IT-Investitionsentscheidungen bzw. historischen Prozessen

1 = trifft gar nicht zu 2 = trifft weniger zu 3 = teils zu - teils nicht zu 4 = trifft eher zu 5 = trifft voll zu					
Bitte geben Sie an, inwieweit die folgenden Aussagen für Ihren Verlag zutreffen.	1	2	3	4	5
1. Technische Abhängigkeiten					
Der gegenwärtige und zukünftige Speicherort unserer Medieninhalte hängt maßgeblich von den IT-Investitionen in Hardware und Software in der Vergangenheit ab.	☐	☐	☐	☐	☐
Durch die bestehende IT-Infrastruktur wird maßgeblich vorgegeben, wo jetzt und in Zukunft unsere Medieninhalte gespeichert werden.	☐	☐	☐	☐	☐
Eine Umstellung der Haltung unserer Medieninhalte wäre mit hohen Umstellungskosten für neue Hardware, Software und Personal verbunden.	☐	☐	☐	☐	☐
2. Historische Entwicklungen					
Die aktuelle Verteilung und Integration von Medieninhalten ist das Ergebnis einer historisch gewachsenen Arbeitsweise unserer Redaktionsmitarbeiter.	☐	☐	☐	☐	☐
Für unsere Mitarbeiter wäre der Aufwand zu groß, sich auf eine neue Art der Haltung und Bereitstellung von Medieninhalten einzustellen.	☐	☐	☐	☐	☐
Die historisch bzw. kulturell gewachsenen Arbeitsweisen innerhalb unseres Verlags werden bei einer Entscheidung über die Verteilung und Integration von Medieninhalten nicht berücksichtigt.	☐	☐	☐	☐	☐

ⓘ Nachfolgend sind Aussagen zur Erfüllung technischer Anforderungen bei zentraler bzw. dezentraler Verteilung von Medieninhalten aufgeführt. Auch hier wurden die Aussagen aufgrund der einfacheren Lesbarkeit so formuliert, dass zentrale Lösungen als vorteilhafter erscheinen. Es soll hier jedoch wiederum nicht suggeriert werden, dass die zentrale Verteilung von Medieninhalten generell vorteilhafter ist. Bitte bewerten Sie deshalb kritisch, inwieweit die folgenden Aussagen für Ihren Verlag zutreffen.

Erfüllung technischer Anforderungen

1 = trifft gar nicht zu 2 = trifft weniger zu 3 = trifft teils zu - teils nicht zu 4 = trifft eher zu 5 = trifft voll zu					
Bitte geben Sie an, inwieweit die folgenden Aussagen für Ihren Verlag zutreffen.	1	2	3	4	5
Der Zugriff auf **zentral gegenüber dezentral** gespeicherten Inhalten ist vorteilhafter, da ...					
... die Verfügbarkeit aller Medieninhalte optimaler ist.	☐	☐	☐	☐	☐
... die Fehleranfälligkeit geringer (bzw. die Robustheit größer) ist.	☐	☐	☐	☐	☐
... die Zugriffsgeschwindigkeit für die Redaktionsmitarbeiter optimaler ist.	☐	☐	☐	☐	☐
... die Skalierbarkeit der Datenverarbeitungskapazitäten optimaler ist.	☐	☐	☐	☐	☐
... da sich auf diese Weise auf Medieninhalte bezogene Sicherheitsmaßnahmen (z.B. Zugriffsrechte, Backups zur Ausfallsicherung) konsequenter umsetzen lassen.	☐	☐	☐	☐	☐
... Medieninhalte besser organisiert (z.B. Content Management), archiviert (z.B. Versionsmanagement) und verwaltet (z.B. Zugriffsmanagement) werden können.	☐	☐	☐	☐	☐
... die Integration einer weiteren Redaktion mit Medieninhalten leichter realisierbar ist.	☐	☐	☐	☐	☐
... da unsere Redaktionsmitarbeiter auf diese Weise optimaler auf die aktuellste Version der Medieninhalte (d.h. weniger Versionskonflikte) zugreifen können.	☐	☐	☐	☐	☐

5) Fragen zur Strategie, Organisation und zu den Produkten Ihres Verlags

Verfolgte Strategie

1 = trifft gar nicht zu 2 = trifft weniger zu 3 = trifft teils zu - teils nicht zu 4 = trifft eher zu 5 = trifft voll zu					
Bitte geben Sie an, inwieweit die folgenden Aussagen für Ihren Verlag zutreffen.	1	2	3	4	5
Unser Verlag verfolgt eine Strategie der Kostenführerschaft, d.h. wir produzieren kostengünstiger als unsere Wettbewerber.	☐	☐	☐	☐	☐
Unser Verlag verfolgt eine Strategie der Differenzierung, d.h. wir heben uns von unseren Wettbewerbern über qualitativ hochwertige Produkte ab.	☐	☐	☐	☐	☐
Unser Verlag verfolgt eine Nischenstrategie, d.h. wir decken nicht den Gesamtmarkt ab, in dem wir uns befinden, sondern konzentrieren uns auf eine enge, spezifische Kundengruppe.	☐	☐	☐	☐	☐

Charakteristika Ihrer Organisationsstruktur

1 = trifft gar nicht zu 2 = trifft weniger zu 3 = trifft teils zu - teils nicht zu 4 = trifft eher zu 5 = trifft voll zu					
Bitte geben Sie an, inwieweit die folgenden Aussagen für Ihren Verlag zutreffen.	1	2	3	4	5
1. Zentralisierungsgrad					
Jede wichtige Entscheidung muss von der Unternehmensleitung genehmigt werden.	☐	☐	☐	☐	☐
Entscheidungen werden strikt von zentraler Stelle getroffen.	☐	☐	☐	☐	☐
Unsere einzelnen Redaktionen genießen weitestgehende Entscheidungsautonomie.	☐	☐	☐	☐	☐
2. Formalisierungsgrad					
Die Produktion unserer Medieninhalte ist durch detaillierte Regeln, Prozeduren und Workflows vorgegeben.	☐	☐	☐	☐	☐
Für jede auftretende Situation in der Produktion von Medieninhalten besitzen wir spezifische Regeln bzw. Vorgaben.	☐	☐	☐	☐	☐
Jeder Schritt in der Produktion unserer Medieninhalte ist genauestens dokumentiert.	☐	☐	☐	☐	☐
3. Spezialisierungsgrad					
Jeder Redaktionsmitarbeiter hat eine spezifische Aufgabe zu verrichten.	☐	☐	☐	☐	☐
Unsere Redaktionsmitarbeiter sind jeweils auf einen Teilschritt in der Bearbeitung von Medieninhalten spezialisiert.	☐	☐	☐	☐	☐
Jeder Redaktionsmitarbeiter muss mehrere Prozessschritte in der Bearbeitung von Medieninhalten abdecken.	☐	☐	☐	☐	☐

Organisationsgröße

Bitte schätzen Sie die jeweilige Höhe des Wertes	
Wie viele einzelne Redaktionen (bitte einzeln werten für unterschiedliche Ressorts, Objekte, Bereiche) bzw. Mitarbeiter gehören Ihrem Verlag an? Wie groß ist die derzeitige Auflagenanzahl Ihres umsatzstärksten Medienproduktes?	
Indikatoren für Organisationsgröße	**Wert (geschätzt)**
Anzahl Redaktionen (in ihrem gesamten Verlag):	
Anzahl vollzeitbeschäftigte Mitarbeiter (in ihrem gesamten Verlag):	
Anzahl teilzeitbeschäftigte Mitarbeiter (in ihrem gesamten Verlag):	
Auflagenanzahl Ihres umsatzstärksten Medienproduktes:	

Medienprodukte

Bitte kreuzen Sie links alle die von Ihrem Verlag abgedeckten Medienprodukte an u. vergeben Sie rechts Rangplätze		
Welche Medienprodukte deckt Ihr Verlag ab?		Stellen Sie nachfolgend bitte eine Rangfolge nach der Umsatzstärke (absteigend von Rang 1) der von Ihrem Verlag abgedeckten Medienprodukte (siehe links) auf:
☐ Buch	(Anzahl Labels/Marken:)	Rang:
☐ Zeitschrift	(Anzahl Titel:)	Rang:
☐ Zeitung	(Anzahl Titel:)	Rang:
☐ Loseblattwerk		Rang:
☐ Nachschlagewerk		Rang:
☐ Hörbuch		Rang:
☐ Katalog		Rang:
☐ Internet/Intranet/Extranet		Rang:
☐ DVD		Rang:
☐ CD-Rom		Rang:
☐ Sonstige:		Rang:

6) Angaben zu Ihrer Person

Wir möchten Sie nochmals darauf hinweisen, dass die Anonymität Ihrer Angaben gewährleistet ist.

Welche Position bekleiden bzw. Funktion erfüllen Sie in Ihrem Verlag?	
Wie viele Jahre arbeiten Sie bereits in Ihrem Verlag?	Jahr(e)

✂--

Um eine Zuordnung der Antworten zu Ihrem Unternehmen auszuschließen, können Sie uns diese letzte Seite **getrennt** zusenden/ faxen:

☐ Ja, wir sind an einer Zusammenfassung wichtiger Ergebnisse interessiert.

☐ Ja, wir möchten an der Verlosung teilnehmen. Hier unsere Kontaktdaten:

Firma:	Ansprechpartner:	
Straße/Postfach:	Abteilung/Position:	
PLZ Ort:	E-Mail:	

Herzlichen Dank für Ihre freundliche Kooperation bei der Beantwortung des Fragebogens!!!

Den Fragebogen bitte zurücksenden an:

Ludwig-Maximilians-Universität München, Institut für Wirtschaftsinformatik und Neue Medien

z. Hd. Herrn Alexander Benlian

Ludwigstr. 28, 80539 München

Fax: 089/2180-13541, Tel.: 089/2180-6395

E-Mail: benlian@bwl.uni-muenchen.de

Appendix C2: Questionnaire in English

Content Reutilization Survey 2005

Technical and infrastructural prerequisites for successful content reutilization in publishing companies

Confidential questionnaire for the chief information officer or IT managers
with both a technical and business background

General Instructions

(Please read before you fill out the questionnaire!)

▷ In the subsequent questions **media content** will be referred to as **digitized editorial content**, explicitly excluding analog and ad content. Some of the following questions also refer to two different types of editorial content in your company. Please try to **distinguish** between **productive and archived content** as described subsequently even if you do not treat them separately in your organization.

▷ A) **Productive content** refers to current editorial content that is either produced or procurred and utilized in daily production and bundling processes (e.g. for the most current issue or edition of a magazine or book).

B) **Archived content** refers to out-of-date content (i.e., which has already been published in a former issue or edition), that is retrieved from an archive during daily production and bundling processes.

▷ In the subsequent questions, **editors** are referred to as employees working in **editorial units** in your publishing organization that produce, bundle, and edit content. If you do not have editorial units in your company, but comparable organizational units in the broadest sense (z.B. departments, objects, etc.), please refer to these in your answers.

▷ The term „**publishing company**" refers to the legally independent publishing organization or subsidiary of a corporate publishing group you are working for and whose management and coordination of IT-related activities you are responsible of. If you are working for a subsidiary of a corporate publishing group, we would very much appreciate it if you could forward the questionnaire to colleagues with a comparable background and function in other subsidiaries.

▷ There are neither right nor wrong answers. We are simply interested in your *personal* opinion. It is very important for us that you answer all of the questions.

All of your answers will be treated anonymously and strictly confidentially!

Thank you very much for your support!

Arbeitskreis
Elektronisches Publizieren
Börsenverein des
Deutschen Buchhandels

Prof. Dr. Thomas Hess
Dipl.-Kfm. Alexander Benlian, M.A.

Arnould de Kemp
Cornelia Waldenmaier

Partake in the raffle
and win one out of five
Apple iPod shuffles (512 MB) or
an iPod (20 GB)!

The questionnaire starts with the next page and comprises 5 pages …

1) Questions regarding content distribution and integration

(i) The **centralization of content** is referred to as storing content in one or few databases that are accessible from throughout the publishing organization (global access). By contrast, the **decentralization of content** describes a situation where content is stored in many separate databases located in different editorial units (only local access).

Please tick only one box per column

Is your archived and productive content stock located inside or outside the boundaries of your company?

Productive content is *primarily* stored …	Archived content is *primarily* stored …
☐ … inside our company	☐ … inside our company
☐ … outside our company (e.g. at a service provider)	☐ … outside our company (e.g. at a service provider)

(i) If your productive and/or archived content is primarily stored outside your company (e.g. at a service provider), please tick the following boxes as if your content base is stored completely at one central location.

Content distribution in your company

Please tick only one box per column

Please indicate for productive and archived content respectively where media content is currently and should ideally be stored in your organization.	Product. content		Archiv. content	
	Curr.	Ideal	Curr.	Ideal
The media content of our company is stored in one central database (i.e. in a central IT department or editorial unit).	☐	☐	☐	☐
The media content of our company is stored in only few central databases (i.e. in a central IT department or in few, but not all editorial units).	☐	☐	☐	☐
The media content of our company is stored in several databases company-wide, but only in one database per editorial unit (e.g. one global database per editorial unit).	☐	☐	☐	☐
The media content of our company is stored in several databases company-wide, but only in few databases per editorial unit.	☐	☐	☐	☐
The media content of our company is stored in several data repositories company-wide and also in nearly all possible data repositories per editorial unit.	☐	☐	☐	☐

Please fill in a value in each field

For both **productive and archived content**, please estimate …	Product. content		Archiv. content	
	Curr.	Ideal	Curr.	Ideal
… the **average percentage of media content** (0-100%) that is currently and should ideally be stored in central databases.	%	%	%	%
… the **number of employees** that are currently and should ideally be responsible for the administration of central databases or network folders.				

Content integration in your company

Please tick only one box per column

Please indicate for productive and archived content respectively in how far editors have currently and should ideally get access to productive and archived content in your organization.	Product. content		Archiv. content	
In order to support their everyday work, editors have access …	Curr.	Ideal	Curr.	Ideal
… to all content that is available throughout the company.	☐	☐	☐	☐
… to content of their own editorial unit and of selected others.	☐	☐	☐	☐
… only to content of their own editorial unit.	☐	☐	☐	☐
… only to content on their own workstations and some others in their own editorial unit.	☐	☐	☐	☐
… only to content on their own workstations.	☐	☐	☐	☐

Bitte in jedes Feld einen Wert eintragen

For both **productive and archived content**, please estimate …	Product. content		Archiv. content	
	Curr.	Ideal	Curr.	Ideal
… the **share of the total content stock** (0-100%) to which editors of your company have currently and should ideally get access to.	%	%	%	%
… the **number of employees** that are currently and should ideally be responsible for the configuration of access rights associated with media content.				
… what **percentage of media content** (0-100%) is currently re-used and should ideally be re-used in various media channels.	%	%	%	%

2) Questions concerning costs of and benefits from content distribution and integration

Production costs

1 = strongly agree 2 = agree 3 = neither agree nor disagree 4 = disagree 5 = strongly disagree	... Productive content ...					... Archived content ...				
Please indicate in how far you agree with the following statements concerning productive and archived content:	1	2	3	4	5	1	2	3	4	5
Our editors work more cost efficiently, if they have access to content that is stored centrally rather than decentrally.	□	□	□	□	□	□	□	□	□	□
Our editors work faster, if they have access to content that is stored centrally rather than decentrally.	□	□	□	□	□	□	□	□	□	□
Media products can be produced at a lower cost if our editors have access to content that is stored centrally rather than decentrally.	□	□	□	□	□	□	□	□	□	□

Coordination costs

(i) Coordination costs are all but direct production costs and are incurred in the form of frictional (z.B. delays in the transmission of content) or management costs (e.g. version or metadata management).

1 = strongly agree 2 = agree 3 = neither agree nor disagree 4 = disagree 5 = strongly disagree	... Productive content ...					... Archived content ...				
Please indicate in how far you agree with the following statements concerning productive and archived content:	1	2	3	4	5	1	2	3	4	5
Search costs incurred are lower if our editors have access to content that is stored centrally rather than decentrally.	□	□	□	□	□	□	□	□	□	□
Coordination problems encountered (e.g. redundant work) occur less, if our editors have access to content that is stored centrally rather than decentrally.	□	□	□	□	□	□	□	□	□	□
Management costs (e.g. version or meta-data management) incurred are lower, if our editors have access to content that is stored centrally rather than decentrally.	□	□	□	□	□	□	□	□	□	□
Frictional costs incurred in the form of waiting time or time delays during the search and exchange of content are lower, if our editors have access to content that is stored centrally rather than decentrally.	□	□	□	□	□	□	□	□	□	□

Strategic benefits

1 = strongly agree 2 = agree 3 = neither agree nor disagree 4 = disagree 5 = strongly disagree	... Productive content ...					... Archived content ...				
Please indicate in how far you agree with the following statements concerning productive and archived content:	1	2	3	4	5	1	2	3	4	5
The achievement of our strategic goals is better strengthened, if our editors access content that is stored centrally rather than decentrally.	□	□	□	□	□	□	□	□	□	□
The ability of our organization to compete successfully against our competitors is better supported, if our editors have access to content that is stored centrally rather than decentrally.	□	□	□	□	□	□	□	□	□	□
The realization of synergy effects (e.g. by the reutilization of content) is better furthered, if our editors have access to content that is stored centrally rather than decentrally.	□	□	□	□	□	□	□	□	□	□

Operational benefits

1 = strongly agree 2 = agree 3 = neither agree nor disagree 4 = disagree 5 = strongly disagree	... Productive content ...					... Archived content ...				
Please indicate in how far you agree with the following statements concerning productive and archived content:	1	2	3	4	5	1	2	3	4	5
The efficiency of our organization's content workflow in our day-to-day business activities is better strengthened, if our editors have access to content that is stored centrally rather than decentrally.	□	□	□	□	□	□	□	□	□	□
The editorial production of content in our day-to-day business operations is more efficient, if our editors have access to content that is stored centrally rather than decentrally.	□	□	□	□	□	□	□	□	□	□
With regard to potentially repurposing content, the editorial production of content in our day-to-day business activities is faster, if our editors have access to content that is stored centrally rather than decentrally.	□	□	□	□	□	□	□	□	□	□
The frictionless operations of our day-to-day business activities is better supported, if our editors have access to content that is stored centrally rather than decentrally.	□	□	□	□	□	□	□	□	□	□

3) Questions regarding the characteristics of your company's content portfolio

Characterize your content portfolio

Please assess your content portfolio on the following criteria							
Media content that is typically part of our best-selling media products can be characterized as follows ...							
	1	2	3	4	5	6	7	
1. With regard to the topic, content that is typically integrated into our media products, can best be described as							
... targeting a very narrow customer group	☐	☐	☐	☐	☐	☐	☐	... targeting a very narrow customer group
... topically specific	☐	☐	☐	☐	☐	☐	☐	... topically unspecific
... badly reutilizable	☐	☐	☐	☐	☐	☐	☐	... easily reutilizable
... rapidly devalued (highly current)	☐	☐	☐	☐	☐	☐	☐	... slowly devalued (timeless)
2. With regard to the structure, content that is typically integrated into our media products, can best be described as							
... monolithic	☐	☐	☐	☐	☐	☐	☐	... modular
... badly structurable	☐	☐	☐	☐	☐	☐	☐	... easily structurable
... complex structure	☐	☐	☐	☐	☐	☐	☐	... simple structure
3. With regard to the layout, content that is typically integrated into our media products, can best be described as							
... badly convertible	☐	☐	☐	☐	☐	☐	☐	... easily convertible
... individualized/customized	☐	☐	☐	☐	☐	☐	☐	... standardized
... layout dependent	☐	☐	☐	☐	☐	☐	☐	... layout independent

Relatedness of content, production processes, and markets across editorial units (e.d.)

1 = unique in all or almost all e.d. 2 = unique in a majority of e.d. 3 = unique in about half of e.d., 4 = common across a majority of e.d. 5 = common across all or almost all e.d. Common across the other half					
Please indicate how related the media products, production processes, and markets are across your editorial units ...	1	2	3	4	5
1. Relatedness of content across editorial units					
Regarding the genre, our content (e.g. articles, pictures, photos, etc.) is ...	☐	☐	☐	☐	☐
The structure and organization of our content is ...	☐	☐	☐	☐	☐
The layout and design of our content is ...	☐	☐	☐	☐	☐
2. Relatedness of production processes and technologies across editorial units					
The complexity of our content production process steps is ...	☐	☐	☐	☐	☐
The time for and number of content production cycles is ...	☐	☐	☐	☐	☐
The technical skills to produce our content are ...	☐	☐	☐	☐	☐
The applied technologies and systems to produce our content are ...	☐	☐	☐	☐	☐
3. Relatedness of markets across editorial units					
The preferences, demands and buying behavior of our customer groups are ...	☐	☐	☐	☐	☐
The characteristics of our customers are ...	☐	☐	☐	☐	☐
The market environment surrounding our products is ...	☐	☐	☐	☐	☐

Intensity of interactions between editorial units of your company

1 = strongly agree 2 = agree 3 = neither agree nor disagree 4 = disagree 5 = strongly disagree					
Please indicate your agreement with the following statements that, with regard to media content, individual editorial units in your company ...	1	2	3	4	5
... work independently of one another (independent workflows).	☐	☐	☐	☐	☐
... cooperate with other editorial units in one-directional input-/output-relationships (sequential workflow).	☐	☐	☐	☐	☐
... cooperate with other editorial units in reciprocal exchange relationships (reciprocal workflow).	☐	☐	☐	☐	☐
... cooperate with other editorial units in projects.	☐	☐	☐	☐	☐

Assessment of the strategic value of your content portfolio

1 = strongly agree 2 = agree 3 = neither agree nor disagree 4 = disagree 5 = strongly disagree					
Please indicate in how far you agree with the following statements:	1	2	3	4	5
Our content stands out against the content of other competitors due to its uniqueness.	☐	☐	☐	☐	☐
Vis-à-vis our competitors, we have the strategic advantage to possess content that is hardly imitable and substitutable.	☐	☐	☐	☐	☐
Our content holds a greater reutilization potential than the content of our competitors.	☐	☐	☐	☐	☐

4) General questions concerning your IT-organization and IT-infrastructure

Organization of the IT function

Please tick only one box
How is the IT function integrated into the organization of your company? Our IT function is organized as …
☐   staff function (just a consulting function without authority).
☐   IT department in its own right next to other departments (e.g., marketing, sales or editorial units).
☐   cross-departmental function (i.e. central IT department and decentralized IT units embedded into one or more editorial units).
☐   line function (i.e. just decentralized IT units embedded into one or more edito-rial units).
☐   external IT service provider inside the corporate publishing group.   ☐   external IT service provider outside the corporate publishing group.

Degree of centralization of IT-related decision-making

1 = strongly agree 2 = agree 3 = neither agree nor disagree 4 = disagree 5 = strongly disagree					
Please indicate in how far you agree with the following statements:	1	2	3	4	5
The management of all IT-related tasks is performed by a central IT department.	☐	☐	☐	☐	☐
Content databases are administered by a central IT department.	☐	☐	☐	☐	☐
Content production and bundling activities are supported and controlled by a central IT department.	☐	☐	☐	☐	☐

Dependence on past decisions on IT investments and historical developments

1 = strongly agree 2 = agree 3 = neither agree nor disagree 4 = disagree 5 = strongly disagree					
Please indicate in how far you agree with the following statements:	1	2	3	4	5
1. Technical dependencies					
The present and future storage location for our content is mainly dependent on prior IT-investments in hardware and software.	☐	☐	☐	☐	☐
The existing IT-infrastructure primarily predetermines the current and future location of our content.	☐	☐	☐	☐	☐
A rearrangement of the current content allocation configuration would entail high switching costs for hardware, software, and personnel.	☐	☐	☐	☐	☐
2. Historical developments					
The current distribution and integration of content is the result of historically grown working structures of our employees.	☐	☐	☐	☐	☐
For our employees, the costs to adjust to new ways in the allocation of content would be too high.	☐	☐	☐	☐	☐
Historically or culturally grown working structures within our organization are not considered when decisions are made on the distribution and integration of content.	☐	☐	☐	☐	☐

ⓘ   Subsequently you will find statements on the fulfillment of technical requirements in centralized vs. decentralized content allocation arrangements. Due to the better readability, the statements were formulated so that centralized content allocation appears to be superior to decentralized content allocation. Please be careful though that this tendency should not be suggested by this research study. For that reason, we ask you to assess critically how the statements apply to your publishing company.

Fulfillment of technical requirements

1 = strongly agree 2 = agree 3 = neither agree nor disagree 4 = disagree 5 = strongly disagree					
Please indicate in how far you agree with the following statements:	1	2	3	4	5
The access to centralized as opposed to decentralized content is advantageous, because …					
… the availability of our entire content stock during production and bundling phases is more optimal.	☐	☐	☐	☐	☐
… the error-proneness of the content provision during production and bundling phases is lower (or: the robustness of the content provision during production and bundling phases is higher).	☐	☐	☐	☐	☐
… the access speed to content for our editors is more optimal during production and bundling phases.	☐	☐	☐	☐	☐
… the scalability of content processing is more optimal during production and bundling phases.	☐	☐	☐	☐	☐
… the management and execution of security measures (e.g. content access rights, daily backups, etc.) can be realized more consistently.	☐	☐	☐	☐	☐
… content can be organized (e.g. content management), archived (e.g. version management) and maintained (e.g. access rights management) more optimally.	☐	☐	☐	☐	☐
… the integration of another editorial unit with additional content is more easily realizable.	☐	☐	☐	☐	☐
… our editors have always access to the most current versions of our content during production and bundling phases (i.e. less version inconsistencies).	☐	☐	☐	☐	☐

5) Questions concerning your strategy, organization, and products

Pursued business strategy

1 = strongly agree 2 = agree 3 = neither agree nor disagree 4 = disagree 5 = strongly disagree					
Please indicate in how far you agree with the following statements:	1	2	3	4	5
Our publishing organization employs a strategy of low-cost, i.e. we strive to produce more cost-efficiently than our competitors do.	☐	☐	☐	☐	☐
Our publishing organization employs a strategy of differentiation, i.e. we seek to differentiate the product offering from rivals' products.	☐	☐	☐	☐	☐
Our publishing organization utilizes a focus strategy, i.e. we don't strive to serve the entire, but a narrow portion of the market.	☐	☐	☐	☐	☐

Characteristics of your organizational structure

1 = strongly agree 2 = agree 3 = neither agree nor disagree 4 = disagree 5 = strongly disagree					
Please indicate in how far you agree with the following statements:	1	2	3	4	5
1. Degree of centralization					
Any decision editors have to make needs the approval of a central organizational unit.	☐	☐	☐	☐	☐
All decisions within our editorial units are strictly made from a central position.	☐	☐	☐	☐	☐
Our single editorial units enjoy extensive decision autonomy in day-to-day business operations.	☐	☐	☐	☐	☐
2. Degree of formalization					
The production and bundling of our content is precisely described in rules, procedures, and work-flows.	☐	☐	☐	☐	☐
For every incident in the production and bundling of content, we have specific rules and guidelines to follow.	☐	☐	☐	☐	☐
Every step in the production and bundling of content is documented in detail.	☐	☐	☐	☐	☐
3. Degree of specialization					
Every editor has a specific job to do.	☐	☐	☐	☐	☐
Our editors are specialized in a specific step in the production and bundling of content.	☐	☐	☐	☐	☐
Every editor has to cover several process steps in the production and bundling of content.	☐	☐	☐	☐	☐

Organization size

Please estimate the folowing values	
How many editorial units and employees does your organization comprise (please count each department, objects, and units separately)? How big is the current circulation of your best-selling media product?	
Indicator of company size	Estimated value
Total number of editorial units (log)	
Total number of full-time workers (log)	
Total number of part-time workers (log)	
Circulation of best-selling media product (log)	

Media products

Please check the products offered by your company and rank them			
Which of the following media products does your company offer?		Please rank the products that you checked on the left in descending order of their sales volume in your company:	
☐ Book	(Number of labels:)	Rank position:	
☐ Magazine	(Number of titels:)	Rank position:	
☐ Newspaper	(Number of titels:)	Rank position:	
☐ Loose-leaf collection		Rank position:	
☐ Encyclopedia		Rank position:	
☐ Audiobook		Rank position:	
☐ Catalog		Rank position:	
☐ Internet/Intranet/Extranet		Rank position:	
☐ DVD		Rank position:	
☐ CD-Rom		Rank position:	
☐ Sonstige:		Rank position:	

6) Information about your person

The anonymity of the information you provide is guaranteed.	
What function do you have in your company?	
How many years do you already work for your company?	Year(s)

✂---

To avoid mapping of answers to your company you can **send / fax** the last page separately:

☐ Yes, we are interested in a summary of major findings of the survey.
☐ Yes, we would like to partake in the raffle. Here is our contact data:

Company:		Contact person:	
Street:		Department/Position:	
City ZIP:		E-Mail:	

Thanks a lot for your cooperation!

Please send the survey back to:

Alexander Benlian **Ludwig Maximilians University of Munich** **Institute for Information Systems and New Media** **Ludwigstr. 28, 80539 Munich** **Fax: 089/2180-13541, Tel.: 089/2180-6395** **E-Mail: benlian@bwl.uni-muenchen.de**

Appendix D: Reliability assessment and cross-loadings

Constructs	Number of items in original scale	Number of items in refined scale
Content distribution	3	2
Content integration	4	2
Production cost advantage	3	3
Transaction cost advantage	4	4
Strategic contribution advantage	3	3
Operational contribution advantage	3	3
Topical specificity	4	3
Structure specificity	3	3
Layout specificity	3	2
Content transaction frequency	1	1
Content relatedness	3	3
Production pocess relatedness	4	4
Market relatedness	3	3
Perceived strategic content value	3	3
Strategy of low cost	1	1
Strategy of differentiation	1	1
Strategy of focus	1	1
Organizational centralization	3	2
Organizational formalization	3	3
Organizational specialization	3	2
Organizational size	4	3
IT organization	1	1
IT governance	3	3
IT investment-related path dependencies	3	3
IT usage-based path dependencies	3	2
Infrastructural IT-imperatives	8	8

Table Appendix-D1: Reliability assessment

Items	Dist	Int	Pc	Tc	Strat	Opera
Dist1	**0.97**	0.81	-0.55	-0.28	-0.32	-0.54
Dist2	**0.98**	0.63	-0.55	-0.32	-0.35	-0.49
Int1	0.60	**0.98**	-0.26	-0.26	-0.46	-0.38
Int2	0.64	**0.98**	-0.31	-0.27	-0.40	-0.43
Pc1	-0.55	-0.29	**0.93**	0.39	0.38	0.52
Pc2	-0.47	-0.24	**0.89**	0.36	0.31	0.46
Pc3	-0.50	-0.25	**0.87**	0.46	0.31	0.56
Tc1	-0.26	-0.25	0.49	**0.81**	0.50	0.48
Tc2	-0.20	-0.21	0.32	**0.81**	0.37	0.36
Tc3	-0.31	-0.21	0.34	**0.89**	0.42	0.48
Tc4	-0.23	-0.23	0.32	**0.81**	0.36	0.51
Strat1	-0.36	-0.47	0.36	0.48	**0.93**	0.44
Strat2	-0.25	-0.31	0.32	0.42	**0.88**	0.30
Strat3	-0.30	-0.39	0.33	0.45	**0.91**	0.37
Opera1	-0.45	-0.35	0.56	0.51	0.38	**0.91**
Opera2	-0.52	-0.41	0.58	0.51	0.42	**0.91**
Opera3	-0.47	-0.36	0.50	0.47	0.35	**0.90**
Opera4	-0.46	-0.37	0.45	0.50	0.36	**0.92**
ConTrans	-0.38	-0.42	0.14	0.20	0.23	0.22
ConRelFac	-0.26	-0.26	0.20	0.28	0.18	0.24
ProRelFac	-0.24	-0.26	0.17	0.39	0.20	0.21
MarkRelFac	-0.10	-0.15	0.17	0.24	0.20	0.11
ConVal1	-0.15	-0.20	0.02	0.13	0.14	0.18
ConVal2	-0.17	-0.14	0.09	0.00	0.00	0.06
ConVal3	-0.10	-0.07	0.04	0.09	0.03	0.08
LowCost	-0.10	-0.04	0.15	-0.01	0.10	0.11
Differ	0.06	0.06	0.07	0.20	0.09	-0.12
Focus	0.10	0.01	0.02	-0.02	0.07	0.12
OrgCent1	0.10	0.05	-0.02	0.07	0.09	0.08
OrgCent3	-0.02	-0.09	-0.03	0.13	-0.10	0.03
OrgForm1	-0.22	-0.15	0.24	0.19	0.25	0.24
OrgForm2	-0.22	-0.04	0.14	0.12	0.15	0.16
OrgForm3	-0.22	-0.09	0.16	0.10	0.16	0.15
OrgSpec2	0.14	0.21	-0.17	-0.06	0.05	0.04
OrgSpec3	0.19	0.25	-0.16	-0.37	-0.30	-0.25
OrgSize1	-0.07	-0.04	0.08	0.13	0.17	0.14
OrgSize2	0.01	0.12	0.02	0.17	0.13	-0.08
OrgSize3	-0.03	0.00	0.03	0.24	0.18	0.05
ITGov1	-0.18	-0.13	0.20	0.30	0.13	0.13
ITGov2	-0.28	-0.19	0.24	0.35	0.17	0.18
ITGov3	-0.19	-0.07	0.21	0.22	0.04	0.12
ITInvest1	0.11	0.10	-0.11	0.01	0.09	-0.16
ITInvest2	-0.03	-0.05	-0.00	-0.05	0.03	-0.16
ITInvest3	0.19	0.20	-0.10	-0.03	-0.02	-0.16
ITUsage1	0.29	0.17	-0.20	-0.19	-0.06	0.00
ITUsage2	0.18	0.19	-0.27	-0.12	-0.01	-0.07

Table Appendix-D2: Cross-loadings for productive content sub-sample (Page 1 of 3)

Items	ConTrans	IntCompl	ConVal	LowCost	Differ	Focus
Dist1	-0.34	-0.26	-0.12	-0.11	0.10	0.10
Dist2	-0.41	-0.24	-0.17	-0.10	0.02	0.10
Int1	-0.39	-0.28	-0.17	-0.05	0.10	0.01
Int2	-0.42	-0.27	-0.19	-0.02	0.02	0.01
Pc1	0.14	0.28	0.02	0.11	0.04	0.03
Pc2	0.08	0.11	0.01	0.11	0.08	0.11
Pc3	0.15	0.19	0.03	0.20	0.07	-0.09
Tc1	0.14	0.31	0.04	-0.03	0.13	0.08
Tc2	0.18	0.35	0.11	-0.02	0.19	-0.04
Tc3	0.13	0.28	0.16	0.03	0.19	-0.04
Tc4	0.23	0.32	0.13	-0.02	0.16	-0.08
Strat1	0.21	0.19	0.22	0.05	0.10	0.08
Strat2	0.16	0.21	0.05	0.14	0.10	0.02
Strat3	0.26	0.27	0.05	0.10	0.05	0.08
Opera1	0.15	0.23	0.15	0.10	-0.07	0.14
Opera2	0.16	0.19	0.18	0.11	-0.12	0.11
Opera3	0.34	0.21	0.20	0.12	-0.10	0.08
Opera4	0.16	0.24	0.11	0.09	-0.14	0.12
ConTrans	**1.00**	0.34	0.25	0.00	0.06	-0.19
ConRelFac	0.32	**0.89**	0.13	0.03	0.00	-0.03
ProRelFac	0.29	**0.83**	0.07	0.18	0.03	-0.17
MarkRelFac	0.21	**0.70**	-0.01	-0.09	0.04	-0.21
ConVal1	0.23	0.06	**0.99**	0.00	0.25	0.13
ConVal2	0.18	-0.03	**0.71**	0.14	0.22	0.15
ConVal3	0.30	0.17	**0.73**	0.14	0.17	0.04
LowCost	0.00	0.07	0.02	**1.00**	-0.10	0.01
Differ	0.06	0.02	0.25	-0.10	**1.00**	-0.04
Focus	-0.19	-0.16	0.13	0.01	-0.04	**1.00**
OrgCent1	0.00	0.10	0.04	0.07	-0.10	0.05
OrgCent3	0.10	0.24	0.09	-0.08	-0.12	-0.15
OrgForm1	0.16	0.18	0.11	0.11	0.03	-0.04
OrgForm2	0.11	0.00	0.18	0.12	0.02	-0.05
OrgForm3	0.12	-0.14	0.07	0.18	-0.07	-0.16
OrgSpec2	-0.26	-0.13	0.08	-0.13	0.10	0.10
OrgSpec3	-0.15	-0.34	-0.18	0.02	-0.03	-0.14
OrgSize1	0.16	0.13	0.09	0.02	0.09	-0.32
OrgSize2	0.08	0.12	-0.02	-0.06	0.14	-0.35
OrgSize3	0.13	0.14	0.16	0.01	0.19	-0.07
ITGov1	0.02	0.19	0.08	0.20	0.27	-0.06
ITGov2	0.12	0.27	0.11	0.16	0.21	-0.18
ITGov3	0.11	0.32	0.07	0.17	0.17	-0.14
ITInvest1	0.15	-0.02	0.02	0.01	0.18	-0.12
ITInvest2	0.15	0.09	0.04	-0.01	0.10	-0.05
ITInvest3	-0.01	-0.06	0.06	-0.16	0.08	-0.10
ITUsage1	-0.26	-0.23	-0.02	0.04	-0.12	0.35
ITUsage2	-0.07	-0.12	0.13	-0.03	-0.02	0.02

Table Appendix-D3: Cross-loadings for productive content sub-sample (Page 2 of 3)

Items	OrgCent	OrgForm	OrgSpec	OrgSize	ITGov	ITInvest	ITUsage
Dist1	0.02	-0.25	0.19	-0.03	-0.24	0.21	0.27
Dist2	0.07	-0.26	0.22	0.00	-0.26	0.20	0.32
Int1	-0.05	-0.11	0.29	0.09	-0.14	0.17	0.22
Int2	-0.02	-0.11	0.26	0.06	-0.18	0.24	0.24
Pc1	-0.04	0.23	-0.22	0.10	0.30	-0.06	-0.28
Pc2	-0.07	0.14	-0.22	-0.03	0.19	-0.12	-0.23
Pc3	0.03	0.22	-0.10	0.02	0.19	-0.18	-0.28
Tc1	0.11	0.10	-0.19	0.12	0.24	-0.02	-0.14
Tc2	0.10	0.10	-0.32	0.19	0.35	0.05	-0.11
Tc3	0.13	0.18	-0.17	0.27	0.41	0.07	-0.19
Tc4	0.08	0.17	-0.30	0.08	0.16	-0.15	-0.22
Strat1	-0.04	0.21	-0.16	0.13	0.12	-0.03	-0.04
Strat2	0.01	0.21	-0.13	0.18	0.18	0.05	-0.04
Strat3	-0.01	0.21	-0.21	0.15	0.11	0.04	-0.05
Opera1	0.08	0.19	-0.09	0.04	0.17	-0.15	0.00
Opera2	0.04	0.19	-0.14	-0.03	0.13	-0.18	-0.09
Opera3	0.02	0.27	-0.17	-0.04	0.12	-0.12	-0.05
Opera4	0.10	0.16	-0.15	-0.01	0.20	-0.19	0.01
ConTrans	0.07	0.16	-0.24	0.12	0.10	0.04	-0.22
ConRelFac	0.26	0.00	-0.21	0.13	0.24	-0.05	-0.18
ProRelFac	0.13	0.10	-0.35	0.15	0.29	-0.07	-0.17
MarkRelFac	0.17	-0.05	-0.16	0.06	0.18	-0.06	-0.21
ConVal1	0.09	0.13	-0.09	0.02	0.10	0.05	0.07
ConVal2	-0.05	0.14	-0.14	-0.07	0.14	-0.05	0.05
ConVal3	0.08	0.15	-0.02	0.14	0.09	0.03	-0.01
LowCost	-0.01	0.16	-0.06	-0.04	0.20	-0.13	0.01
Differ	-0.15	-0.01	0.03	0.16	0.25	0.13	-0.09
Focus	-0.08	-0.10	-0.04	-0.33	-0.15	-0.13	0.26
OrgCent1	**0.71**	0.02	-0.07	0.18	-0.07	-0.01	0.14
OrgCent3	**0.81**	-0.05	-0.08	0.22	0.15	-0.10	-0.33
OrgForm1	0.06	**0.87**	-0.15	0.18	0.25	0.18	-0.20
OrgForm2	-0.07	**0.83**	-0.06	0.19	0.27	0.17	-0.08
OrgForm3	-0.06	**0.81**	-0.02	0.28	0.13	0.08	-0.13
OrgSpec2	-0.03	-0.03	**0.76**	0.13	-0.01	0.07	0.25
OrgSpec3	-0.12	-0.11	**0.86**	-0.05	-0.13	-0.06	0.03
OrgSize1	0.28	0.21	-0.02	**0.82**	0.19	0.13	-0.21
OrgSize2	0.27	0.26	0.06	**0.96**	0.20	0.16	-0.25
OrgSize3	0.05	0.12	-0.01	**0.67**	0.18	0.10	-0.13
ITGov1	0.01	0.22	-0.09	0.21	**0.87**	0.12	-0.07
ITGov2	0.09	0.21	-0.11	0.19	**0.94**	0.01	-0.17
ITGov3	0.04	0.25	-0.03	0.17	**0.75**	0.15	-0.18
ITInvest1	-0.10	0.20	0.03	0.23	0.19	**0.71**	0.16
ITInvest2	-0.04	0.19	-0.07	0.01	0.09	**0.51**	0.08
ITInvest3	-0.05	0.13	-0.03	0.08	0.03	**0.94**	0.21
ITUsage1	-0.17	-0.28	0.08	-0.44	-0.27	0.08	**0.83**
ITUsage2	-0.07	0.05	0.17	0.10	0.05	0.31	**0.74**

Table Appendix-D4: Cross-loadings for productive content sub-sample (Page 3 of 3)

Items	Dist	Int	Pc	Tc	Strat	Opera
Dist1	**0.98**	0.60	-0.50	-0.24	-0.49	-0.54
Dist2	**0.98**	0.55	-0.54	-0.24	-0.43	-0.54
Int1	0.58	**0.98**	-0.29	-0.18	-0.56	-0.43
Int2	0.58	**0.98**	-0.32	-0.21	-0.54	-0.44
Pc1	-0.57	-0.35	**0.94**	0.39	0.28	0.56
Pc2	-0.42	-0.24	**0.90**	0.28	0.27	0.51
Pc3	-0.44	-0.25	**0.89**	0.45	0.27	0.58
Tc1	-0.22	-0.22	0.40	**0.83**	0.35	0.51
Tc2	-0.22	-0.18	0.36	**0.85**	0.28	0.45
Tc3	-0.20	-0.12	0.33	**0.90**	0.21	0.45
Tc4	-0.19	-0.17	0.34	**0.86**	0.26	0.58
Strat1	-0.41	-0.51	0.31	0.39	**0.89**	0.48
Strat2	-0.42	-0.41	0.30	0.23	**0.84**	0.41
Strat3	-0.39	-0.53	0.17	0.21	**0.88**	0.39
Opera1	-0.53	-0.41	0.57	0.53	0.47	**0.91**
Opera2	-0.51	-0.41	0.59	0.51	0.44	**0.93**
Opera3	-0.47	-0.43	0.54	0.54	0.47	**0.93**
Opera4	-0.50	-0.38	0.53	0.54	0.44	**0.90**
ConTrans	-0.24	-0.38	0.26	0.14	0.14	0.25
ConRelFac	-0.23	-0.22	0.27	0.20	0.25	0.22
ProRelFac	-0.05	-0.19	0.16	0.18	0.22	0.13
MarkRelFac	-0.19	-0.32	0.22	0.34	0.26	0.23
ConVal1	-0.06	-0.24	-0.03	0.15	0.08	0.13
ConVal2	-0.10	-0.19	0.05	0.01	0.05	0.08
ConVal3	-0.03	-0.12	0.02	0.03	0.02	0.08
LowCost	-0.01	0.00	0.10	-0.03	0.07	0.00
Differ	-0.02	0.04	0.02	0.12	0.01	-0.04
Focus	0.06	0.07	-0.14	0.06	0.00	0.06
OrgCent1	0.00	-0.02	-0.08	0.09	0.26	0.10
OrgCent3	0.07	-0.08	0.02	0.12	0.18	0.07
OrgForm1	-0.19	-0.23	0.21	0.14	0.27	0.29
OrgForm2	-0.15	-0.11	0.19	0.16	0.10	0.17
OrgForm3	-0.20	-0.13	0.15	0.08	0.13	0.15
OrgSpec2	0.05	0.21	-0.06	0.01	-0.24	-0.02
OrgSpec3	0.19	0.29	-0.10	-0.34	-0.34	-0.24
OrgSize1	-0.01	-0.05	0.08	0.21	0.13	0.04
OrgSize2	0.01	0.07	0.06	0.13	0.11	-0.09
OrgSize3	-0.04	-0.04	-0.03	0.07	0.05	-0.09
ITGov1	-0.19	-0.11	0.18	0.25	0.17	0.09
ITGov2	-0.26	-0.19	0.27	0.30	0.27	0.19
ITGov3	-0.22	-0.12	0.29	0.20	0.22	0.17
ITInvest1	0.03	0.06	-0.05	-0.03	-0.05	-0.16
ITInvest2	-0.07	-0.02	0.08	-0.08	-0.07	-0.11
ITInvest3	0.17	0.15	-0.08	-0.02	-0.17	-0.12
ITUsage1	0.22	0.18	-0.16	-0.09	-0.17	-0.07
ITUsage2	0.17	0.18	-0.17	-0.02	-0.10	-0.15

Table Appendix-D5: Cross-loadings for archived content sub-sample (Page 1 of 3)

Items	ConTrans	IntCompl	ConVal	LowCost	Differ	Focus
Dist1	-0.21	-0.19	-0.09	0.03	-0.02	0.05
Dist2	-0.25	-0.22	-0.07	-0.04	-0.01	0.07
Int1	-0.39	-0.3	-0.2	0.01	0.07	0.08
Int2	-0.37	-0.3	-0.26	0	0.01	0.06
Pc1	0.25	0.33	-0.03	0.1	0.02	-0.18
Pc2	0.16	0.19	0.05	0.09	0.08	-0.06
Pc3	0.29	0.2	0.01	0.1	-0.04	-0.12
Tc1	0.1	0.32	0.08	-0.08	0.06	0.11
Tc2	0.12	0.27	0.1	0.01	0.17	0
Tc3	0.12	0.24	0.09	0	0.15	0.03
Tc4	0.16	0.22	0.08	-0.02	0.03	0.06
Strat1	0.12	0.26	0.08	0.03	0.11	0.01
Strat2	0.06	0.26	0.04	0.09	-0.06	-0.01
Strat3	0.17	0.26	0.06	0.07	-0.03	0.01
Opera1	0.15	0.19	0.07	-0.01	-0.02	0.09
Opera2	0.22	0.24	0.07	-0.05	-0.03	0.03
Opera3	0.31	0.26	0.17	0.02	0.02	0.02
Opera4	0.24	0.22	0.14	0.06	-0.13	0.07
ConTrans	**1**	0.34	0.25	0	0.06	-0.19
ConRelFac	0.32	**0.88**	0.09	0.03	0	-0.03
ProRelFac	0.29	**0.84**	0.03	0.18	0.03	-0.17
MarkRelFac	0.21	**0.69**	-0.01	-0.09	0.04	-0.21
ConVal1	0.23	0.06	**0.95**	0	0.25	0.13
ConVal2	0.18	-0.03	**0.87**	0.14	0.22	0.15
ConVal3	0.3	0.17	**0.72**	0.14	0.17	0.04
LowCost	0	0.07	0.07	**1**	-0.1	0.01
Differ	0.06	0.02	0.26	-0.1	**1**	-0.04
Focus	-0.19	-0.16	0.14	0.01	-0.04	**1**
OrgCent1	0	0.1	0.03	0.07	-0.1	0.05
OrgCent3	0.1	0.24	0.04	-0.08	-0.12	-0.15
OrgForm1	0.16	0.18	0.12	0.11	0.03	-0.04
OrgForm2	0.11	0	0.19	0.12	0.02	-0.05
OrgForm3	0.12	-0.14	0.08	0.18	-0.07	-0.16
OrgSpec2	-0.26	-0.13	0.02	-0.13	0.1	0.1
OrgSpec3	-0.15	-0.34	-0.17	0.02	-0.03	-0.14
OrgSize1	0.16	0.13	0.06	0.02	0.09	-0.32
OrgSize2	0.08	0.12	-0.05	-0.06	0.14	-0.35
OrgSize3	0.13	0.13	0.13	0.01	0.19	-0.07
ITGov1	0.02	0.19	0.09	0.2	0.27	-0.06
ITGov2	0.12	0.27	0.14	0.16	0.21	-0.18
ITGov3	0.11	0.32	0.07	0.17	0.17	-0.14
ITInvest1	0.15	-0.02	-0.01	0.01	0.18	-0.12
ITInvest2	0.15	0.09	0.07	-0.01	0.1	-0.05
ITInvest3	-0.01	-0.06	0.04	-0.16	0.08	-0.1
ITUsage1	-0.26	-0.23	-0.02	0.04	-0.12	0.35
ITUsage2	-0.07	-0.12	0.14	-0.03	-0.02	0.02

Table Appendix-D6: Cross-loadings for archived content sub-sample (Page 2 of 3)

Items	OrgCent	OrgForm	OrgSpec	OrgSize	ITGov	ITInvest	ITUsage
Dist1	0.05	-0.21	0.2	-0.06	-0.25	0.2	0.27
Dist2	0.09	-0.22	0.13	-0.06	-0.27	0.16	0.22
Int1	-0.1	-0.2	0.31	-0.12	-0.16	0.13	0.22
Int2	-0.06	-0.19	0.31	-0.19	-0.17	0.19	0.22
Pc1	0.01	0.2	-0.11	0.05	0.36	-0.05	-0.25
Pc2	-0.01	0.13	-0.1	-0.08	0.2	-0.11	-0.14
Pc3	0.03	0.26	-0.08	-0.09	0.22	-0.09	-0.15
Tc1	0.18	0.1	-0.18	0.08	0.23	-0.04	-0.03
Tc2	0.06	0.1	-0.26	0.09	0.29	-0.02	-0.04
Tc3	0.07	0.16	-0.2	0.11	0.36	0.12	-0.06
Tc4	0.12	0.15	-0.27	0.02	0.12	-0.08	-0.11
Strat1	0.16	0.15	-0.33	-0.01	0.23	-0.21	-0.15
Strat2	0.19	0.18	-0.3	-0.01	0.25	-0.08	-0.16
Strat3	0.2	0.23	-0.33	0.09	0.22	-0.11	-0.13
Opera1	0.08	0.23	-0.12	0.01	0.19	-0.08	-0.06
Opera2	0.07	0.22	-0.21	0.08	0.17	-0.11	-0.19
Opera3	0.07	0.28	-0.25	0.09	0.17	-0.17	-0.15
Opera4	0.08	0.21	-0.16	-0.01	0.14	-0.11	-0.08
ConTrans	0.09	0.16	-0.22	0.17	0.1	0	-0.21
ConRelFac	0.26	0.01	-0.23	0.11	0.25	-0.08	-0.18
ProRelFac	0.14	0.11	-0.36	0.05	0.3	-0.08	-0.17
MarkRelFac	0.21	-0.05	-0.17	0.08	0.19	-0.07	-0.21
ConVal1	0.09	0.13	-0.12	0.24	0.1	0.05	0.07
ConVal2	-0.06	0.14	-0.14	0.11	0.13	-0.05	0.06
ConVal3	0.08	0.15	-0.01	0.16	0.1	0.02	0
LowCost	-0.07	0.16	-0.04	0.09	0.2	-0.15	0
Differ	-0.13	-0.01	0.02	0.1	0.25	0.1	-0.09
Focus	-0.14	-0.1	-0.07	0.05	-0.15	-0.12	0.25
OrgCent1	**0.75**	0.03	-0.08	-0.01	-0.07	-0.03	0.14
OrgCent3	**0.99**	-0.05	-0.08	-0.01	0.14	-0.07	-0.33
OrgForm1	0.02	**0.88**	-0.16	0.06	0.26	0.15	-0.2
OrgForm2	-0.05	**0.82**	-0.07	-0.06	0.27	0.15	-0.07
OrgForm3	-0.09	**0.81**	-0.01	-0.01	0.13	0.05	-0.13
OrgSpec2	-0.05	-0.04	**0.66**	0.05	-0.01	0.09	0.25
OrgSpec3	-0.08	-0.11	**0.92**	-0.16	-0.13	-0.07	0.03
OrgSize1	0.23	0.21	-0.04	**0.44**	0.19	0.13	-0.2
OrgSize2	0.24	0.26	0.04	**0.59**	0.2	0.14	-0.24
OrgSize3	0.06	0.13	-0.04	**0.69**	0.18	0.07	-0.12
ITGov1	0.07	0.22	-0.11	0.09	**0.86**	0.08	-0.07
ITGov2	0.17	0.21	-0.12	0.12	**0.92**	-0.01	-0.17
ITGov3	0.07	0.25	-0.03	0.04	**0.79**	0.11	-0.17
ITInvest1	-0.17	0.2	0.02	-0.01	0.19	**0.55**	0.17
ITInvest2	-0.09	0.19	-0.05	-0.07	0.1	**0.37**	0.08
ITInvest3	-0.05	0.14	-0.04	0.01	0.03	**0.97**	0.21
ITUsage1	-0.28	-0.28	0.06	0	-0.28	0.12	**0.82**
ITUsage2	-0.19	0.04	0.14	-0.04	0.04	0.27	**0.76**

Table Appendix-D7: Cross-loadings for archived content sub-sample (Page 3 of 3)

Index